WILD WEASEL
FIGHTER
ATTACK

WILD WEASEL
FIGHTER
ATTACK

The Story of the Suppression
of Enemy Air Defences

Thomas Withington

Pen & Sword
AVIATION

First published in Great Britain in 2008 by
Pen & Sword Aviation
an imprint of
Pen & Sword Books Ltd
47 Church Street
Barnsley
South Yorkshire
S70 2AS

ISBN 978 1 84415 668 9

A CIP catalogue record for this book is
available from the British Library.

Typeset in Palatino by
Phoenix Typesetting, Auldgirth, Dumfriesshire

Printed and bound in England by
CPI UK

Pen & Sword Books Ltd incorporates the imprints of Pen & Sword Aviation,
Pen & Sword Maritime, Pen & Sword Military, Wharncliffe Local History,
Pen & Sword Select, Pen & Sword Military Classics and Leo Cooper.

For a complete list of Pen & Sword titles please contact
PEN & SWORD BOOKS LIMITED
47 Church Street, Barnsley, South Yorkshire, S70 2AS, England
E-mail: enquiries@pen-and-sword.co.uk
Website: www.pen-and-sword.co.uk

Contents

Dedication   vi

Acknowledgements   vii

Chapter One
The Mission Defined   1

Chapter Two
Vietnam and SEAD   33

Chapter Three
SEAD Operations in the Middle East   66

Chapter Four
Cold War SEAD   92

Chapter Five
Non Cold-War SEAD Operations 1965–1987   116
Chapter Six
Desert Storm SEAD   146

Chapter Seven
SEAD in the Balkans   162

Chapter Eight
SEAD During the Global War on Terror   189

Chapter Nine
Future SEAD   215

Glossary   236

Index   241

For Dr. Chris Smith and Dr. Ahron Bregman;
both mentors *extraordinaire*, great friends and suppliers of
inexhaustible wisdom, motivation and enthusiasm!

Acknowledgements

Researching a book which covers such a huge swathe of military aviation history is both a highly rewarding and, at times, frustrating business. That said, several individuals were kind enough to give me their time, suggestions and knowledge which helped me understand the complex nature of the air defence suppression mission. Dr. Gerald 'Gerry' Stiles provided me with an excellent overview of the principles behind Suppression of Enemy Air Defence (SEAD) and the mission's history. I am grateful to Major General Len Le Roux at the Institute for Security Studies who kindly put me in touch with Brigadier General Richard Lord, formerly of the South African Air Force, from whom I gathered much information regarding South Africa's SEAD missions during the Angolan Wars. Similarly, Colonel Pierre Alain Antoine gave a very valuable account of French Air Force SEAD operations during the Chad civil war. Major Anthony Roberson of the United States Air Force supplied first-rate information on the SEAD effort during Operation Iraqi Freedom, while Tom Newdick gave me the benefit of his considerable knowledge of Soviet Air Force SEAD doctrine and platforms. Philippe Wodka-Gallien was an eleventh-hour hero for providing some fascinating information regarding French SEAD operations, pictures and also an infectious motivation with his love of military aviation. My thanks also to Mike Gibbons of Boeing who provided me with a superb overview of the EA-18G Growler programme. Captain Mark Gibson at the Public Affairs office at Shaw AFB helped immeasurably in sorting out interviews, while Sergeant Rebecca Danet at the National Media Outreach Center of the USAF also helped to a great extent in this regard. Darren Lake, Editor of Unmanned Vehicles Magazine, provided me with some very useful contacts.

Special thanks must go to Peter Coles, Editor of Pen and Sword military aviation, for believing in this project and also for being so patient when deadlines were outstripping my interview schedule! My friends and family were patient, enthusiastic and happy to hear me whittling on about surface-to-air missiles on a regular basis. Last but by no means least my partner Dr. Nathalie Rivere de Carles was a source of endless encouragement and motivation, patient in the extreme during my long hours at the computer, but with a keen eye and perceptive mind. There may be others who assisted me who I have omitted to thank and if that is so, please accept my humble apologies and deep gratitude. Needless to say, the responsibility for any errors or omissions lies solely with the author.

Thomas Withington,
South-west France.

CHAPTER ONE

The Mission Defined

It would be an exaggeration to say that the mission is suicidal, yet an understatement to say that it is dangerous. However, in almost seventy years, the effort to suppress and destroy enemy air defences has pitted the determined wit and cunning of the combat pilot against the dogged tenacity of the air defender manning either Anti-Aircraft Artillery (AAA) weapons, Surface-to-Air Missiles (SAMs) or gazing at radar; whether as part of an Integrated Air Defence System (IADS) or as part of an individual battery.

For as long aircraft have been used for military purposes there have been efforts to frustrate and defeat their desires. In peacetime, pilots face dangers from the whims of the weather, the slack hand of inadequate maintenance and design, or the simple yet deadly risk of human frailty; all of which can lead to accidents. In wartime, these dangers are in addition to those of the gun and the missile whose operators seek, with all intent and purpose, to down the aircraft that is bringing ordnance to a target, performing a reconnaissance sortie or a Combat Air Patrol (CAP).

The way to defeat the latter risk is to take the war directly to the defenders, to make anti-aircraft defences a key target of airpower and also, in some instances, land forces. Thus, the Suppression of Enemy Air Defence (SEAD) mission has evolved from World War II as an adjunct to a larger air or ground operation, to a complicated mission in its own right encompassing specialist aircraft and munitions, Electronic Intelligence (ELINT) and ground forces in a carefully scripted, destructive concerto aimed at wiping out the air defences of an adversary with decisive blows.

1

Always a good starting point for definitions and descriptions is the United States Department of Defense (DoD) *Dictionary of Military Terms* which defines SEAD as: 'That activity which neutralizes, destroys, or temporarily degrades surface-based enemy air defenses by destructive and/or disruptive means. This definition is corroborated by the Royal Australian Air Force's Air Power Development Centre's *Air Power Terminology* dictionary which reinforces the importance of the mission, while also stressing the result that successful SEAD operations can have on the conduct of wider air operations: 'The suppression of enemy air defences is a major role in the application of air power. It is the neutralisation, destruction or temporary degradation of enemy air defence systems so that aircraft have the freedom of action to complete their mission without interference from ground-based anti-aircraft systems.' So there we have it. The importance of the mission defined; to allow other aircraft the freedom of action to roam the skies unhindered by the radar that may see them and the communications links that may transmit information on their whereabouts and the weaponry that might shoot them down. In short, the SEAD mission is as integral to establishing air superiority as CAPs of fighter aircraft looking for and attacking their opposite numbers. They are indivisible, one and the same in sanitizing the skies.

The importance of the mission also transcends the air force. If an army on the ground or the warship at sea is to obtain aerial reconnaissance data on potential targets or to benefit from the provision of Close Air Support (CAS), then the aircraft which provide these capabilities must be able to do so with the minimum of harassment from the ground.

Up until the American withdrawal from the Vietnam War in 1975 the SEAD mission had primarily been the preserve of specialist aircraft that were outfitted at first with cannon, and then rockets and missiles, together with sophisticated radar-seeking electronics and Electronic Counter Measures (ECMs). However, since then the SEAD mission has evolved to encompass all elements of a modern armed force. Certainly, the specialist platforms dedicated to SEAD still exist and are vitally important, the United States Air Force (USAF) F-16CJ Wild Weasels and their accompanying AGM-88 High-speed Anti Radiation Missiles

(HARMs) being two examples. However, these aircraft are joined by sophisticated ECM-equipped planes such as the US Navy (USN) and US Marine Corps (USMC) EA-6B Prowler aircraft which can blast the radar and communications net of an IADS with torrents of hostile electrons rendering the eyes and ears of the system deaf and blind. In addition, conventional 'dumb' bombs, rockets and gunfire can all find their way onto a radar or SAM site. Attack helicopters can unleash their not-inconsiderable cannon, rockets and air-to-surface missiles on radar, SAMs and hardened command centres. Meanwhile, artillery can take apart similar targets, as can raiding parties of Special Operations Forces (SOF) commandos. Even long-range heavy bombers can play their part in decimating hardened IADS Command and Control (C2) centres. For example, the attack aircraft that strafes a convoy of vehicles carrying Man-Portable Air Defence System (MANPADS) hand-held launchers illicitly across a border into a neighbouring country gripped by insurgency is arguably playing as useful a role in the SEAD operation as a Wild Weasel sending an AGM-88 into an IS-91 Straight Flush ZRK-SD Kub 3M9 (NATO codename SA-6 Gainful) SAM fire-control radar.

However, it is not just the weaponry that makes a SEAD operation. Modern technology has wondrous attributes but it is nothing more than dead metal and sleeping circuits without rigorous campaign planning and highly skilled individuals who can apply the kit to the mission in an innovative and decisive fashion. No longer does the SEAD effort begin and end with specialist planes riding shotgun for a larger package of attack aircraft as it did in the Vietnam War. This campaign, as we shall see, was vital in helping to develop incredibly sophisticated and complex tactics, which has allowed SEAD to evolve as a meticulously planned effort in its own right.

SEAD Principles

SURPRISE
Careful planning of a SEAD operation is an unsurprising prerequisite, given the mortal dangers that modern IADS present. The USAF air power theorist, Colonel John A. Warden III, stressed the two important elements of surprise and mass when

performing SEAD. Like two relatively benign chemicals, when these tactical characteristics are united they can produce a reaction disastrous for its intended victim. Surprise denies the enemy the means adequately to prepare their own air defences. The blow takes them by surprise and they struggle to prepare a response in kind to the opening salvo that may have seriously disrupted the nervous system of their IADS by crashing communications links and filling radar screens with white noise. Meanwhile, several SAM and radar sites may have been reduced to smouldering pyres after a visit from a HARM.

FORCE WEIGHT

Surprise on its own can only do so much. It must be supplemented with force weight. This ensures that the opening blow is as decisive as possible. To use a martial arts analogy, there is little point in a kick-boxer giving his opponent a slap on the cheek as an opening gambit, unless they want to suffer a knee in the face as a response. Better instead to deliver a weighty uppercut at the start and hope that it puts your opponent on the canvas, or even better, out for the count. It is this principle that characterises the use of force weight for SEAD. Go in with surprise and hit with everything you can: HARMs, bombs, electrons, gunfire, artillery and SOF. The harder the strike the harder for the enemy to consolidate any remaining air defences that may be left to pose a subsequent threat to follow-on sorties, be they SEAD, ground attack or reconnaissance.

PERSISTENCE

Major Stanley J. Dougherty (USAF) in his article *Defense Suppression: Building Some Operational Concepts* adds another important element to the surprise and weight equation: persistence. This latter aspect is, of course, one of airpower's strongest suits. For SEAD it is essential, returning to the boxing analogy, that the fighter, having thrown the felling punch, does not turn his back and walk away. He must remain vigilant in case his opponent dusts himself off and returns to the fray. SEAD operations are no different. The opening surprise-weight mixture may smash some major parts of an IADS but may not kill it in one fell swoop. Other parts may remain operational and therefore still a threat and air power must remain vigilant to respond with fresh attacks, be they hard- (using missiles, gunfire or bombs) or soft-kill (using ECM) against those elements that survive.

INTELLIGENCE
To appreciate fully the Surprise-Weight-Persistence (SWP) approach we have to backtrack somewhat. There is little point in unleashing these three horsemen unless they know what to fight. A famous car advertisement once said that 'power is nothing without control' and SEAD is no different. For the above mix to work, the SEAD commander has to know as much as he can about his enemy's IADS. He has to know his order-of-battle including the AAA, SAM, radar, communication links, C2 centres, power sources; logistics depots and organisation; and leadership. He has to know the age of the system, its level of maintenance and its level of redundancy. He has to understand how it is staffed (with either conscripts or highly trained air defenders), how its leadership thinks and how it has performed in combat before. He has to think like his enemy, get into their mindset to anticipate their decisions. It is by doing this that the SEAD professional will find that tell-tale chink in the armour; that one, or many, weaknesses that could cause the system to fall like a house of cards when surprise, weight and persistence are applied with vigour.

This is not a new trick, and it harks back to the very essence of Clausewitzian theory; that is the identification of the Centres of Gravity (CoGs). The great Prussian military thinker Carl von Clausewitz (1780-1831) extolled the importance of attacking CoGs. These, he said, were the hubs 'of all power and movement, on which everything depends. That is the point against which all our energies should be directed. Clausewitz was, of course, writing before the dawn of airpower, but his thoughts are highly relevant to the SEAD battle. True, they may arguably be more relevant to SEAD efforts against an enemy with a sophisticated air defence network where attacks against a few hardened command centres and Early Warning (EW) radar systems may cause the wider network to lose its senses and the SAM and AAA operators to be unable to fire with anything like the accuracy they had expected. Yet, the centre of gravity in the case of disparate militia groups armed with MANPADS which can exact a heavy toll on attack helicopters, low-flying attack aircraft and transport planes entering and exiting an airfield may well be the covert cross-border supply networks which get these weapons into theatre. Without these networks, as for the command centres and radar of the IADS at the other end of the spectrum, the air defence system cannot function effectively. Once these key points, or CoGs, are identified then the SWP approach can be applied to the SEAD effort.

However, it almost goes without saying that robust and comprehensive Intelligence, Surveillance and Reconnaissance (ISR) capabilities are a prerequisite for the identification of CoGs to be properly undertaken. Thus, Human Intelligence (HUMINT), space-based and aerial reconnaissance must all be brought to bear for this task. The possession of adequate ISR capabilities is allied to adequate planning time. If a comprehensive understanding of an enemy's air defence capabilities is to be acquired then SEAD planners need enough time to gain a proper understanding of where these centres of gravity are located and how they are interlinked. Without this, the task of SEAD, while not impossible, will become more difficult. This can present problems when a country is plunged into a so-called 'come-as-you-are' war where its forces have little time to build up an operational picture of their enemy's air defences due to the need to respond suddenly in support of national, or multinational, objectives. That said, one way around this is for an air force to maintain a comprehensive peacetime record of the operational air-defence systems of possible adversaries and this is no doubt something that defence intelligence agencies around the world turn their talents to on a regular basis.

DECEPTION

Allied to the SWP approach is deception. This is one of the oldest military tricks in the book, its age betrays its utility, and it is a highly useful tool for the SEAD planner. Give the air defences something to concentrate on; namely a feint. Convince the enemy's network, the SAM/AAA sites or the MANPADS operator that the attack is coming from elsewhere and then sneak in either using stealth or an unexpected route of entry and hit them and their CoGs with overwhelming, focused violence. The key is to preserve the avenue of attack: either the route that the opening SEAD strike package will take or the ingress of the individual SEAD aircraft by either low-level flight or stealth, to deny the adversary reaction time, or preferably any reaction at all.

TACTICS AND TECHNIQUES
There are several ways in which the SEAD SWP operation may be performed and they can largely depend on which weapons, aircraft and capabilities a particular air force may have available, as well as the quantity of these assets and the overall objectives of the military campaign that the SEAD effort is being executed to support. Dougherty's excellent paper discussing SEAD draws attention to several approaches that the SEAD planner may choose:

The Manoeuvrist Approach
The first technique uses the so-called Manoeuvrist approach. Returning to our trusty DoD Dictionary, we are told that the principle of manoeuvre is defined as the 'employment of forces on the battlefield through movement in combination with fire, or fire potential, to achieve a position of advantage in respect to the enemy in order to accomplish the mission. This echoes back to the work of the British military theorist Basil Liddell Hart (1885–1970) and his 'indirect approach' which suggested that armies should advance along the most unexpected route to attack at the most weakly defended point.

So, how does this relate to SEAD? Well, it is to use those SEAD assets that you have at hand, namely the specialist anti-radar weaponry, ECM aircraft and ground forces (which for the sake of argument we shall say in the SEAD context includes SOF, artillery and attack helicopters) judiciously in such a way as to achieve an advantageous position (by establishing a sanitized air corridor) over the enemy from where surprise, weight and persistence can be brought to bear. Crucially, with the Manoeuvrist approach, weight can be directed over the entirety of the air defences, disparate CoGs or instead directed at a finite number of CoGs whose destruction may cause irreparable damage to the adversary's air defence. This must be done from an unexpected route of advance towards a weak point in the air defences.

Dougherty stresses that for the Manoeuvrist approach to yield its desired results, it is imperative to: 'use intelligence information to construct and update a near real-time, three dimensional "aerial terrain" map of the enemy's integrated air defence system, and (use) manoeuvre to traverse this aerial terrain safely, improving the penetrability of non-stealth aircraft for deep attack'. Not only is ISR imperative for providing knowledge of the CoGs, but Dougherty also notes that it is essential to use 'the aerial terrain map to determine the best penetration route (line of least resistance). IADS are normally finite with flanks, have a directional orientation, and are rarely strong in both depth and width – several preferred routes of penetration should be evident'.

This takes us back to the realms of Liddell Hart. In layman's terms, if country 'A' has oriented its air defence radar and weaponry to point in the direction of approaches from its neighbour, country 'B', which is to the north, then the SEAD commander can plan ingress and egress routes for the SEAD force to attack the key targets from the south which may necessitate the use of aerial refuelling caused by the longer sorties required to go 'through the backdoor', but will provide the necessary surprise and present less danger than attacking directly. Therefore, we can see that in the SEAD context, the famed outflanking action beloved of land commanders on the ground, can have as much utility in the air. If over-flight rights above a third party country for an unexpected ingress into country 'A' are denied, then stealth aircraft can attack directly into the hornet's nest with accompanying ECM aircraft shooting their electrons from beyond the air defence's lethal reach. If stealth aircraft are unavailable, then the Manoeuvrist approach may call for a deception to come into play to keep the air defenders looking at something else while the SEAD force sneaks in to attack the CoGs. Whatever the tactic, the same rules apply; the least expected route against the least defended point.

The Manoeuvrist approach is not risk-free. It may reduce dangers, but it has its own shortcomings: availability of appropriate ISR means aircraft and weaponry and, above all, people. Dougherty argues that the Manoeuvrist approach is at risk from that most intangible of factors: knowing how the enemy will react. The old military adage that 'no plan survives contact with the enemy' penned by Field Marshall Helmuth von Moltke the Elder (1800-1891) is founded on a general, if not absolute, truth. Yes, the SEAD planners can use deception and flanking motions to outwit their opponents, but that does not mean that their opponents will take the bait. The opponents can respond to the deception realising what it is, while at the same time reinforcing their defences in other areas, particularly those from where a SEAD attack is most unlikely to come. For example, they can create redundancy in their networks, ensuring that the destruction of their critical CoGs does not bring the entire air defence system to its knees. They can use deceptions of their own: dummy command centres, looking like bunkers on the outside, but empty inside, radar vans that are little more than dishes, and pipe arrangements looking not unlike SAMs. These go their own way into forcing the attackers to expend precious aircrews, sorties, munitions and time on false targets, while at the same time helping to preserve those CoGs whose destruction could herald the crippling of the air defences. Furthermore, the very electronic barrage which is intended to reduce circuitry to jelly before the SEAD effort gets underway may alert the defenders that something is amiss. They might not be able to use their air defences effectively, but in the case of a sophisticated enemy, that would not stop them getting their fighter aircraft airborne to meet the attackers when they arrive.

The Manoeuvrist approach has another shortcoming. It is arguably most effective against large and mainly static IADS. Those networks which are designed for national defence and feature SAMs and AAA around key centres networked to command centres stand the most risk from the Manoeuvrist approach. Their very immobility can place them in view for the ISR effort and allow them to be plotted accurately in Dougherty's 'aerial map' before the SEAD attack begins.

What is more difficult to prosecute is a SEAD attack against mobile targets. Whether they are humble MANPADS or a vehicle with its own air search and tracking radar, SAM/AAA and operators; all can be hidden or disguised. Obviously, the smaller the weapon the easier it is to conceal, but this does not make it less of a danger. Plotting the position of MANPADS, as the Soviets found during their invasion of Afghanistan, is nigh on impossible. The only assertive defence is to interdict their avenues of supply. However, the only reactive defence is to hunt the weapons and their operators down after an attack, and given that the 'guerrilla is the fish that swims in the ocean of the population' as Mao-Tse-Tung once said, this can be difficult: Rules Of Engagement (ROE) can preclude attacks on civilian houses and buildings where the MANPADS operators and weapons stocks may be located. In the case of the larger vehicles like mobile SAM launchers, these can stay on the move using the so-called 'shoot-and-scoot' tactic. They can also be disguised as civilian vehicles, although the larger the mobile SAM system the harder it is to pass off as a furniture truck. Another technique afforded to mobile systems is that they can be parked next to off-limits civilian targets, such as schools, hospitals and places of worship in full view of the SEAD planner; out-of-bounds yet still able to inflict significant damage.

Furthermore, it is a prerequisite of the Manoeuvrist approach that it requires a large supporting cast. According to Dougherty not only should there be a handsome inventory of specialist SEAD weaponry, aircraft to carry these weapons and ECM aircraft, but there also needs to be a significant fleet of ISR gathering platforms and legions of personnel to interpret the data, coordinate the reconnaissance effort to identify the weak points, plan the campaign and ultimately support its execution. All of these requirements cost considerable amounts of money. All but the largest air forces may lack these assets in the required numbers to perform anything more than a moderately-sized SEAD effort, i.e. neutralising air defences for a finite period in support of a specific mission, as opposed to the wholesale degradation and ultimate destruction of an IADS network for the duration of a prolonged campaign. Small- and medium-sized air forces may have competing funding priorities, for example, paying for new multi-role combat aircraft, or paying for a campaign that they are engaged in abroad. There may not be the political will or inclination to fund the acquisition of equipment necessary for a large-scale SEAD campaign and they may also lack the personnel required for such an effort.

The Mass Approach

Total saturation of enemy air defences through massed SEAD is arguably the antithesis of the Manoeuvrist approach. There is much to be said for pouring in as many SEAD assets as you can get your hands on. Not only does this place as many of the enemy's air defences as possible at risk, but it may have the added effect of simply overwhelming these air defences. Josef Stalin, while waxing lyrical on his legions of tanks and soldiers that had rolled back the Barbarossa invasion of the USSR, unwittingly or otherwise noted the importance of numbers to other military operations when he said that 'quantity has a quality all of its own.' An adversary may have a superb IADS network, but with what threat in mind was this network designed? Was it designed to cope with isolated air attacks from a neighbour? Is it configured to protect key strategic sites such as political or military command centres and bases? Is it modern and comprehensive, but spread over a huge area, and therefore spread too thinly? This takes us back into the realm of establishing CoGs for the opening SEAD effort to be effective. Are the answers to the above questions the weak points in the system?

Mass SEAD attack hands the defenders another dilemma. Faced with an overwhelming assault on their air defences by an armada of supporting aircraft they are forced to make an unpalatable decision over *what* to defend. Should their air defences be clustered around key targets or hidden as best they can to avoid destruction, allowing them to live to fight another day? Should the air defences be unleashed to maximum effect to meet the attackers head-on in battle? Moreover, mass also gives the attackers choice. It allows them to attack a wide range of targets, or key targets of huge importance which will mortally wound the defenders' defences. In essence, mass allows the attackers to strike from almost anywhere at almost anything. The defenders have to try to protect everywhere and everything if they want to remain damage-free and this is simply impossible. Thus the advantage, and most importantly the initiative, is handed to the attackers. However for the larger air forces around the world, the use of mass may be a consideration, but unless part of a Coalition operation, this approach may be beyond the reach of smaller and medium-sized air forces.

The Balanced Approach

However, for such nations help may be at hand. Improvements in stealth-aircraft technology over the past two decades have given rise to a situation where low-observable aircraft such as the F-35 Lightning-II may well be in the hands of many air forces around the world over the next twenty years. With its impressively low radar-signature, the F-35 may provide a SEAD platform that can sneak into considerably robust air defences to deliver anti-radar ordnance or conventional attacks on IADS command and control systems. What is more, a stealth aircraft is an asset that can be used repeatedly, and can provide a SEAD escort to other planes as they perform attack missions. In the future, stealthy Unmanned Combat Aerial Vehicles (UCAVs) may provide a similar function, but their development and fielding is probably at least two decades away by conservative estimates and their employment will raise a host of questions regarding the legality of such aircraft using hard-kill weapons.

Importantly, though, stealth does have its limitations. It is arguably only as good as the most modern air defence radar that it encounters, and with the best will in the world, it is impossible to predict whether technology will evolve to allow stealth aircraft to be detected by more sophisticated radar or by other means, thus rendering their previous advantage void. Legend has it that current stealth aircraft, notably the USAF's B-2A Spirit stealth bomber, the recently-retired F-117A Nighthawk and the F-22A Raptor that replaces it, are not invisible to radar in the conventional sense and that they do produce a radar signature but one that cannot be used in any meaningful fashion, i.e. to provide a firing solution for a SAM. Moreover, in broad daylight stealth aircraft may become as vulnerable to visually-guided AAA or MANPADS as their unstealthy brethren.

Another solution, according to Dougherty, could be the use of stand-off attack missiles; that is, weapons with an adequate range which can be fired from beyond the lethal reach of an adversary's air defences but with sufficient accuracy to hit key CoGs and produce deadly results. Cruise missiles are the obvious candidate here, but they too have their shortcomings. Firstly, unless they can be reprogrammed in flight, they are only useful against static sites. Secondly, unlike aircraft, they can only be used once and are not always that cheap. Stocks can be finite and can be used up quickly once a SEAD operation gets underway, especially if the weapon's production line has long-since closed or the factory cannot produce the weapons quickly enough to satisfy the appetite.

For these smaller air forces, perhaps the balanced approach may be more appropriate for the SEAD battle. Small- and medium-sized air forces often have a versatile capability which can be brought to bear, namely the Multi-Role Combat Aircraft (MRCA). Primarily a feature of the later Cold War and post Cold-War years, the MRCA can be configured for a host of tasks: reconnaissance, ground attack, ARM deployment and air-superiority missions which are all firmly within its grasp. Furthermore, given that they are a veritable flying Swiss army knife of capabilities, an air force does not need huge numbers of them to provide a force of fast jets that can be configured for that day's mission priorities.

Dougherty notes that in the SEAD context, the MRCA can be outfitted with ARMs at an early stage of an air campaign to hit the air defences. There may not be enough aircraft to perform a mass attack of the type outlined above, but that does not mean that they cannot deliver a hard-hitting punch in a Manoeuvrist fashion, particularly if they operate in concert with other capabilities such as Air- or Sea-Launched Cruise Missiles (ALCMs/SLCMs), naval gunfire and land forces. These combinations of capabilities can operate together at the start of a campaign delivering a major punch against an identifiable weak point in an IADS. This can open an entry route into the enemy's airspace and provide a subsequent ingress and egress path for following waves of combat aircraft which are tasked with either hitting other air defence targets or other targets relevant to the overall campaign. Alternatively, the MRCAs can press home the attacks on the critical IADS weak points, while the other assets (the land and naval forces, and the cruise missiles) hit other air defence targets either to keep the defenders off balance with deception or to 'soften up' other SEAD targets so that they can be attacked at a later point by ARM-equipped MRCAs to open new avenues of entry and exit. What is more, once the SEAD objectives have been accomplished, the MRCAs can be re-roled to perform other missions such as reconnaissance or ground attack. If the IADS recovers or continues to pose a major threat then the aircraft can be re-roled once again and fitted with ARMs for a renewed attack.

There are disadvantages with this approach. While the same aircraft can be used for a variety of different missions, this may mean that they experience a higher than average rate of attrition and damage which could thus increase their maintenance burden putting them out of service for longer periods while essential maintenance is performed. At the operational level, the *balanced* as opposed to *mass* SEAD approach may not decisively degrade or destroy an air defence system early in a campaign and risks leaving some parts of it operational and some airspace still off-limits or at the very least extremely dangerous for other aircraft.

In truth, no single approach offers a panacea and individual techniques can be as much tailored to the air force as to the overall objectives of an air campaign. Neither do techniques need to be exclusive. A Manoeuvrist approach may be ideal at the start of a campaign, but only to open up avenues of attack so that a massed SEAD strike can begin. Similarly, a balanced approach may be more appropriate if the objective is to provide a SEAD escort for a package of aircraft performing a few isolated air strikes. Perhaps all three approaches may be performed simultaneously in different parts of the theatre. With SEAD, there is no 'one size fits all' and the tactics and techniques which are brought to bear will be largely dictated by prevailing campaign objectives and the aircraft, munitions, supporting capabilities and personnel available to the SEAD commander.

Integration
The history of SEAD has taught an important lesson to the air campaign planners and commanders. SEAD has to be an integrated part of any air campaign. As long as air defences are unchallenged aircraft are at risk. SEAD cannot be brought into the fray as an afterthought, but instead must be tightly intertwined with the overwhelming campaign objectives from the start. For example, if the objective of an air campaign is to destroy a country's nuclear weapons production, storage and deployment facilities then the air defences which are located around those

targets and on the possible routes to and from the aimpoints must be understood.

At the other end of the spectrum, if the campaign objectives are to stop the killing, rape and dislocation of a particular ethnic group by a rag-tag militia, then what defences against air attack does this militia have, or what air defence protection could they draw upon from a sponsoring state? Where are these defences located? Are they static or mobile? A population may applaud a government's efforts to attack the militia, but their support may ebb if even a couple of the aircraft sent to fight the bullies don't return. The Western media is generally unforgiving as far as casualties are concerned, particularly if they are one's own military or civilians in the field and in this context SEAD is as much part of the battle for domestic support as it is to protect the aircrews on the front line.

It is imperative that SEAD is a key priority at the very start and for the entire duration of a campaign. A threat may be dealt a mortal blow at the onset of hostilities but that does not mean that it is destroyed once and for all. As we have seen in the aftermath of Operation Iraqi Freedom, one of the world's most sophisticated air defence systems was comprehensively destroyed in two wars and ten years of sanctions and no-fly zone enforcement. Instead, the hi-tech communications links and missiles have been swapped for devastatingly simple rocket-propelled grenades and even rifle fire. The fast, high-flying jets that traverse Iraqi airspace may be a whole lot safer than they were at the start of Operation Desert Storm in 1991, but the helicopters that are taking the war and the troops to the insurgents, and the injured to the operating theatre, are not. The knights of yesteryear would never have fought without their armour, and neither must the air forces of today.

World War II

It is hard to say when SEAD began. Undoubtedly during World War I early combat aircraft probably fired bullets at those taking pot shots at them, but it seems that the first dedicated application of a SEAD effort occurred during the early stages of the Battle of Britain between the Royal Air Force (RAF) and the *Luftwaffe* in 1940.

The early development and advances in Radio Direction Finding and Ranging, which became better known as radar, were not lost on the RAF. The efforts of Sir Robert Watson Watt, considered to be the inventor of radar, yielded a network of EW stations positioned around the United Kingdom and given the code-name Chain Home. Chain Home was intended to provide long-range 'eyes' for the RAF to warn them of approaching *Luftwaffe* aircraft. The system was a breakthrough. It gave the RAF as much as 30 minute's advanced notice of an incoming formation of German bombers, enough time for fighters to be scrambled to meet the aircraft as they neared the British Isles. The Germans of course, put two-and-two together and realised that Chain Home was a *de facto* force multiplier which could exact a heavy toll on their aircraft. If future missions over the UK were to succeed then Chain Home would need to be destroyed.

The *Luftwaffe* began their attacks on the radar stations on the 12 August when destruction arrived from a fine and misty sky onto radar stations at Dover in Kent, Dunkirk in northern France, and Pevensey and Rye in East Sussex. The attack was enough to put all but Dunkirk out of action for 6 hours and would herald the *Luftwaffe*'s battle for air superiority, known as *Adler Tag* (Eagle Day); the prelude to Operation Sea Lion, the invasion of the British Isles. Yet, despite these successful attacks *Luftwaffe* commander Hermann Göring called off further strikes believing them to be somewhat lacking in effectiveness. Göring's lack of tactical understanding was perhaps not surprising, he did after all, famously switch the *Luftwaffe*'s priorities from hitting RAF airfields to bombing London, raining hell on the civilians below but leaving the airfields relatively untouched and the RAF free to destroy his bombers. This unwittingly ignited a debate over the virtues of strategic bombing which has raged ever since. Our Prussian friend would have been appalled, the Chain Homes were a perfect example of a CoG as they allowed fighters to be directed towards the bombers, and their comprehensive destruction could have made the outcome of the Battle of Britain, and the Second World War, very different.

That said, the Allies were also at risk from German air defences. Before the Battle of Britain had begun, the RAF had started to take the war to the Third Reich, performing a bombing raid on Berlin in August 1940. The dangers of AAA increased throughout the war. As such, formations of Allied bombers had to become larger to ensure that, to paraphrase British Prime Minister Stanley Baldwin, at least some of the bombers always got through to their target. The AAA was exacting a heavy loss on aircrew and aircraft, and subsequently degrading the effectiveness of the Allied bombing campaign against Nazi Germany. One report by the United States Army Air Force (USAAF) as it was known until 1947, notes that while the damage from enemy fighters wrought on its bombers operating over Europe had been reduced, the devastation caused by AAA or 'flak' (an acronym for *Flugabwehrkanone*; 'anti-aircraft cannon') had increased damage ten-fold for bombers compared to damage inflicted by enemy fighters. The puffs of black smoke that exploded around the B-17 Flying Fortresses and Avro Lancasters which threaded their dangerous paths to their targets, were much more harmful than their pint-sized explosions would suggest. Well-placed rounds could damage an aircraft, preventing it from dropping its bombs and, at worse shoot the aircraft out of the sky. Realising the effectiveness of flak, the *Luftwaffe* saturated its AAA coverage, clustering the weapons in citadel-like structures known as *Flaktürme* or Flak Towers, their forbidding, slab-like appearance leaving little doubt as to their destructive purpose.

The Germans had also developed the *Würzberg* gun-laying radar during World War II which was deployed from 1941 and used to connect flak batteries for guiding AAA. The *Würzburg* had a range of around 18 miles (29 km) and could pick up targets after they had been detected at long range by the *Freya* system. The fire control radar allegedly got its name from Wilhelm Runge, its inventor, blindly sticking a pin into a map and hitting the city of *Würzburg*. Production of *Würzburg* began in 1940 and around 3,000 would be built in three versions; 'A', 'B' and 'C' with the accuracy of the system steadily improving as time went by. The accuracy of the *Würzburg* was particularly good up to a range of around ten miles (16 km) and could give the radar operator an accurate picture as to the location of an incoming formation of aircraft.

Würzburg was joined by the *Freya* long-range EW radar system which had a range of 100 miles (160 km), and over 1,000 were constructed during the war. The radar was linked to Germany's network of ground observers to provide an embryonic Integrated Air Defence System (IADS). The first engagement that the RAF had with a *Freya* radar was on 18 December 1939, when eighteen RAF Wellington bombers were performing a daylight bombing attack on Germany. The radar was able to detect the bombers and direct fighter aircraft to intercept them.

The long-range radar could detect the incoming formation of aircraft and alert the *Würzburg* operators as to their expected avenue of attack. *Würzburg* would then watch the skies and once it had detected the formation, hand the targets off to flak batteries which could bring accurate fire to bear on the formation. The Germans invested heavily in radar technology, and it would not be long before networks of radar were positioned throughout occupied Europe covering many directions of possible advance.

The British took strenuous efforts to seek and destroy German radar and a high priority was placed on the *Würzburg* sets. During a reconnaissance sortie on 22 November 1941, an RAF photo-reconnaissance unit (PRU) Spitfire had taken a picture of a German radar installation at Bruneval near Le Havre on the French coast. Reginald Victor Jones, the British Assistant Director of Intelligence (Science) and radar expert, had stressed the need for an intensive effort to hunt down German radar systems after the acquisition of the famous Oslo Report by the British in 1939 which, amongst other things, detailed the characteristics of German EW radar technology.

The installation at Bruneval prompted further interest and another PRU sortie was performed on 5 December, this time with Flight Lieutenant Tony Hill at the Spitfire's controls. Flt. Lt. Hill's pictures revealed a 10 ft (3 m) diameter radar dish which resembled the *Würzburg* design. The British government decided that the Bruneval site would be attacked (codenamed Operation Biting) by a commando force of 120 troops from C Company, 2nd Battalion of the Parachute Regiment led by Major John Frost and including Flight Sergeant Charles Cox, a technician, who would assist with dismantling and carrying any parts of the *Würzburg* that the force could carry. The troops would parachute from twelve Armstrong-Whitley-V bombers commanded by Wing Commander PC Pickard from RAF 51 Squadron.

Once on the ground the force met some heavy resistance and suffered two killed and four taken prisoner. That said, Major Frost's force was able to photograph the radar and take some components back to the United Kingdom for examination. One of the most important things revealed by the analysis was that the radar was susceptible to countermeasures. However, one unwanted side-effect of the raid was that the Germans fortified their radar sites, determined that they would not be attacked in this way a second time. However, the positive side of this was that the fortified structure made enemy radar installations easier to locate. Operation Biting was notable in its use of commandos to assist the defence suppression task and was arguably the first example of the joint approach to SEAD, something that would later be utilised by the Israelis with great effect during the 1960s.

While the British performed commando raids to assist the defence suppression fight, aircraft were also brought to the fray, particularly hitting the factories which produced the *Würzburgs*. On 20 June 1943, RAF bombers were sent to attack the Zeppelin factory at Friedrichshafen which was thought to house a *Würzburg* production line. This was following photographs that had been taken in June 1943 which appeared to show a collection of radar reflectors outside the factory. Two days after Winston Churchill had personally viewed the photographs at RAF Medmenham, home of the RAF PRU, orders were sent to the RAF's No.5 Group to attack the Zeppelin works with their Lancaster bombers during the next full moon. The raid, which occurred on 20 June 1943, was a success and the *Würzburg* assembly line was smashed.

Thoughts also turned to defensive methods. This was still the early days of defence suppression, before the principles of surprise, weight, mass, balance and persistence were defined for the mission, but the germ of these ideas were present in how the Allies chose to confront the flak menace. True, the Germans had robust air defences around their cities and their key targets, but they were just as susceptible as any other defender to the rule that you cannot protect everywhere at once. Those prosecuting the bombing campaign therefore realised that one solution could be to fly around the flak emplacements on their way to and from the target. Another recommendation was for the crews to fly their

bombers as high as possible. However, the use of altitude to frustrate flak also had to be squared with the need to see the target
being attacked, so hiding behind cloud cover could not be an
option. A major railway marshalling yard may be quite visible
and characteristic from a considerable height, but a ball-bearings
factory may not and what is more, the latter may look rather like
surrounding buildings which do not have a military function.
The other idea was to space bombers at certain intervals or within
designated sections of airspace that would enable them to take
full advantage of the emerging radar countermeasures that the
Allies were starting to field.

A snapshot of the losses suffered by the Eighth Air Force over
one month, August 1944, illustrates how devastating radar-
guided flak could be. The USAAF sent almost 45,600 aircraft over
their targets. Of those aircraft, almost 11,700 suffered hits from
flak, around 26 per cent of the total. In 250 cases, the flak was sufficient to destroy the aircraft. Of all Eighth Air Force aircraft lost
during August 1944 in the European theatre to all causes, flak
claimed 70 per cent. In terms of damage suffered to Eighth Air
Force aircraft in theatre, flak was responsible for 84 per cent of
that damage. The fighter menace may have begun to dissipate as
the Allies smashed up the *Luftwaffe*, but undoubtedly ground-
based air defence was still a considerable force to be reckoned
with.

However help was at hand from a surprisingly simple in-
vention. Chaff, or Window as it was initially called by the British,
was used from 1943; initially as part of Operation Gomorrah, the
bombing of Hamburg. It was dispensed by aircraft and would
provide a confetti of thousands of tiny metallic strips of
aluminium foil which would lazily drift around the air and eventually down to earth. As they did this, they would reflect radar
beams back on themselves. The result was that these millions
of metal strips would show up as a series of returns on the
radar operator's scope. Situated well-away from the action, the
operator could not be sure if the strips were a deception or a
formation of bombers heading for a target. Window was
famously used on the eve of D-Day on the 4 June 1944 to create
a phantom bomber force attacking in the direction of Calais
rather than Normandy to fool the Germans as to the locations of

the Allied landings by convincing the operators of the *Würzburg* and *Freya* radar that a huge force of bombers was heading in that direction.

Window gave bomber crews protection from radar provided that they flew within 2,000 ft (609 m) of the cloud of metallic foil. Guidance to the bomber crews of the USAAF Eighth Air Force directed that they should not attack on a heading of more than five degrees difference from the Window dispensing aircraft to ensure that they did not appear as a separate radar return and thus a lucrative target. However, the system worked for a while, but eventually German radar operators got wise to Window and learned to differentiate between the cloud of foil and the bomber formations. Initially, The British Government's Chief Scientific Advisor, Professor Alexander Lindemann had counselled against employing Window on raids over Germany fearing that once the Germans realised that the foil strips were accompanying bombing raids where their air defence radar was being disrupted, they would see the ruse and use similar techniques during their raids on the UK. Ironically, the Germans had developed their own version of Window called *Düppel*, and held off using it over the UK for very similar reasons.

Window was not the only defence against radar, it was joined by Carpet. Unlike its cousin, this was not a physical counter-measure, but was instead one of the first ECMs to be used by attacking aircraft. In essence, Carpet transmitted radio waves to jam the *Würzburgs* thus depriving the flak batteries of their eyes which told them where the attacking bomber formation was located. However, like Window, the efficacy of Carpet was degraded the farther a bomber was operating from the aircraft carrying the equipment. Therefore, the spacing of the bomber formation *vis-à-vis* the Carpet-equipped aircraft became a matter for dextrous handling.

Carpet was the product of the rigorous research that both British and American scientists were performing to defeat the radar menace. The effort was two-fold: not only were counter-measures designed, but for these countermeasures to be effective, the scientists had to develop a comprehensive understanding of how German air-search radar actually worked as part of getting inside the German air-defence network's mindset. In modern parlance, this is known as building an understanding of the enemy's Electronic Order of Battle.

One of the methods of doing this was to use specially-equipped aircraft, known as Ferrets. These aircraft, were modified B-17F Flying Fortresses which carried no bombs, but were instead fitted with an APA-24 Direction Finding antenna which would listen and record the radio frequencies that German radar used. This enabled the Carpet system, and later the Mandrell radar jamming equipment, then to be tuned to that wavelength to produce interference to disrupt the radar and thus make the flak inaccurate. The equipment would be mounted in the lead aircraft of a bomber formation and was credited with some considerable success in spoofing the *Luftwaffe*'s radar. The USAAF had the 16th Reconnaissance Squadron based at Foch airfield, Tunisia, and used Boeing B-17F Ferrets on bombing raids into Europe.

B-17F Ferret missions began in 1943 and had several objectives in mind. The first was to monitor the radar stations and locate their position which could then be attacked by other bombers. The immediate effect would be to cost the Germans precision in their flak direction, thus rendering it less effective. However, the destruction of the radar would have other effects. Radar was a time-consuming and intricate thing to build. Line replacement units could not be mass produced like artillery shells and, therefore, it would take time to replace equipment that had been destroyed and would lead to a subsequent gap in coverage which the Allies could then exploit. Secondly, once they realised that they were the target, the morale of the German radar operators was bound to suffer, as was the morale of the personnel manning the flak emplacements as they realised that their fire would be increasingly inaccurate. Finally, the strikes on the radar stations would kill experienced German radar operators, thus depriving the *Luftwaffe* of the training cadre who could pass their wisdom onto younger generations who would need to learn the mysteries of radar afresh. Moreover, radar and personnel which survived the attacks would become increasingly overloaded as other units were lost and therefore less effective. Thus, the German air search radar was the CoG in their flak system.

The first Ferret missions by the 16th Reconnaissance Squadron were performed on 21 April 1943 from Tunisia and the unit continued to perform its missions notably supporting Operation Avalanche, the Allied invasion of Italy, when it supported landing operations on the island of Salerno in September 1943. As the year drew to a close, the squadron would have a total of thirty-five B-17F Ferret aircraft at its disposal. The unit came to the fore during the Big Week bombing campaign of 20-25 February 1944 which unleashed a massive campaign against the German aviation industry and helped the Allies to achieve air superiority prior to Operation Overlord in 1944.

The USAAF was not alone in developing specially equipped aircraft for radar hunting. The RAF was working on Project Abdullah by 1944. Abdullah was the codename for an electronic radar hunting device that was fitted to three Hawker Typhoon aircraft which belonged to 1320 Special Duty Flight in May 1944. Abdullah consisted of a Cathode Ray Tube (CRT) which was connected to a radar homing receiver. This receiver could be tuned to the known operating frequencies of German radar. The equipment would be switched on and the Typhoon would fly around the area where radar was suspected and wait for the Abdullah equipment to pick up the radar transmissions. Once Abdullah alerted the pilot that radar was active, the pilot would visually try to acquire the target. They would then fly towards it and fire smoke rockets to mark the target for their accompanying escort of ground-attack aircraft. These tactics were not unlike those which would be used by the earliest Wild Weasel aircraft in the Vietnam War.

The initiative was an impressive step forward but, as with Sir Issac Newton's dictum that every reaction has an equal and opposite reaction, the presence of the Abdullah aircraft would lead the German radar operators to switch off their radar once they had learned that keeping it switched on invited attack. The Germans pioneered this technique which would be used time and again by radar operators in every conflict henceforth. Keeping radar activated invites attack, switching it off invites safety. However, Abdullah had other shortcomings. The radar receiving equipment had to be preset to a particular German radar frequency before the aircraft took off for its mission. If the Germans changed their radar frequency, then the Abdullah aircraft would have no way of locating the radar.

One of the most notable SEAD raids occurred during Operation Market Garden in September 1944, made famous by Cornelius Ryan's book *A Bridge Too Far*, which relates the brave Allied attempts to seize the bridges over the Waal and Rhine rivers at Njimegen and Arnhem respectively to open the next stage of a land route into Germany following the liberation of Belgium and France. The operation was to feature a significant effort by the Eighth Air Force to perform SEAD against German flak emplacements posing a grave threat to the airborne landings of the First Allied Airborne Army and their accompanying 1,438 C-47 Dakotas, and over 3,000 gliders which were to dispense the American, British and Polish airborne forces to take bridges at Son, Veghel, Grave, Njimegan, Arnhem and Oosterbrook across a north-east/south-west axis. The airborne operation to seize the bridge was absolutely imperative to the overall success of Market Garden as they awaited the arrival and reinforcements of the British XXX Corps. The flak emplacements were a clear and present danger.

The Eighth Air Force's orders were to bombard 'the anti-aircraft installations along the routes to be followed by the troop carrier aircraft and in the areas surrounding the drop and landing zones. The B-17s belonging to the 1st and 3rd Bombardment Divisions based in the UK, were earmarked for the task. Photographic reconnaissance had provided those planning the operation with up to 112 targets for the B-17s. Needless to say, this was to be a classic example of the mass approach to SEAD. The aircraft were to carry fragmentation bombs as they would be attacking from altitude and thus area attacks to hit the flak emplacements would be more appropriate. Low-level attacks were the preserve of the faster, more agile fighter-bombers.

Prior to the airborne operation on 17 September, an armada of 872 bombers heaved themselves into the late summer air and made their way to towards their targets in the Netherlands. Over the bombardment area, these aircraft dispensed their ordnance onto the AAA emplacements below, but that did not stop them suffering damage from their indented victims.

The Flying Fortresses were not alone; they were joined by P-47 Thunderbolts from the Eighth Air Force. Their task was to get in close and hit flak emplacements which covered the southern ingress routes for the Dakotas. These aircraft were joined by a further four groups of P-47s from the Ninth Air Force. The P-47 was the ideal tool for the task. With its rugged, sturdy construction the aircraft could take a fair degree of punishment which was very important given the strength of German anti-aircraft artillery in the area of operations. But these aircraft gave as good as they got. They were outfitted with eight 0.5-in (12.7-mm) M2 Browning machine guns and they could also dispense up to 2,000 lb (907 kg) of bombs on the emplacements. During the Market Garden anti-flak operations they dispensed a total of 287 x 260 lb (118 kg) bombs and fired over 122,600 rounds. The tally for the Thunderbolt pilots was eighty flak positions damaged and fifty-nine destroyed.

Market Garden was not the success that was hoped for and still remains a subject of controversy. There is not the space here to discuss the merits and shortcomings of this operation, which can be left to other historians, but there is room to look at the SEAD lessons learned from the operation. The USAAF 56th Fighter Group, which flew Thunderbolts in the operation, noted that thirty-nine of its aircraft began a mission to attack flak targets in the vicinity of Turnhout, south of the Belgian-Dutch border. Weather over the target area, which included fairly low cloud cover and a haze which frustrated the pilot's visibility scotched hopes of locating the AAA targets from higher altitudes. Moreover, the flak bombardment being suffered by the unit dispersed the formation and claimed the scalps over sixteen aircraft as they were forced down into the weeds both to locate their targets and to press home their attacks. The lesson was obvious, but it was also instructive. The closer the attacking aircraft got to the flak, the more intense the fire became and the likelihood that the aircraft would be shot down increased. Yet, for the bombers the higher altitude the aircraft flew, the less accurate was their bombardment against the flak emplacements unless area weapons were used and these aircraft also had to contend with significant anti-aircraft fire.

The results of AAA suppression during Operation Market Garden were 118 anti-aircraft gun emplacements destroyed and around 127 damaged. However, the cost of this was 104 aircraft lost to flak over 4,320 sorties. AAA suppression sorties, of which the Allies performed 646, cost thirty-seven aircraft. The conclusion from Market Garden was that the use of low-flying attack aircraft for AAA suppression was largely curtailed in favour of passive measures such as chaff and evasive manoeuvres. Another approach was to use artillery to suppress the flak positions before aircraft approached a target. Such measures had already been put into operation during the encirclement of Cherbourg, France, following the Operation Overlord invasion of June 1944. However, the results of the artillery-AAA suppression were mixed. That said, artillery would be used for defence suppression in other conflicts over the next sixty years, notably in the Middle East and later during Operation Desert Storm in 1992.

This joint approach was taken to the issue of flak suppression in March 1945, as the Allies began their Operation Varsity offensive to cross the Rhine at Wesel. The area was surrounded by 922 AAA gun barrels and the Allies suppression efforts saw 8,100 tons of bombs dropped on German AAA emplacements during 3,741 sorties spread over three days. Of these German AAA positions, ninety-five were attacked with 24,000 rounds of artillery though only a few hits were scored using this method. The German flak was not completely suppressed and still claimed 381 American and 160 British gliders of the airborne assault out of a total of 1,125 gliders: over 50 per cent. In addition, AAA also claimed sixteen transport aircraft and fifty-two towing planes. Despite the all-out joint offensive against the German air defences, flak had managed to exact a heavy toll on the Allies. Before the advent of the high-speed Anti-Radiation Missile, SEAD would be a mass affair which would consume large numbers of aircraft and artillery for often limited results.

Major strides were made in defeating AAA along with locating air defence radar as the curtains drew on the Second World War. However, the end of the conflict also betrayed another danger which was waiting in the wings. As the horrors visited on continental Europe by Nazi Germany were being uncovered, so were the technological advances that the Germans had made in the fields of rocketry. Londoners knew to their cost the destruction that these advancements would bring having suffered attacks from the V-1 Flying Bomb proto-cruise missiles, and later V-2 ballistic missiles. However Dr. Werner Von Braun, who led the

Nazi rocket research programme, together with his scientists and an army of press-ganged slave labourers had made other key advances in the world of missiles. These included anti-shipping missiles such as the 'Fritz-X' but most ominously for pilots, guided anti-aircraft rockets. History tells us that German scientists had perfected the *Wasserfall* SAM but that Adolf Hitler's arrogance had scoffed at the project claiming an interest only in offensive weapons, causing it to be neglected until 1943.

It was in this year that the project was revived in the face of increasing Allied bombardment against Germany and the slow death of *Luftwaffe* air superiority. So it was that on 8 January 1944 that the *Wasserfall* took to the skies for a test flight. The missile was huge, standing over 25 ft (7.6 m) in height and weighing a staggering 7 tons, yet its speed was in the region of 1,600 ft (500 m) per second and it had a range of 12 miles (20 km). The weapon's guidance system had been based on the *Rheintochter* SAM which had been ordered by the German Army in November 1942. The test firings of the weapon, named after the mythical maidens of the Rhine from Wagner's *Der Ring des Nibelungen* opera, had begun in August 1943, making the weapon the world's first SAM and eighty-two test firings were completed and an air-to-air version was also developed, but the weapon would never equip the Army and the project was cancelled on 6 February 1945.

Wasserfall had a radar-based guidance systems. Once in the thick of a formation of aircraft it would detonate. The logic of the weapon was not unlike the later nuclear-tipped anti-aircraft missiles such as the American MIM-14 Nike Hercules which appeared during the Cold War and was designed to use a shotgun approach by detonating a huge quantity of, in this case nuclear, explosive in the middle of a formation to destroy as many enemy bombers or incoming missile warheads as possible. Certainly, *Wasserfall* was far ahead of its time, but none were ever fired against Allied aircraft. Yet the importance of *Wasserfall* was that it demonstrated that the Surface-to-Air Missile was a viable concept. This was not lost on the United States and Soviet Union which would use captured German technical documents and German scientists to kick start the development of Cold War missile technology.

Pacific Theatre

Early SEAD efforts were not confined to Europe during World War II. The USAAF focused on methods of defeating Japanese anti-aircraft radar and protecting their own aircraft. As the 1930s drew to a close, Japan pioneered a radar system which could detect aircraft but which could not provide any information on the aircraft's height or bearing. This radar became known as the IJA Type-A ('Imperial Japanese Army Type-A') with around 100 IJA-Type-A stations constructed in China. Interestingly, both the Japanese Army and Navy were working on radar designs, but inter-service rivalry prevented them from discussing their work with each other. Similarly, the Japanese received scant assistance from the Germans on radar development with the latter zealously guarding the technological advances they had made. Each side also believed that they had little to teach the other; for instance during official inspections of radar equipment by the Japanese in Germany, the Germans would not discuss the *Freya* radar.

That said, Japanese radar design did develop during the war. The Navy developed the Imperial Japanese Navy (IJN) Mark 1 Model 1 EW radar with a range of 90 miles (145 km), with around eighty sets being constructed. The Japanese Army meanwhile built the IJA Tachi-6 system which could search out to 185 miles (300 km). The radar entered service in 1942 and around 350 were built.

The Japanese Army deployed its radar throughout the empire to provide warning of Allied air attack and also for the guidance of AAA triggering the anti-radar war in the Pacific theatre. In many ways, the radar war in the Far East mirrored what was happening in Europe, and the USAAF made use of the Ferret equipment, this time fitted to Consolidated B-24H Liberator aircraft and modified Boeing B-29 Superfortress Ferret-equipped bombers. However, because of the long ranges involved in the Pacific theatre these aircraft were termed Ravens. Yet it was the Douglas B-25B Invaders which were the first dedicated, self-contained SEAD aircraft of the war. They possessed the APA-24 radar-locating equipment and eight cannons in the nose. It was a lethal and terrifying combination. The aircraft would use their equipment for radar location, acquire the target visually and then blast it to pieces with guns. The approach was not unlike that used by the RAF Typhoons, but unlike the Typhoons these aircraft were armed and therefore extremely dangerous. Unwittingly, the USAAF had drawn the template for the later Wild Weasel SEAD aircraft which would appear during the Vietnam War.

A game of cat-and-mouse developed between the United States and Japan as far as the latter's radar was concerned. Realising that they could be attacked, Japanese scientists improved the quality and sophistication of their radar and the Americans responded by improving the sophistication of their radar detection equipment. Much of the expertise developed by the 16th Reconnaissance Squadron in Europe was leveraged into the battle against Japanese radar. The B-25Bs operated in conjunction with the B-29 Ravens. The latter located and jammed the Japanese radar and the B-25s would press home the attack.

Korea

No sooner had the Pacific War ended than the United States found itself embroiled in war once again in the Far East, this time alongside seventeen other Allied nations as part of a United Nations force raised to repulse the Communist takeover of the Korean peninsula which began on 25 June 1950 as North Korean forces crossed the 38th parallel into the South. The Korean peninsula had been partitioned following the end of World War II and Japan's eviction from the peninsula. The Soviet Union occupied the northern part and the United States occupied the south. Once again, American and Allied aircraft would face the scourge of radar directed anti-aircraft fire.

By early 1952, the United States Marine Corps (USMC) was hitting AAA positions. Spotter aircraft looked for North Korean flak emplacements and then strike aircraft were called in to attack them. Later that year, the USMC published procedures regarding the attack of AAA positions which called for suppressive fire to be directed at AAA emplacements half a minute before attack aircraft hit their target.

On 6 August 1952, the US Army and USAF published their *Suppress* plan which detailed how artillery was to support the fight against AAA during air attacks. Proximity-fused artillery fire would be used to attack AAA positions before attack aircraft arrived, with the end of the bombardment being signalled by a smoke or illumination round. The experiment, which was trialled between 25 September – 25 October 1952, saw one USAF aircraft being lost for every 1,816 CAS sorties; this was in contrast to the average losses of one aircraft per 380 CAS sorties. What made these results even more impressive was the fact that the North Korean Communist forces had tripled the number of AAA positions they had in the US Army's IX Corps (the unit performing the experiment) sector as the trial was conducted.

Needless to say, the success of the experiment resulted in it becoming standard defence suppression doctrine from 2 December 1952. A North American Aviation T-6 Mosquito aircraft would lead a formation of fighter-bombers towards their target. Once the target had been verified by the fighter-bomber pilots, all AAA positions within 2,500 yards (2,286 m) of the target were engaged before and during the fighter-bombers' attack. The effect was that one aircraft was lost per 917 CAS sorties in December 1952, decreasing to one aircraft per 1,285 CAS sorties in January 1953 and one aircraft per 2,581 CAS sorties in March. Clearly the new procedures were having a positive impact.

As they had been five years before, the familiar countermeasures saw the light of day once more with ECMs and chaff working to foil the Soviet-supplied radar. Once again, the SEAD aircraft were modified Douglas TB-26J Marauders with their APA-24 systems listening for Soviet radar frequencies using their windscreen-mounted antennae. Crucially, these B-26s would be used to provide SEAD support for the B-29 bombing raids on targets in the north. The missions were organised by the respective bomb groups in theatre, but from 18 September 1953 as the conflict drew to a close, they became the preserve of the 11th Tactical Reconnaissance Squadron/67th Tactical Reconnaissance Wing (11th TRS/67th TRW) which operated RB-26 reconnaissance aircraft from Kimpo, Seoul. This was an echo of the Ferret- and Window-equipped aircraft of World War II which escorted bombers over Germany, but this time the Marauders were armed and could prosecute radar and flak targets as they were discovered, along with the search-lights and sound locators which were also used by the North Korean Communist forces. As well as using mass, a balanced approach to SEAD was also utilised by the Allies.

Fortunately, the United States did not have to face the levels of AAA attrition that it had suffered during World War II but that said, it could not ignore the danger and radar-guided flak exacted its toll. Altogether the USAF flew 721,000 sorties during the conflict, which cost 1,465 aircraft. However, of these losses, around 140 were the victims of air-to-air combat. A further 500 crashed because of non-combat related reasons while the balance of 825 were victims of AAA.

The Korean War ceasefire took hold on 27 July 1953 and the 11th TRS/67th TRW returned to its home at Itami AFB, Japan. The SEAD lessons-learned were taken on by the 9th TRS which was established at Shaw AFB, South Carolina. This would be the first electronic warfare squadron of Tactical Air Command and was tasked with the location of enemy radar and direction of strike aircraft for their destruction. An exercise in 1955 called Sage Bush noted the role that radar-jamming aircraft could play in support of a wider air campaign. The final report on the exercise urged 'that the tactics and techniques of radar-busting operations be exploited to the fullest. The capability, when incorporated in high performance aircraft, will greatly aid the theatre commander in the effective execution of operations'. However, the USAF was slow to act on these observations. The country was settling down to a time of peace following Korea, albeit in the tense atmosphere of the Cold War with the Soviets and the risk of Armageddon therein. The 9th TRS, which had done so much to advance the radar hunter-killer team, lost the latter part of their mission, after they re-equipped with Douglas RB-66 Destroyer photo-reconnaissance aircraft which were bereft of an attack function.

Meanwhile, the air defence threat remained. Such was the tension of the Cold War that the USAF began reconnaissance flights on the edges of Soviet airspace to gain an insight into the country's air defences and their reaction time. However, in 1953 North Atlantic Treaty Organisation (NATO) Intelligence had discovered the existence of a new Soviet weapons system which would go on to plague the lives of USAF pilots, namely the C-75 (NATO reporting name SA-2 Guideline) SAM. This weapon would famously claim the Lockheed U-2 aircraft of Central Intelligence Agency (CIA) pilot Francis Gary Powers on 1 May 1960 as he flew over Sverdlovsk in the southern USSR, after departing from Badaber AFB, Peshawar in Pakistan on a CIA over-flight of the Soviet Union. The whole sorry affair severally chilled already frigid relations between the United States and Soviet Union. The SA-2 would claim another U-2 during the Cuban Missile Crisis of 1962 when Major Richard S. Heyser's aircraft was knocked out of the sky on 14 October 1962. The U-2 was the aircraft which revealed to the world the Soviet preparations to station Intermediate Range Ballistic Missiles on the Caribbean Island of Cuba. Another life was claimed when Major Rudolph Anderson's U-2 was shot down over Cuba on 27 October 1962.

The SAM age had dramatically announced itself to the world flying at speeds of Mach 3 through a clear blue sky. The SA-2 was a terrifying new weapon which the United States Air Force viewed with foreboding. Three years after Major Anderson's life was cut short (Gary Powers survived being shot down), pilots from across the United States would be meeting the Guideline in the skies over Vietnam. Anti-aircraft warfare would never be the same again, and SEAD would come of age.

CHAPTER TWO

Vietnam and SEAD

Amerian involvement in Vietnam had begun under the administration of President Dwight D. Eisenhower, following the French withdrawal from Indochina in 1954 amid mounting violence and then open civil war after the French struggled to keep hold of their precarious possession in southeast Asia. The Japanese had occupied the French colony from 1941 to 1945 during World War II, but with the yoke of imperialism thrown off, the Vietnamese were now anxious to discard French rule. The resistance movement was led by Ho Chi Minh and had a decidedly Marxist bent. The country was effectively split down the middle following the Geneva Accords between the UK, USA, Soviet Union, China, Laos and Cambodia which saw Vietnam divided between North and South with Ngo Dinh Diem as Prime Minister of the south and the communist North under President Ho Chi Minh, with its respective capitals of Saigon and Hanoi. In keeping with the prevailing American policy of containing the expansion of Communism around the world, US military advisers trickled into the country along with financial support to assist the South Vietnamese authorities in resisting the infiltration of the North Vietnamese-backed National Front for the Liberation of South Vietnam (a.k.a. Viet Cong or VC) from the North. By 1963 that trickle had become a flood and the number of US military advisers in the country under the United States Military Assistance Advisory Group grew from between 746 in 1961 to 9,430 in 1968.

The catalyst for full-scale US involvement was the infamous Gulf of Tonkin incident. On 2 August 1964 two US Navy destroyers, USS *Maddox* and USS *Turner Joy* were attacked by

North Vietnamese P-4 torpedo boats. American President
Lyndon B. Johnson authorised an attack on the docks of the
torpedo boats and a Petrol-Oil-Lubrication facility at Vinh in
North Vietnam. As a response on Capital Hill, the Tonkin Gulf
Resolution was pushed through Congress and approved on 7
August 1964, stipulating support to 'the determination of the
President, as Commander-in-Chief, to take all necessary
measures to repel any armed attack against the forces of the
United States and to prevent further aggression'. Around 3,000
US troops from the US Army's 173rd Airborne Division were
despatched to provide security at Da Nang AFB in the central
coastal area of South Vietnam. The Joint Chiefs of Staff led by
General Earle Gilmore Wheeler drafted a plan of attack to include
over ninety targets in North Vietnam which could be hit from the
air. This would form the basis for the now legendary Operation
Rolling Thunder, which began on 2 March 1965 with the USAF
and Navy hitting the supply depot at Xom Bang north of the 17th
Parallel, the border between the two Vietnams.

   Rolling Thunder caught North Vietnamese air defences largely
unaware and unprepared. The defences that the North possessed
almost seemed an afterthought; little more than a handful of
visually-guided anti-aircraft guns and radar-directed search-
lights for guidance. These systems were of Soviet designs and
were leftovers from, most recently, the war in Korea and also
World War II. Even by 1964, the air defences of the People's Army
of Vietnam (PAVN), as the Northern forces were known,
included 500 AAA pieces. SAMs were not something that the
early Rolling Thunder attacks had to worry about. North
Vietnam had, after all, been called a 'raggedy-assed fourth-rate
country' by President Johnson. How wrong he was. The North
would develop one of the most sophisticated air defence systems
in the world using both SAMs and artillery connected to radar.
The air defence system operators would develop equally innovative tactics. Ho Chi Minh was able to call on assistance from the
Soviet Union and paraphrasing a later hit single of the time they
would get by with a little help from their friends.

   However, the *Politburo* was still smarting from their eye-
blinking which ended the Cuban Missile Crisis and were
determined that their South-east Asian protégés would not take

a beating from the evil Yankee imperialists and prepared to bolster their friends with the latest air defence technology that they had to offer. So the North Vietnamese air defences had an impressive make-over, radar-directed AAA was despatched along with the infamous SA-2 Guideline which arrived in theatre in the Spring of 1965, with a pair of SA-2 regiments located at Hanoi and Haiphong in central North Vietnam on the North Vietnamese coast, with six batteries each of which could be deployed to over thirty-two prepared sites around North Vietnam. The pre-prepared sites included launching pads positioned in a so-called 'Star of David' pattern with networks of tracks surrounding each pad for either a launcher or accompanying equipment such as radar. Of course this made the design relatively easy to spot from the air. Because of this, the NVA took efforts to conceal their location. That said the Star of David pattern was not the only site layout that was used. Under Soviet advice, the SA-2s were also arranged in a fan pattern concealed behind ridge lines or alternatively, perhaps only one or two launchers would be located under jungle canopy making their detection difficult. Moreover, the NVA also pressed local labour into service using carpenters to build fake launchers to confuse American reconnaissance efforts.

The Americans first got wind of the Guideline's arrival from reconnaissance flights which yielded pictures of SA-2 sites being constructed around Hanoi and Haiphong. The fun and games over Cuba in 1962 had taught photo-intelligence interpreters how to recognise an SA-2 site. Scores of sites were created throughout the north which could host SA-2 systems and accompanying radar. The danger was there but the sites had not yet downed any American aircraft. US Defense Secretary Robert McNamara insisted that no pre-emptive strikes be performed on the sites, fearing that this would antagonise the Soviets and force them to escalate the conflict. NcNamara was no doubt following his dictum that he explains in the 2004 *Fog of War* documentary in which he stresses the importance of giving one's opponent room to negotiate, but the result was that these sites remained functioning and ready to unleash death.

Some individuals in the intelligence community felt that the SA-2s were an insurance policy for Ho Chi Minh and that the north would desist from using them unless it felt truly threat-ened. In mid June 1964 a reconnaissance flight by a Douglas EB-66 Destroyer detected the telltale emissions of the Guideline's P12 'Spoon Rest' 171 mile (275 km) target acquisition radar and by 23rd Signals from the Fan Song tracking radar had also been detected. However, disaster struck on 24 July 1965: F-4C Phantom-IIs of the 15th Tactical Fighter Wing were about 55 miles (88 km) north-west of the capital over rolling terrain. Out from below an SA-2 rushed into the sky exploding its 430 lb (195 kg) warhead into the formation of aircraft and causing the destruc-tion of one of the Phantoms and damage to all the other aircraft in the package. The retaliation came in the form of forty-six F-105Ds hitting the SAM site north-west of Hanoi which had shot the Phantom out of the sky. A cause and effect pattern evolved where every time an American plane was lost, the offending SAM site was attacked by a large group of aircraft. The problem was that this was not an efficient use of airpower given that between July and November 1965 three Republic F-105 Thunderchiefs, two Vought F-8 Crusaders, the same number of Phantoms and a Douglas A-4 Skyhawk were lost for the destruction of eight SAM sites. This was working out at one aircraft per SAM site and the air force was determined to find a better way of doing business. In 1965 alone the NVA hit one aircraft for every thirteen missiles expended and by that point they had sixty SAM sites positioned across the North.

The objective of the Rolling Thunder campaign was to restrict the supplies coming across the North-South Vietnamese border for the Vietcong. From December 1964 until mid-1968, the USAF and the US Navy was permitted to perform SEAD missions, but the problem was that due to political interference from the highest levels in the White House there was considerable control exercised over what could and could not be hit. Until the summer of '68 the SEAD attacks followed a highly piecemeal approach. They were performed primarily in support of other packages of aircraft conducting air-to-ground missions and not as part of an overall campaign to subdue and destroy the PAVN's air defences. While the SEAD attacks were remaining fragmented, the PAVNs missiles, radar and guns were anything but, and were steadily growing in size, sophistication and connectivity as the campaign dragged on. The problem was that this built redundancy into the system, by which a single, or even several, attacks on isolated air-defence targets would not sufficiently degrade the system as a whole.

The US Navy was already performing SEAD during Rolling Thunder using A-4 and A-6 aircraft which were equipped with Radar Warning Receivers (RWRs). Ironically, the USAF had been offered RWRs and locator technology which had been produced by the Bendix Corporation but this was not pursued as, at the time, the USAF did not perceive a requirement for it. The company had originally suggested fitting a Radar Homing and Warning System (RHAWS) to an F-100F, but this idea was rejected again, as the USAF did not have a formal requirement for it, despite the damage that the force was sustaining from SAMs. The Thunderchief was a good choice for the RHAWS given that these aircraft were already operating with the QRC-253-2 radar homing systems which had been fitted to a small number of aircraft during Exercise Goldfire in 1964, which studied the aircraft's ability to detect a Hawk SAM site

The US Navy would perform SEAD by flying so-called Alpha Strikes with formations of aircraft which originally included Douglas A-1 Skyraiders; although these were later phased out of Navy service and transferred to the South Vietnam Air Force from 1970. The Skyraiders were replaced by the Grumman A-6 Intruder for Rolling Thunder missions soon after their commencement. For suppressing PAVN flak, the Douglas A-4 Skyhawk became the aircraft of choice. Their task was to lead the Alpha Strike package and engage the AAA emplacements.

But it was in the wake of the Phantom shootdown that Brigadier General KC Dempster was directed by General John P. McConnell, USAF Chief of Staff, to find a method of countering the SAMs. The Air Staff Dempster Committee reported back to its boss. The committee made several recommendations. Firstly, a number of aircraft were to be modified with specialist electronics to allow them to seek out SAM sites which could then be destroyed be accompanying aircraft carrying air-to-ground munitions. Secondly, the committee advised that a dedicated anti-radar missile should be developed along with electronic jamming equipment which would be able to disrupt the radar.

However, they stressed that the immediate priority was for an RHAWS to alert an aircrew that they were being painted by enemy radar.

On the recommendations of the Dempster Committee, the USAF purchased a number of different systems. The committee had already reviewed the results of the Goldfire experiments and took proposals for RHAWS equipment from both Bendix King and Applied Technologies Incorporated. It would be the latter which won the contract, and the committee recommended that purchases be made of the company's off-the-shelf Vector IV RHAWS, IR-133 panoramic scan receiver and the WR-300 receiver, the latter tuned to the guidance and control frequencies for the SA-2 which would alert the crew that a missile had been launched by the flashing of a large red light, marked 'launch' in front of the backseat crew member (who was known in the Wild Weasel community as the 'Bear'). Amazingly, the WR-300 system had been developed entirely on the basis of electronic emissions obtained from a single SA-2 launch, but the main thing was that the system worked. This piece of kit later became known as the AN/APR-26 in USAF nomenclature. The Vector IV could listen for hostile radar signals across the S, C and X-band frequencies upon which EW, fire control and SAM radar operated. Once this system picked up a telltale radar emission, it would display the information on a CRT in the aircraft's cockpit, giving an indication of the direction of the radar with a strobe. What is more, the Vector could also alert the crew to the type of radar that was tracking them, be it EW, fire control or SAM. The technology was undoubtedly a major step forward and would finally give the Air Force a degree of situational awareness as regards the radar threat. Also fitted to the aircraft was a Mohawk Midgetape 400 tape recorder. Following the downing of the Phantom on 24 July, the need for the technology was becoming very pressing. Since that incident, the PAVN succeeded in bringing down twenty-five aircraft out of the 171 which were lost over North Vietnam in 1965, this translated roughly into a single hit for every thirteen missiles that the North fired.

With the equipment in the bag, the next stage was to find an aircraft. Four F-100Fs had already been used as the test beds for the electronics requested by Dempster. The aircraft had several benefits; it was already available and as a two-seater it could accommodate a Bear to monitor the radar warning equipment. Testing of the aircraft and its electronics was completed by 19 November 1965 at the Air Proving Ground Center at Eglin Air Force Base (AFB) Florida following testing at Edwards AFB, California. By now the initiative had acquired the moniker Project Wild Weasel.

Flight testing of the four aircraft with their new equipment moved forward at Edwards AFB. Minor tweaks were required for the Super Sabre because of problems that were caused by buffeting attributed to the antenna installation for the new equipment, although this was later attributed to the gun system in the nose and legend has it that a crew chief remedied the problem by fitting some Golf tees to the gun assembly to stop it rattling around. Additional flight testing was completed at Eglin before the aircraft were handed over to their first crews.

The evolution and development of the PAVN IADS did not remain static from the first Soviet donation of Guidelines and AAA. It was following the Gulf of Tonkin incident that North Vietnam began a significant investment into its air defences including both ground-based systems and also interceptor aircraft. It continued as the war unfolded and by August of 1966 the system was fully integrated. What that meant in practice was that the NVA could share radar data across its SAM and AAA sites; the latter of which would eventually include 0.57 in (14 5 mm), 1.4 in (37 mm), 2.2 in (57 mm), 3.3 in (85 mm) and 3.9 in (100 mm) guns. Connectivity would allow radar in one location to spot an incoming formation of aircraft, plot its position and likely direction, and then pass that information to either a SAM or AAA site which could then attack the formation. In short, it made the IADS far more responsive and coordinated, and made the lives of American pilots that bit more difficult. By the summer of 1967, the vision of the NVA had improved still further, with 270 S-75 Fan Song 93 mile (150 km) range fire control radar arrayed throughout the North. This was the Soviets most advanced radar for the time, and these were linked to an astonishing number of AAA pieces which may have numbered up to 7,000 guns; including 3.9 in (100 mm) radar-guided weapons such as the KS-19 AAA gun system.

Training

With the development of the first four test aircraft completed it was time to train the crews. Taking over from Colonel Kim Kropuik, Major Garry Wiliard began to assemble crews of pilots and weapons systems officers who would perform the first missions. It was absolutely imperative that the crews worked well together, understood, and above all, trusted each other because of the danger of the sorties. The anti-SAM strikes would be very risky. There was precious room for error and the tactical situation could change very quickly. In October, the crews would begin flying against the Soviet Air Defense Simulator (SADS) which was positioned on the Eglin Range and was essentially composed of a beacon which could be tuned to known Soviet air defence radar frequencies. The training focused on flying towards the Eglin beacon until it appeared on the AN/APR-25 scope. The Bear would describe the location of the radar to the pilot and talk them onto its position. The pilot would then make a standard attack run before pulling aloft and attacking from a different direction. Once the aircraft had been deployed to theatre and the programme moved forward, the course for those training to become Wild Weasels was to fly twenty-one sorties against the SADS beacon, one of which was also located on the Hawthorne Test Range in Nevada.

From 1966, the crews would also practice firing an inert AGM-45 Shrike anti-radar missile (ARM), and from 1968, the AGM-78 Standard ARM, which superseded the Shrike. From early 1968, the Wild Weasel backseat crew were able to benefit from a North American T-39F training aircraft, nicknamed 'Teeny Weeny Weasel', which carried the electronic equipment that they would use for the mission. Three crew members could be trained on each flight and these training sorties were flown against the Soviet radar simulators. Pilots would also fly on the T-39F to gain an understanding of the Bear's task.

Regarding the 'backseater's' nickname one adage says that it was derived from an arcade shooting game where a metal bear would stop and roar every time it was shot. Alternatively, it was said that some of the backseat crew members would place their hands on the back of the pilot's seat and roar every time that a SAM missed their aircraft. Other explanations include brown bears being used in the first ejector seat tests during which they were propelled out of the rear seat in a tandem cockpit by the pilot.

Wild Weasel I

Four crews would perform the first Wild Weasel missions and they had been paired-up at Eglin during their training. They included Captains Al Lamb and Jack Donovan; Ed Sandilius and Ed White; John Pitchford and Bob Trier; George Kerr and Donald Madden, and Maurice Fricke and Walt Lifsey. Interestingly, when the officers volunteered for the mission they were not sure what they were letting themselves in for due to the intense secrecy that surrounded the programme. The crews were told that Wild Weasel was the codename for a flying command post mission using the F-100F. In 1965 November the first four F-100Fs left Eglin for Hickham AFB, Hawaii, and from there to Anderson AFB, Guam. Air Force Secretary Harold Brown famously told the crews that; 'if the SAMs don't get you, they at least force you down from your attack to within altitude of North Vietnamese AAA; the strike forces are taking a beating. And with these hopeful, encouraging words ringing in their ears, the crews departed for South East Asia. On 25 November, the aircraft left Anderson AFB and made an almost six hour flight to Korat AFB, Thailand arriving in time for Thanksgiving dinner.

At Korat, the aircraft were bedded down with the 355th and 388th Tactical Fighter Wings (TFWs), with the F-100Fs under the operational control of the latter as part of a new unit called the 6234th TFW Wild Weasel Detachment. The two fighter wings had briefings with the Weasel flyers regarding the F-100F's capabilities and how it could support the strike force. By 28 November, it was time to begin orientation missions close to the North Vietnamese border, alongside EB-66 aircraft. The routine called for the F-100Fs to take off, then rendezvous with a tanker and then, with the EB-66, fly up and down the border to listen for radar emissions. During these flights, it was possible to test the AN/APR-25 and IR-133 systems which worked well, but the proof of the AN/APR-26s capabilities would not come until the aircraft was actually under attack from a SAM.

The experiences of using the F-100Fs alongside the EB-66 aircraft for electronic reconnaissance were such that during the orientation flights both aircraft types recorded a total of 109 radar intercepts of which eighty-four signals were received simultaneously by the Weasel and the Destroyer and of these seventy-one were identified as the same by the crews of both aircraft. The orientation flights concluded on the 1 December and it was now time to take the war to the SAM sites. Wild Weasel missions were codenamed Iron Hand and the F-100Fs would lead a formation of Republic F-105D Thunderchiefs looking for launchers. The Super Sabres were armed with a combination of 0.78 in (20 mm) rounds, two drop tanks and up to twenty-four LAU-3 rockets. The F-100Fs could launch their rockets to attack the SAM radar once it had been detected, but this would not always result in the target's destruction. However, this was where the accompanying F-105Ds came in to finish the job with their own ordnance.

The first kill for the F-100F/F-105D mixed force, the former belonging to the 6234th TFW Wild Weasel Detachment, occurred on 20 December during a mission to escort a Rolling Thunder strike on Kep airfield, north-west of Hanoi. Twelve F-105Ds were led by one F-100F while another eight were led by a second Super Sabre. The force of twelve F-105Ds led by Captains John Pitchford and Bob Trier and the second force of eight led by Captains Bob Schwartz and Jack Donovan. As Pitchford and Trier's F-100F rolled in northwards to Kep they received signals from the Fan Song and Fire Can radar defending the base and were engaged by AAA, taking some hits. Both Pitchford and Trier ejected out of their aircraft, with Pitchford remaining a Prisoner of War until 1973 and tragically Trier was killed by the PAVN. Despite the tragedy, a second mission went ahead on 22 December against the Yen Bai rail yard to the north-west of Hanoi with Captains Al Lamb and Jack Donovan leading a flight of four F-105Ds for the attack. Despite being picked up by Fan Song radar, the F-100F ducked down towards the deck and used terrain-masking to hide their presence until the RWR showed a second Fan Song. Lamb and Donovan spotted the radar located near a small village after pulling up to gain some altitude. A rocket attack from the F-100F was followed by a burst of gunfire from the aircraft's four-barrelled cannon hitting the radar and a SAM launcher. Both flyers were awarded the Distinguished Flying Cross for their exploits.

Wild Weasel-1 would see the 6234th flying 112 scheduled sorties with forty-four of these being strike missions; this was out of a total of 135 sorties which were scheduled for the test phase of the Wild Weasel programme. These flights amassed a total of 250 hours. The Weasel crews could claim nine SAM sites destroyed and scores more scared off the air by their antics. At the time, it was thought that the PAVN had up to twenty-four SAM systems operational throughout this first Wild Weasel deployment. The electronic equipment onboard the Weasels had performed as well as had been hoped. The concept had been proven to work. The only sticking point was translating the electronic location of the offending radar or SAM system to a visual target marking which could be actioned by the rest of the strike formation. The other important requirement was ranging equipment to tell the crews just how close they were to the offending radar. The only other requirements was for a higher performance aircraft and also sharper weaponry to blast the SAM site and radar. While rockets, bombs and machine gun fire were all well and good, they could not always guarantee a first-strike kill. Fortunately for the Weasels, help was on the way in the form of a new ship and missile.

In 1966, the Wild Weasel-I crews would receive AGM-78 Shrikes from March of that year, performing their first strikes with the weapon on 18 April. New F-100Fs were also received to replace aircraft which had been lost in combat. Losses included an aircraft destroyed in a training accident on 13 March 1966 and another shot down by AAA on 23 March claiming the lives of Captains Clyde Dawson and Donald Clark. This was in addition to the aircraft of Trier and Pitchford

On 8 January 1966, a decision was made by the Air Staff to equip the Wild Weasel crews with a more powerful aircraft, namely the Republic F-105F Thunderchief with the F-100s continuing to perform the mission even after the F-105Fs had begun arriving on 28 May. By then, the Wild Weasels were being used in two distinct fashions, either as part of the strike force assigned to destroy targets nominated by the Chiefs of Staff or those assigned by the 2nd Air Division. The emphasis would be placed on either destroying or neutralising SAM launchers and their radar on the way to or from a strike. Wild Weasels could also be sent on search and destroy missions during which they would hunt for air defence targets in a particular area. More often than not, these attacks were executed in support of other strike missions that were performed in the area at the time. The preparations for the missions were very much adapted as time went on, with weapons load-outs, timings, feint and support tactics being evolved on the basis of what worked and what did not.

On strike missions, the Wild Weasel aircraft could assume the temporary lead of a flight once the F-100F had picked up emissions from hostile radar. The F-100F would move to the front of the package and cruise at 400 knots (740 km/h), listening for the radar while the rest of the package of aircraft would follow. The Wild Weasel would watch the ground and listen at altitudes between 4,500–14,000 ft (1,219–4,267 m) which would keep the aircraft within range of the Fan Song radar, but beyond the reach of small arms fire. With radar detected, the F-100F would turn towards the radar and begin a descent. It would then be for the F-105F crew to determine whether they could gain an accurate bearing to the radar, if so then the fight would begin. If it was being painted by the radar, the Weasel could always try terrain-masking to prevent the radar from gaining a lock on to the aircraft, although the disadvantage in this respect was that such a manoeuvre would break the aircraft's radar tracking if there was terrain in the line of sight. If a SAM was in the air, then the F-105F would transmit this information to the rest of the formation and they would then begin evasive manoeuvres to break the missile's lock by flying below its minimum engagement altitude. As we have seen earlier, the down side of this was that it put the formation straight into the range of AAA that could inflict some serious damage.

If the Bear had established a positive location on the offending radar system, then the pilot would have to scan the ground visually for the radar and SAM site given that the RHAWS equipment on the aircraft was unable to give ranging information to the radar. If the pilot obtained a good fix on the target, he would transmit this to the rest of the formation and they would begin their attack. However, if the aircraft over-flew the target, something that was always a good possibility given the PAVN's good use of camouflage, then the Bear would have to rely on the equipment to indicate that the signal was now behind them with the pilot performing a steep turn in an attempt to re-acquire the target once again. However, if a good visual sighting of the SAM installation had been made, then the Wild Weasel could fire marking rockets, usually 2.75 in (69 mm) High Explosive Anti-Tank or High Explosive Anti-Personnel weapons which were effective in reducing the target to ashes. The Weasels could carry two pods each of twenty-four rockets and a full load of machine-gun rounds. The Thunderchiefs in their formation would usually carry the four rocket pods or two rocket pods and up to six 750 lb (340 kg) bombs each, more than enough to deal with any SAM site. CBU-24 Cluster Munitions were another weapon of choice to deal with the SAM launchers and were often carried on the F-105Ds along with up to six Mk.82 500 lb (226 kg) weapons; these being earmarked for follow-on attacks on the air defence site or attacks on targets of opportunity.

These Iron Hand missions had two important effects. The first was psychological given that the presence of the Wild Weasels and the destruction that they could unleash could be effective in distracting the PAVN air defenders from other aircraft in the strike package, allowing them to perform their mission while the missile operators tangled with the Wild Weasels. Secondly, the actually destruction of an air defence site was important, although it's destruction was refrained from if this endangered the attacking Wild Weasel and strike force therein. This made sense as the USAF was clearly not going to return to the horrendous loss rates that it was suffering in the SAM battle prior to the arrival of its Wild Weasels in South East Asia in 1965. That said it was recognised that the best and most permanent form of defence suppression was destruction. Something that is now very much reflected in today's Destruction of Enemy Air Defence (DEAD) doctrines. Timing was an important matter for the Wild Weasel crews and their aircraft would usually arrive in the target area around 20–30 minutes before the rest of an attack formation in order to draw out enemy radar emissions and SAM site locations so that they could be dealt with prior the arrival of the main strike package, thus helping to enhance the safety of these aircraft. In addition, the attacking formation may also have some suppression aircraft to lend SEAD support as the main air-to-ground attacks were being performed. The priority was, however, to build as much of a sanitised area as possible before the main attack.

With the advent of Shrike, the crews had to develop new tactics. Shrike could be unleashed up to 13 miles (20 km) from the radar target during the Wild Weasel's usual ingress as it began its attack. However, the lack of ranging information in the cockpit would make life difficult for the crews. To get around this, crews could pre-plan where they would fire the missile although that would depend on knowing the general area where the radar was operating.

Shrike could trace its birth back to 1958 and it was developed in response to the Soviet deployment of the SA-2 with the AGM-45 intended as a means to counter it. The development of the missile was performed by the Naval Ordnance Test Station at China Lake, California. The idea was to fit a missile with a seeker that could home in on the Fan Song's radar transmissions and then destroy the radar. The theory being that the SA-2s would be all but useless without their tracking radar, thus receiving no guidance commands via UHF transmission on the way to their target. The Shrike had borrowed the AIM-7 Sparrow air-to-air missile which was fitted with a blast-fragmentation warhead.

The development of the missile received added impetus following the Cuban missile crisis and the loss of the U-2 and attacks on US Navy F-8U Crusader aircraft. The result was that the AGM-45-1 Shrike became a reality and Texas Instruments, along with Sperry Rand/Univac would eventually produce over 16,600 rounds, along with the ATM-45 training rounds which were indispensable for getting the Weasel crews accustomed to this missile. The destructive effect of the Shrike was centred on the 23,000 steel fragments which would be sprayed by the blast; this explosion was initiated by either a proximity or contact fuse and the guidance section for the missile could be changed according to the threat that the crews expected to encounter.

The first Shrikes arrived with the Wild Weasel-I crews in March 1966 and would enter action on 18 April 1965. The Shrike did have one drawback in that it was vulnerable should the enemy switch off its radar after the Shrike had been launched. The missile's relatively slow speed of Mach 2 was another problem, given that the Guideline could touch Mach 3.5. This meant that it was theoretically possible for the PAVN air defenders to get a fix on the Shrike once it had been launched and then to get a fix on an enemy aircraft with their radar, fire their missile with radar guidance to the target aircraft and then switch off the radar; even with the AGM-45 in the air, causing the latter to break lock. The only way for the Wild Weasel crews to hedge against this was to get in closer to the radar and SAM launcher. The other short-coming of the missile was that its warhead was relatively small and could not always be guaranteed to destroy the radar site. In some incidences, the same site could be radiating again within 24 hours if it had only suffered damage to the antenna, which was relatively easy to replace.

Tactics

The PAVN improved their air defence technology and tactics as the war dragged on. A favourite technique was for AAA opera-tors to maintain tight fire-discipline, keeping their guns silent until the moment a fighter-bomber began its attack run. At this point the attacking aircraft would have to keep a predictable flight profile in order to ensure that the ordnance got onto the target. One account by a journalist who witnessed PAVN AAA in action talked of fire being unleashed without warning and being sustained at full rate before it abruptly stopped following the attack, their analogy was 'as if a conductor had slashed down his baton'. In order to frustrate the radar-seeking missiles, the PAVN would switch on and switch off their radar in much the same way as the German *Würzburg* operators two decades before. This would allow them to perform intermittent radar surveillance while also breaking the lock of the ARM. A variation of this tactic was termed 'Dr. Pepper' by US fighter pilots where the radar would be active and a Wild Weasel would begin its attack, the site would shutdown and another would come on the air. This would bring the response of another ARM before it too shut down and a third would activate. Then all three sites would switch their radar on and launch missiles at the Wild Weasel from three different directions. The pilots who experienced this maddeningly frustrating tactic would no doubt disagree fervently with the soft drink's slogan that 'to try it is to love it'.

The PAVN would also fire their SAMs at long range into an aircraft formation. This was designed to break up the package of aircraft which would then be attacked individually as they entered the engagement zones of other missile systems. Other tactics included manually changing the frequencies that the radar used which in turn would frustrate electronic jamming efforts as the operators on the jamming aircraft struggled to keep abreast of the changing PAVN frequencies. Moreover, the firing of SAMs could be used to push aircraft down from high altitudes where they would be vulnerable to the weapons closer to the deck where they could in turn be engaged by AAA. Favourite AAA tactics included shooting a wall of flak from several AAA guns towards an incoming strike package, and AAA would be especially effective if the cloud base was below 8,000 ft (2,548 m), given that cloud cover would restrict the attacking aircraft's manoeuvring.

The PAVN were also able to deal with the electronic counter-measure systems adopted by US aircraft, particularly the AN/ALQ ECM pod which arrived in 1967. The crux of the problem was that for these pods to be effective, the aircraft using them had to fly in formation. To counter this, the PAVN would fire a barrage of SAMs at long range from the incoming forma-tion. This would force them to break and thus degrade the efficiency of the pods. With the aircraft in separate locations, they could now be engaged individually by other SAM launchers. Allied to this was the PAVN's ability to spoof the electronic warfare techniques of the USAF. For example, the Douglas EA-1 Skyraider electronic countermeasure aircraft that were in theatre required the countermeasures operators to tune their jamming equipment to the frequency of the radar system that they wished to spoof. The PAVN radar operator would then move their frequency forcing the EA-1 jamming operator into a game of catch-up as they struggled to keep tabs on the radar frequency. The PAVN were even able to track the offending aircraft based on the inference of its location by analysing its jamming energy.

In terms of hard kill, the PAVN also exploited a technique which would be used time and again by air defenders. High-altitude systems such as the SA-2s would be fired which would in turn force a formation of aircraft down from altitude to avoid the impact. This would then force the package squarely into the jaws of the AAA systems such as the ZSU-23-4s. To increase the chaos, the NVA would also send in interceptor aircraft to chase the formation. Staying out of the danger of the AAA, SAMs and interceptors required some tight-flying skills on the part of the American pilots and supreme vigilance to prevent 'blue-on-blue' fratricide.

Training
Selection for Wild Weasel training had originally focused on pilots with over 1,000 hours in the Thunderchief, although this was later reduced to 500 hours and was subsequently opened across the USAF jet community. As far as the Bears were concerned, they were originally drawn from the B-52 and EB-66 worlds, but later, Weapons Systems Officers (or 'Whizzos') could be taken directly from Air Force Electronic Warfare School graduation. The first step for the trainees was for the would-be crews to go to McConnell AFB, Kansas to qualify on the Thunderchief and in particular to learn the principles of bombing using the aircraft's R14-A radar system. Following the successful completion of this course, the pilots and Bears would be grouped and sent to Nellis for full Wild Weasel training.

The first early flights in Vietnam during the Wild Weasel-I programme taught the USAF a number of important lessons about training. The basic syllabus called for twenty-one missions to be flown against the SADS at either the St. George or the Hawthorne ranges in Utah. The missions could also include practice AGM-45 Shrike launches and as a requirement, all missions included evasive manoeuvre practice which could include the use of terrain-masking and out-turning a missile. As well as performing a live Shrike firing, the crews would practice dive-bombing. From 1968, as well as getting their heads around the Shrike, the crews had to learn how to handle the AGM-78 Standard ARM with its range of 56 miles (90 km) and 223 lb (100 kg) warhead compared to the 25 miles (46 km) and 149 lb (68 kg) blast-fragmentation warhead of the AGM-45.

In the same year that the AGM-78 was entering service, the Wild Weasel course phased in a new training method for the Bears which would use a modified T-39F Sabreliner business jet.

The cabin had the passenger seats ripped out and replaced by the equipment that they would find in the back seat of their jet, namely the console for the AN/APR-25 RHAWS, the AN/APR 26 Launch Warning Receiver and the IR-133 panoramic receiver. Three Bears could be trained on each flight, although standard practice was for two students to fly with an instructor. As they learned to use their backseat equipment Wild Weasel pilots would sometimes join the flight to get an understanding of how their back-seat colleagues worked and the equipment they operated.

Those with experience of the Wild Weasel world brought their experience with them to Nellis. Jack Donovan, Maurice Fricks, Al Lamb, Ed White, Walt Lifsey and George Kerr, by now all Majors, were on the staff with Colonel Garry Willard as the head of school officially known as the 4537th Fighter Weapons School.

Wild Weasel-II/III

The delivery of the F-105F to the USAF marked the beginning of the Wild Weasel III missions. The reason why the numerical designation appears to have been skipped was because the Joint Chiefs of Staff evaluated two airframes to pick up the WW mission from the Super Sabres. Along with the F-105F, the F-4C Phantom was also evaluated, but rejected in favour of the former. Ironically, the F-4 would later be chosen as a WW airframe and would go on to win some illustrious battle honours. The F-105F was ordered by General Dempster on the 8 January 1966 and it took just eight more days to install all the electronics into the F-105F and for the aircraft to make its first flight; a procurement cycle unthinkable in today's world.

Confusingly, the aircraft had two designations, also being known as the EF-105F, the 'E' prefix denoting Electronic but that said, the aircraft was almost always known as the F-105F Wild Weasel-III. The first aircraft arrived in theatre on 28 May and featured the same AN/APR-25, IR-133 and AN/APR-26 systems which had been in the Wild Weasel-I F-100Fs, but with the addition of the AZ-EL kit which would tell the Bear the bearing and elevation of the hostile radar. The previous tape recorder was replaced by a Stancil-Hoffman two channel system and a KA-71 motion picture camera for capturing the details of the strike for the debrief. The M61 Gatling gun was retained in the aircraft with up to 1,028 rounds to shred a target, but these Thuds could also carry the AGM-45. Where the F-100F had begun, these new kids on the block truly followed.

However, as it turned out, the eight-day installation was the easy part. With the black boxes added at Eglin, the aircraft was taken down to McClellan AFB in California so that ground and aircrews could be trained on the F-105F. Those who were training on the Wild Weasel-III would have a course lasting over six weeks, although they were the first to benefit from the trickle down of skills from those 'Weaselers' who had returned from combat; Jack Donovan joining the school at Nellis in February of 1966 for example. The flight test programme also ran into difficulties: all six F-105F aircraft had to undergo repairs because of problems with the installation of the aircraft's specialist equipment. However, as of May the first six aircraft made the hop across the Pacific to Korat followed by another five aircraft. With all eleven aircraft on the flight line, it was not long before four of the airframes were modified with the addition of the North American Aviation QRC-317A SEE-SAMs system, which would later become known as the AN/ALR-31. Designed as a supplement to the AN/APR-25/26 systems, SEE-SAMS shared their antenna and was designed as a passive missile launch detection system.

Teething problems to one side, the F-105Fs were a major leap forward. The F-100Fs, with their top speed of 864 mph (1,390 km/h) were slow in comparison to the 1,372 mph (2,208 km/h) which could be squeezed out of the Thuds. This meant that a mixed F-100F/F-105D package could only travel as fast as the Super Sabres in order to benefit from the SEAD protection. In the fast-jet world, speed equals life, and having to slow down over an area of acute danger was a serious shortcoming for the F-100/F-105 combination. With the Thud now working as a Weasel, these concerns were largely negated. The other side-effect was that it was one less aircraft type that had to be sustained in theatre. But no benefit comes without costs. The problem with the Thud was that Republic had stopped production of the aircraft in 1964 and, to put it bluntly, when an airframe was gone it would be gone forever and thoughts turned once again back to the Phantom as the successor Wild Weasel.

When they arrived in theatre, F-105F crews were intensively prepared for the missions they would undertake. Despite the fact that they had completed their six weeks at Nellis they were back in the school house learning the ROEs, the threats they would face, the enemy's air defence order of battle and jungle survival techniques in case one of the NVA's missiles did get the benefit of the doubt. The crews were required to have an exemplary record on all the courses that they undertook at Korat and 100 per cent was said to be the only acceptable pass mark. With the Thuds, the days of the 6234th had passed and the new aircraft were shoehorned into the 13th TFS, 388th TFW. Orientation flights began on 3 June 1966.

In fact it was on this first flight that more problems with the Thud's black boxes were encountered. The bright South East Asian sunlight played havoc with the Bears' view of their scope although a jury-rigged piece of cardboard as a sun visor over the CRT saved the day. There were also visibility issues with the Launch light on the AN/APR-26 which was also not so easy to see and the IR-133 panoramic receiver could be difficult to hear. The orientation missions went on, with F-100Fs flying the lead, although on this first flight the F-105F had to abort its mission after mechanical problems on departure from Korat. One of the new aircraft took over and encountered a weak Fan Song emission. A second flight later in the day picked up a much stronger signal although no missiles were seen by the aircraft's crew despite the AN/APR-26 flashing the Launch light.

The standard weapons load-out for the F-105Fs included the AGM-45 and two LAU-3 rocket canisters. When they were flying with F-105Fs, the F-105Ds would benefit from enhanced SEAD support as some of the Deltas would also carry the Shrike. Because of the missile's guidance system, the aircraft could pick up a radar warning using its own RWR and the missile could be launched to engage the radar. This allowed the SEAD effort to be organised into teams of Deltas and Foxtrots. The Foxtrots would act as the ears and eyes listening for the radar emissions with their sensors with the Delta then launching its Shrike against the radar. The first kill for the F-105F came a day after the first orientation flight when an F-105D smashed a radar with a rocket attack.

Ten days later, the USAF began night operations with the Wild

Weasels. If the backseat system's lighting was too dim during the day, then it was too bright during the night. A remedy was found with the installation of a control to alter the brightness of the console, along with a volume control for the audible warning of the AN/APR-25. The makeshift cardboard screen was replaced by a rubber hood which improved clarity. Another important addition was a switch which allowed the Bear to concentrate on the immediate tactical situation, i.e. scan for other threats while the pilot rolled in for a Shrike attack

On 14 June, a pre-planned strike bagged a radar which was operating in the southern part of North Vietnam in Route Pack 1. On 21 June, a Fan Song radar was obliterated as an SA-2 site was being established in Route Pack 6 towards the north and in the most heavily defended North Vietnamese air space. Further strikes in Route Pack 6 followed on 29 June when another radar van was wasted and before the day was out 'Tico Flight' had bashed one Fan Song causing serious damage and destroyed another.

The best day so far for WW-III came on 5 July. Route Pack 6A SEAD was to be the order of the day with Majors Bill Robinson and Peter Tsouprake homing in on a Fan Song using the APR-25 before firing off a Shrike when the hostile radar signal was indicated as strong, but the missile missed its target. Major Robinson realised that he was out of range with the first shot, so he got in closer just as two SA-2s were launched at their 'Eagle Flight'.

Despite the performance of the Thud time was not on the Air Force's side. Even by 1967 the lowest-houred F-105Fs were still logging around 1,500 flying hours while older airframes had up to 2,000. The lifespan of the airframe was reckoned to be in the region of 4,000 hours by the manufacturer. Spares were sometimes in short supply which meant that aircraft were cannibalized and the Pratt and Whitney J75 was heavily taxed with the demands of fast combat. Moreover, if the aircraft took a hit in either of the two hydraulic systems, then more often than not the flight controls would give up, given that all of these systems were located close together in the airframe.

As the US improved its SEAD capabilities, the PAVN did not stay idle and beefed up their air defences. By 1 August estimates talked of in excess of 100 SAM sites operational in North Vietnam, set against the twenty-five Wild Weasel crews which could attack them. There were by now two F-105F squadrons: in addition to the aircraft of the 13th TFS, there was a detachment with the 354th TFS which was located at Takhli AFB north-west of Bangkok in Thailand. What did not help was the loss rate that the Weasels were suffering. There is no doubt that they were enjoying success against the missile batteries but that was at the cost of eleven F-105Fs.

Help would eventually arrive from six A-6A Intruders of the US Navy which had been modified for defence suppression. The aircraft were fitted with an AN/APS-107B RHAWS along with an ER-142 receiver. These aircraft could also carry the AGM-78. The aircraft were despatched to the 357th TFS. Although the PAVN were up-gunning their defences, the F-105Fs and their A-6A brethren could still hit the air defenders where it hurt. As December 1967 turned into January 1968, the Thuds and Intruders had notched up eighty-nine SAM site kills as the Beatles 'Hello, Goodbye' scored a number one chart position on both sides of the Atlantic in the last week of December; a fitting song for the Weasel's treatment of a SAM site. However, these figures do not include the countless number of sites that performed switch-offs once the Weasels were in their locale and the EF-105Fs did not just stick to shooting up missile sites. In April 1968 Major Leo Thorsness and Captain Harold Johnson shot their way into the record books as the first Weasels to bag a MiG-17 using their M61 gun. This was the first of two more MiGs which would be splashed by Weasel crews during 1967. Thorsness was later shot down and was awarded the Medal of Honor. His misfortune highlighted the dangerous nature of the mission: the technology and airframes may have improved but the risks remained and forty-two Wild Weasel crew had either been killed in action, were missing or were POWs, along with the loss of twenty-six aircraft.

As they were making life difficult for NVA radar operators with their Shrikes, the WW-III crews would receive the AGM-78 Standard ARM from early 1968. While the Shrike had taken its ancestry from the Sparrow, the Standard evolved from the Tartar SAM used by the US Navy for fleet air defence. The finished product weighed in at 1,350 lb (612 kg) and was 15 ft (4.5 m) long and dedicated launch rails were designed for the F-105F/G and the A-6B Intruder which would carry the missile for the Navy. With the rail, the whole lot weighed in at 1,600 lb (725 kg) and that was before the missile's black boxes were installed!

The missile would be first used in combat on 6 March 1968 carried by A-6B Intruders of the VA-75 The Sunday Punchers Navy attack squadron being catapulted off the USS *Kitty Hawk*. Results of the first use remain unknown. Three days later EF-105Fs carrying Shrikes and Standards left Korat to escort a flight of F-4s during an attack on a rail target, but the Weasels could not get permission to use the missile. Finally the official nod was forthcoming on the 11 May and EF-105Fs from the 357th TFS, four aircraft in total, escorted an F-4 package operating near Hanoi. The actual target was scrubbed and instead the Phantoms and the Weasels stayed downtown looking for trouble in the form of SAM sites and their radar while the F-4s watched the skies for MiGs.

The combination of the Phantoms and the Thuds illustrated the amount of team work that would go into SEAD. It is tempting to think of SEAD as a one aircraft show, but this is not the case. History showed that aircraft types and indeed service arms would operate together in the destruction of air defences with Commandos and artillery in the fight as well as fast jets and anti-radiation missiles. In Vietnam, jamming support was vital to a mission's success and the Lockheed EC-121Q Warning Stars, EB-66Es and the Douglas EA-3B were all brought to the fight to bash electrons and disrupt the performance of the radar and in 1967 the USAF stipulated that all tactical aircraft entering North Vietnamese airspace must have an ECM pod. The decision rested uneasily with the Weasel crews as the fitting of a pod would occupy a hardpoint which translated into less ordnance to take to the fight, notably costing one Shrike. The other side effect in addition to the loss of ordnance was that the ECM pods which were fitted actually interfered with the Weasel's ability to listen for hostile radar emissions. Notably the proximity of an EB-66 could also have the same effect.

The hardpoint issue was a concern to the Weasel crews. The F-105F had many attributes but space was not one of them; one of the consequences of the aircraft having originally been designed as a tactical nuclear bomber. The normal load-out for a

SEAD mission up north could include two Shrikes along with two 450 gallon (1,703 litres) fuel tanks beneath each wing. On the centreline, the aircraft could carry up to six bombs or two Shrikes and two Standards plus a 600 gallon (2,271 litres) fuel tank. Alternatively, two Shrikes could be carried along with a pair of CBU-24 cluster bombs and the 600 gallon tank on the aircraft's belly. As if the ECM pod was not enough of a headache another USAF decree had originally stipulated that the Thuds had to carry at least one AIM-9 Sidewinder for self-defence against MiGs, but just as the Weasels had won this battle and the air force had relented, the ECM requirement arrived.

Air and ground crew are nothing if not inventive, after all their very survival depends on that. Several schemes were tried regarding the pod. One solution was to borrow some dual Shrike launcher rails that the Navy had developed which could allow two Shrikes to be carried on a single hardpoint. This kept the number of Shrikes on the Thud the same *and* allowed for the ECM pod to be carried beneath a hardpoint on the other wing. So far so good, but the only problem with this arrangement was that if the aircraft launched one of its Shrikes, the remaining missile on the dual rail would cause some serious vibration for the aircraft. Another clever ruse fitted a Thud with a dual launcher carrying two Shrikes beneath each wing and an additional two Standards, one under each wing; the cumulative destructive power of six anti-radar missiles. Photgraphs were taken of this fearsome creation that was sprung from hell's very drawing boards and in a psychological operation, the photos were distributed throughout North Vietnam, no doubt giving more than a few radar operators pause for thought as to what might be visiting them in the future.

Yet the problems with hardpoints, flying hours, losses and maintenance issues compelled the USAF once more to look for a new SEAD solution, but the solution would rest with the same airframe, leading to the development of the F-105G. As summer had turned to Autumn in 1967, a cabal of Eglin AFB's Air Warfare Center, Republic and Westinghouse were busy transforming the F-105G into a SEAD platform. The immediate priority was to move as much equipment as possible into the airframe and off the hardpoints to free-up weapons space and hopefully go some way to quietening the gripes of the crews regarding their weapons space. The AN/ALQ-101 ECM pod had received particularly vociferous complaints and this was cut in half with each part located in a fairing on either side of the fuselage. This system later received its own AN/ALQ-105 designation and was fitted onto an F-105F to trial the concept. Meanwhile, out came the AN/APR-25/-26 system which had given such sterling service and in went the AN/APR-35/36 RHAWS. Also removed was the ER-142 panoramic receiver, and it was the AN/APR-25 half of the RHAWS that replaced this. Also destined for retirement was the QRC-317 SEE-SAMS which was substituted with the AN/APR-31.

The new black boxes greatly increased the number of radar frequencies that the Weasel crews could listen for and in turn offered greater protection to the aircraft that they would be escorting. By now SA-3s were operating in theatre as a medium-altitude SAM. They were guided by Flat Face radar and a PRV-11 Side Net height finding radar which had a tracking range of up to 52 miles (85 km). However, the arrival of the S-125/SA-3 (NATO codename 'Goa') surface-to-air missile was a worry. This was a missile dedicated to medium altitude interception with a 12.5 mile (7.7 km) kill radius. While the Guideline had claimed more than its fair share of victims it was still ostensibly a strategic system, designed for the homeland defence of the USSR against big lumbering bomber formations, and less adapted to the rapid twists and turns of the fighter jock. The arrival of the Goa would definitely up the ante.

There was another danger lurking for the US aircraft. The PAVN were not just getting new missiles and guns. They had realised the cardinal importance of connectivity. Hooking SAMs, guns and radar up to each other allowed fire to be controlled in a responsive manner and concentrated or dispersed when necessary. A networked air defence system suddenly has millions of pairs of eyes connected to the same brain rather than millions of both operating separately. Along with the missiles and guns, the NVA had acquired 250 Ground Control Intercept radars to vector their fighters onto ingressing packages of American aircraft; ground control of fighters was very much in keeping with Soviet doctrine in contrast to the Airborne

Warning and Control doctrines and technologies which emerged from the United States during the Vietnam War. This was reinforced with networks of EW radar. The upshot of the integration of this technology was such that it would make surprise, that vital prerequisite of not only SEAD but all military operations, harder to obtain while also giving PAVN air defence a clearer picture of the tactical situation above them; both highly undesirable outcomes for the Americans.

However, the new equipment in the F-105G would accommodate the frequencies used by the Flat Face and Low Blow and afford added protection. Fortunately, radar emissions were hoovered-up by the Navy and Air Force ELINT effort as EC-121s, RC-135Vs and EA-3Bs listened hard to the electromagnetic spectrum. Where a new frequency was found, it was logged and the information filtered down to the scientists who would tweak the Weasel electronics accordingly.

New electronics were not the only addition to the F-105G. The aircraft was also outfitted with a new weapon, the AGM-78B Standard. An updated version of the original, the Bravo boasted a Maxim Seeker head which could listen for radar operating in the E and G bands with one seeker and I bands with the other, along with red smoke for target marking, and two fuse types; proximity and impact. Further improvements were enshrined in the AGM-78B-2 which had a single seeker which could listen across bandwidths, while the Charlie and Delta designations for the AGM-78 denoted the seeker-head manufacturer (Bendix or General Dynamics).

The year 1968 had as much drama on the home front as it did in theatre with the Vietnam War dictating the domestic and international political agendas. Johnson, appearing in photographs looking visibly exhausted told the Democratic Party that "I will not seek or accept my party's nomination for President of the United States" on the last day of March halting bombing of North Vietnamese targets north of the 17th Parallel and beginning talks in Paris with the North Vietnamese. LBJ was seeking a way out of both the crisis and politics. As the bombs briefly fell silent, the Wild Weasels waited.

The Vietnamization policy of President Richard M. Nixon's administration, which followed Johnson, was predicated on progressively handing the security and defence burden for the South to the South Vietnamese Army, in much the same way that the Coalition in Iraq is keen to transfer the security burden to the Iraqi armed forces to facilitate a gradual withdrawal. Vietnamization hit the Wild Weasels hard. The 355th TFW at Takhli was stood down leaving only the 44th and 354th in Thailand consolidating the Wild Weasel units which had been spread across the 355th under one banner. Two squadrons were created with surplus F-105F and, by now F-105G aircraft being raised as the 12th TFS at Korat and just to add to the confusion was then re-designated as the 6010th Provisional Wild Weasel Squadron under the command of the 388th TFW.

Problems with aircraft numbers caused the unit to be re-designated a second time on 12 January 1971, this time as the 17th Wild Weasel Squadron (WWS). However, within three months of the designation the 354th and 44th WW squadrons were de-activated and the USAF SEAD burden landed on the shoulders of the 17th WWS. This lonesome unit stayed in theatre. They received their F-105Gs (Golfs) from April 1968 with a steady trickle of EF-105Fs which had been transformed into F-105Gs thanks to the new equipment additions. Once in theatre, the Weaselers soon discovered the foibles of the Golfs. While the new equipment gave the aircraft added capability, there was a weight penalty and the short Korat runway coupled with the summer humidity caused more than a few rejected take-offs. One way around this was to take off with almost barren tanks and take a drink once airborne.

But while they waited the 17th WWS did fly missions during the intermittent bombing pauses as Johnson and later Nixon tried to bomb the North Vietnamese to the negotiating table, The USAF would keep tabs on the border areas using RF-4 Phantom recon-naissance aircraft while the fearful AC-130 Spectre and AC-119K Stinger gunships would go on the prowl over Laos and Cambodia checking for infiltration. The stipulation was that no bombing missions were to be performed north of the 20th Parallel. The result was that the NVA took advantage of the respite to reinforce their air defences acquiring artillery and SAMs. Prior to 1972 the lower numbered Route Packs towards the North-South border had were more sparsely defended compared to the Route Packs up north near the capital. When bombing did resume above the parallel in April 1972 the NVA were waiting and claimed six F-105Fs and eight F-105Gs.

One dramatic event really shook things up in Vietnam and that was the Tet Offensive that was launched on 30 January 1968. This was a series of attacks mounted by the Viet Cong and PAVN around the South on a public holiday, when the American and South Vietnamese operational readiness was expected to be at its lowest ebb. Tet occurred as Wild Weasel units were thin on the ground in South East Asia with the 355th TFW having left for the United States, the 12th TFW based at Cam Rahn Bay was withdrawn and the 366th TFW also scheduled to leave. The only unit operational in the region was the 17th WWS based at Korat.

The Wild Weasels had one more major assignment before they would leave South East Asia. On 30 March 1972, PAVN launched the Easter Offensive against South Vietnam. The response was Operation Linebacker, the first major bombing offensive on the North since Johnson's bombing halt of 1968, which was designed to stop the North driving into the South by using heavy air power in the form of B-52D Stratofortresses flying north to hit targets with the 17th WWS performing an exhausting two-missions-per-day, two-missions-per-night schedule to escort the bombers. The 17th was supplemented with additional SEAD power in the guise of the 561st TFS from McConnell AFB, Kansas which was despatched to Korat, not only were the reinforcements welcome, but they also brought with them shiny new Golfs; this unit being subsequently joined by the 67th TFS which was flying the new F-4C Phantom Wild Weasel-IV. The new aircraft was a response to the loss of Thuds which had been out of production since 1964. This was the second time that the Americans had used the Phantom as a USAF SEAD platform, the first being back in 1966 when the F-105F was ultimately chosen. A total of thirty-six F-4C Phantoms (also known unofficially as the EF-4C) had been designated F-4C Wild Weasel-IV which had been customised with the AN/APR-25/-26 systems and ER-142 panoramic receivers. Yet the Phantoms birth as a Weasel was a troubled one. The perennial issue of space caused bad vibrations and also resulted in interference between electronics systems which were too close for comfort. That said the aircraft eventually entered service with the 4537th Fighter Weapons Squadron at Nellis; this unit would later become known as the 66th Fighter Weapons School after its parent unit, the 4525th Fighter Weapons Wing was re-designated as the 57th Fighter Weapons Wing. A second unit, the 67th TFS, was raised from the 80th TFS, 347th TFW at Kadena AFB, Japan.

During the Linebacker-I operations, the pre-emptive launch of the AGM-45 Shrike was the favoured means of suppression. This was designed to keep the radar down regardless of whether any were operating in a given area, the logic being that the PAVN would desist from activating their radar once they realised that the Shrike was in the air and thus able to home-in on their position. It was said that from the end of October 1972, this technique was sufficient to keep the PAVN radar off the air while the Shrike was in their area.

The bombing missions of Linebacker 1 were sufficient to force the North Vietnamese to return to talks having seen their offensive blunted and the North suffering intense damage, and bombing north of the 20th Parallel was once again halted. Talks broke down once more on 14 December with Nixon ordering a renewed bombing offensive against the North called Linebacker II which began on 16 December. Once again the B-52s were brought to the fray, but like the F-100Fs seven years earlier, this time it was the turn of the Weasels and not the strikers to suffer the speed burden. These relatively slow and not very manoeuvrable bombers were flying deep into the heart of the enemy and had to be escorted by nimble fighters as they struck an array of targets around Hanoi and Haiphong including rail yards, airfields, factories and transportation links. To make matters worse, the PAVN air defence enhancement initiative meant that the aircraft were now facing a hyperactive hornets' nest of defences. On 20 December, for example, two days after the first Linebacker bombing raids were flown, the PAVN was able to attack the formation with 220 SAMs, bagging six B-52s. The following two days saw the loss of another five bombers with an accumulative loss of 120 crewmembers.

Part of the problem appeared to be that the B-52s were using tactics that they had learned to employ for nuclear raids into the Soviet Union, jamming specific radar rather than the huge array of radar and missiles that they faced when flying into the Route Pack 6A/6B areas. For their part, the Tactical Air Force was said to have transferred little of its wisdom on how to deal with the PAVN air defence threat to the B-52 crews. Above all, the issue seemed to be integrating the Weasels and the Statofortresses together in employing SEAD techniques. A tactical rethink caused the B-52s to make more use of their organic ECM systems which had been installed during the Rivet Rambler programme and which included the addition of an AN/ALR-18 receiver system, AN/ALR-20 panoramic receiver, AN/APR-25 RHAWS system, either four AN/ALT-6B or AN/ALT-22 continuous wave-jamming systems, a pair of AN/ALT-16 barrage-jamming systems and the same number of AN/ALT-32H and a single AN/ALT-32L high- and low-band jamming system, six AN/ALE-20 flare dispensers totalling ninety-six flares and 1,125 chaff bundles in the AN/ALE-24 system. Prior to the re-evaluation, the bombers had flown predictable routes into their target areas, and the ECM mix-up had seen the B-52s ECM systems jamming friendly aircraft radar and the EB-66 aircraft jamming the radios of the bombers. Tactical problems included a 100 degree turn that the bombers had to make to leave North Vietnam after they had hit their targets. It was this turn that helped greatly to enlarge the aircraft's radar cross section and that the chaff corridor that was sown for their protection did not always hold in un-forecast winds. The air force had also forbade the bombers to take evasive action on their way to and from the bomb run in order to maximise the mutual ECM support that the bombers could offer to one another .

Meanwhile, during the Linebacker-II strikes, the F-105Gs and the F-4s would work together in teams with the latter force unleashing a dramatic and hard-hitting campaign against PAVN air defences as the bombers went north, using the benefit of the eight years' experience that they had be now accrued against the air defence systems. This all-out campaign was important and had a major effect on the resilience of the air defences that the United States faced, it also greatly assisted the survival of the bomber force. The USAF made an important discovery in Linebacker-II. It applied the principle of mass in the SEAD fight right at the end of its involvement in Vietnam and this had a decisive effect. These lessons taught the SEAD community of the importance of striking the IADS with a heavy punch right at the beginning of a campaign to aid the work of other aircraft further down the line. Following Vietnam, SEAD operations over the Bekaa Valley, Iraq, the Balkans and even Afghanistan during Operation Enduring Freedom, would apply this principle time and again. The arrival of the Weasel Phantoms in theatre had made the USAF SEAD force even more robust and translated into double the number of air defence targets that the force could engage. Following a halt to the bombing ordered by Nixon over Christmas, a massive force of B-52s, totalling up to 116 aircraft attacked a total of ten targets around Haiphong and Hanoi with a Wild Weasel escort. This time, the combination of the counter-measures on the bombers and the EF-4C/F-105G team helped to reduce losses with two bombers being shot down, but the PAVN elected to fire their missiles ballistically rather than use the radar and invite an attack. While the salvo-firing of the telegraph-pole-like SA-2s were still a hazard as they zoomed through the air, a lack of radar guidance greatly reduced their accuracy.

The war was also taken directly to the PAVN SAM infra-structure. While radar bombing of the SAM sites was not always a great success, a B-52 strike on a SAM storage site, along with attacks on the Vietnamese transportation network which hampered the transit of missiles and their components, and the mining of the harbour at Haiphong directly affected the missile stocks that the PAVN had available. A focused raid by Phantoms against a SAM assembly line also had a dramatic effect in reducing the missiles that the PAVN had available.

The Strategic Air Command (SAC) and Tactical Air Command (TAC) aircraft had devised a technique by which waves of up to fifty bombers in each package were flown on the first three nights with gaps between the packages of up to 5 hours. Within the waves of bombers, the aircraft would operate in three-ship formations with gaps of 2 minutes between each formation. Up to an hour before the first formation of bombers arrived over their targets, packages of tactical USAF, Navy and Marine aircraft would perform SEAD operations by hitting airfields, SAM launchers, AAA and radar. Five minutes before the first bomber formation arrived, the Wild Weasels would perform their Iron

Hand missions against any radar sites that were still active around the bomber's target area. These bombing missions were heralding the final moments of the war and on 29 December, bombing was once again halted north of the 20th Parallel and negotiations continued.

The last Wild Weasel mission of the Vietnam War was flown on the 3 August 1973. The Weasel units which were in theatre for Linebacker-II, including the 17th and 561st TFS, made their way back home to George AFB, California. In the case of the 561st TFW, they joined the 35th TFW and were followed by the 17th TFS; subsequently re-designated as the 562nd TFS. The squadrons went back to training and refining their mission against the SADS at Nellis and also preparing for the retirement of their F-105Gs in preference for the new F-4G Advanced Wild Weasel. Neither the F-100F nor the F-105F/G had been permanent solutions to the SEAD issue, but they had performed their role admirably during the conflict. The USAF, Marines and Navy sat back and counted the cost in blood and treasure for the war. In Wild Weasel terms, forty-eight aircraft were lost between December 1965–August 1973 which included a pair of F-100Fs and forty-six F-105Gs. In terms of suppressive effect, ten Guidelines could claim ten aircraft for every 150 that were launched after the Weasels had arrived in theatre in 1965. Figures for November 1968 show an aircraft being lost for every forty-eight missile launches, while this improved to an aircraft lost for every fifty launches by the time that Linebacker-II kicked off. This does not measure the psychological effect of the Wild Weasels and the SEAD effort in general.

The Air Force Electronic Warfare Centre concluded that as much as 95 per cent of the SEAD effect was psychological in encouraging the radar operator to switch off, rendering their missile launchers pretty much useless and allowing the strike package of aircraft to get to and from their target relatively unhindered. The Vietnam conflict also showed SEAD to have both a strategic and tactical impact. The use of SEAD diminished the enemy's ability to pursue their overarching campaign aims i.e. safeguarding the war-making potential in the north to support the operations of the VC in the south. Yet SEAD also had a tactical effect in helping to protect other strike aircraft as they took these attacks to the North's war-making infrastructure.

Moreover, the SEAD fight doctrinally further enhanced its position as an all-arms and capabilities battle with the Marine Corps, Navy and Air Force all performing SEAD operations and the panoply of electronic attack and strike aircraft working towards the common end of defeating the enemy's air defences both in terms of ground-based systems and fighters. Perhaps this should have been done at the beginning of the war rather than waging an all-out effort during its last days, but to be fair that was not a military decision. Fearful of escalation with the Soviet Union, the war had been controversially micro-managed by politicians thousands of miles away in Washington who decided exactly what could and could not be hit and until Linebacker-II, SEAD would remain as the adjunct in support of air-strikes against politically acceptable targets cleared by the White House.

CHAPTER THREE

SEAD Operations in the Middle East

The Middle East since the end of World War II has been characterised by both uneasy peace and open war. Israel and its neighbours of Egypt, Syria, Iraq and Jordan have been locked together in conflict on two major occasions (1967 and 1973), while the intervening years witnessed an undercurrent of violence and skirmishes. Furthermore, Israel performed a major action against Syria in 1982 in a bid to halt attacks by Palestinian guerrillas against northern Israel known as Operation Peace for Galilee. Throughout the period from the Six Day War of 1967 to Operation Peace for Galilee, the *Tsvah Haganah Le Israel\Heyl Ha'Avir* (Israeli Defence Force/Air Force IDF/AF) honed its Suppression of Enemy Air Defence skills to a point where during the 1982 operation, the SEAD task became *the* initial and overriding objective of the air campaign prior to the commencement of CAS missions.

After the USAF and Navy, the IDF/AF is now arguably the most experienced SEAD force in the world. What is more, they have fought the SEAD fight by matching available weapons with tactical ingenuity. The Israelis may have one of the world's smaller armed forces, but the influence that it has had on SEAD, amongst other military tactics and operations, far outstrips its size. This chapter will explain how the IDF/AF and other parts of the Israeli armed forces, notably the *Tsvah Haganah le Israel* (Israeli Army), have consistently punched above their weight when taking the SEAD fight to their opponents.

The Six Day War

The conflict which became known as the Six Day War commenced on the morning of 5 June 1967, beginning with *Mivtza Moked*, or Operation Focus, as it was known. The build-up to the conflict had seen relations between Israel and Egypt deteriorating. The motivations for Israel's attack have been extensively analysed by historians in the intervening years since the conflict, but broadly speaking, the Israeli attack was launched as a response to concerns that Egypt was preparing for an invasion of southern Israel.

Moked was aimed at catching the *Al Quwwat Al Jawwiya Il Misriya* (Arab Republic of Egypt Air Force/EAF) on the ground by attacking important airbases which included El Arish, Jebel Libni, Bir Thamada, Bir Gifgafa, Kabrit, Inchas, Cairo West, Abu Suweir and Fayid. Prior to the attack, the IDF/AF had used its C-47 transport aircraft to traverse the Israeli-Egypt border to sow chaff corridors to mask the movement of Israeli aircraft behind the border. The Israelis also made much use of electronic countermeasures not only to disrupt Egypt's air defences, but also to prevent the Egyptian air defence system from sharing its information with other air forces around the region, an important consideration given that Syria, Jordan, Iraq and Saudi Arabia's armed forces were also involved in the conflict to a greater or lesser degree. The Israelis were fully aware of the size of forces arrayed against them in the Arab world and were prepared to hamper the chances of other countries entering the conflict on Egypt's side. The runways of Egypt's air bases were destroyed with BLU-107 Durandel bombs, and anti-aircraft emplacements around the airfields were strafed. The Israelis were said to have been unwittingly assisted by Field Marshal Abdel-Hakim Amer, Egypt's Vice President, and Lieutenant-General Sidqi Mahmoud, the EAF head, flying across the Sinai Desert for a conference with other military commanders. Because of this, Egyptian air defences were ordered to stay idle to reduce the risk of fratricide in case the aircraft was mistaken for an Israeli warplane. That said the IDF/AF went to great pains to ingress well below Egyptian air search radar cover and also below the effective range of the Egyptian SA-2 Guideline SAMs. As well as the vast majority of the EAF combat aircraft that were wiped out in the first few hours of the operation, which saw the destruction of 197 planes, it also saw the first SEAD action of the war, in which eight Egyptian radar stations were destroyed.

A follow-up strike at 12.45 hrs on 6 June, saw the Royal Jordanian Air Force also being targeted in a pre-emptive strike in which air bases at Mafraq, eastern Jordan and Amman, the capital, were hit wiping out eighteen Hawker Hunters in the process, with one aircraft shot down for the loss of one Israeli Dassault Mystere. The SEAD effort included an attack on radar at Ajlun, northern Jordan. The SEAD battle continued into the afternoon when the IDF/AF attacked other airfields at Mansura, Cairo International, Helwan, Al Minya, Bilbeis, Herghada, Luxor and Ras Banas along with twenty-five accompanying radar sites in the Sinai and west of the Suez Canal.

The IDF/AF took the fight to the Egyptian SAM systems the following day. SA-2 sites which had been positioned close to the Suez Canal came under attack, while the air force flew combat air patrols to interdict Egyptian, Jordanian and Iraqi combat aircraft. The latter would lead to claims at the end of the day that over 400 Arab aircraft had been destroyed; with fifty shot down in dogfights and the rest smashed up before they even got into the air.

The losses Egypt suffered from the Six Day War prompted much soul-searching within the Egyptian High Command. One of the lessons that they had learnt from the conflict was that air defence had to be consolidated under a single *Quwwat il Difaa Al Jawwi* (Air Defence Command or ADC) which would include missiles, radar, command and control, and fast-jet interceptors. The Egyptians very much followed Soviet air defence doctrine in this regard.

As well reorganising the country's air defences, Egypt approached the Soviet Union for new equipment to strengthen its missiles and AAA systems. The country already had the Guideline, but these could be attacked by the IDF/AF and they could also be spoofed by the Israelis flying below their radar coverage. A rearmament programme was engineered by Egyptian President Gamal Abdel Nasser. Defences along the Suez Canal were beefed-up by the Egyptians with 150,000 troops deployed to the area. At their disposal were 500 tanks and around 1,000 artillery pieces. The ADF began to receive MiG-19 and MiG-21 fighters and crucially, the Ground Based Air Defence (GBAD) environment began to be networked with radar, SAMs and anti-aircraft guns linked together and clustered around strategic targets such as Cairo.

The War of Attrition

However, the end of the Six Day War did not bring peace to the region. Military operations between Israel and Egypt continued to bubble away in what became known as the War of Attrition.

It was the F-4E that became the potent weapon against Egyptian Air Defences in the War of Attrition. Israel began to receive the aircraft from the United States in 1969 under the Peace Echo-I initiative. The aircraft had an impressive bomb load, able to lift up to 18,650 lb (8,480 kg) of ordnance, earning it the nickname of *Kurnass* (Sledgehammer) by the IDF/AF. The first two squadrons to receiver the Phantom were the 201 *Ahat* at Hatzor, central Israel, and the 69 *H'patishim* at Ramat David, south-east of Haifa in northern Israel. At 17.30 on 5 September 1969, the Phantoms showed their worth, being unleashed against an SA-2 battery at Abu Suweit, causing its destruction.

Israel performed one of its most audacious attacks on 7 September 1969. Egyptian Navy patrol boats were destroyed by Israeli commandos at the Gulf of Suez port at Ras el Sadat. This act was a prelude to the Israelis landing a small force of captured Egyptian vehicles to perform an amphibious raid on Egyptian defences on the western bank of the Suez Canal. While this was occurring, the IDF/AF took the opportunity to press home attacks on Egyptian SA-2 emplacements. Two days later, the Israelis performed another attack, this time on Egyptian radar further south near the Gulf of Suez.

Such was the IDF/AF pressure that, although the Egyptians had enthusiastically invested in air defence technology, almost all the SA-2s positioned around the Suez Canal were destroyed by November 1969. Jordanian air defences were similarly degraded and on 17 November: the IDF/AF performed a robust attack against Jordanian SAM and radar targets with an attack on a radar site at Mazar, eastern Jordan that cost one Israeli aircraft; the seventh to be lost over Jordan since the 1967 war.

The icing on the cake for the Israelis came via another audacious attack on 26 December 1969 when a Special Forces raid netted a Spoon Rest EW radar positioned at Ras Gharib on the western bank of the Suez Canal. The seizure operation had two prongs; the commando force landed after sunset, while IDF/AF aircraft, along with Israeli artillery, hit areas around the radar site to provide a diversion to keep nearby Egyptian Army units distracted. The entire radar and its command centre were dismantled after the guards were overpowered and two Sikorsky CH-53D helicopters airlifted the system back to Israel for analysis. The find would no doubt go some way in helping the Israelis to get the inside track on the workings of the radar and most importantly how to spoof it; information which was shared with the United States.

Israeli actions throughout 1969 had cost Egypt the lives of many pilots sent up to meet incoming Israeli warplanes, sixty aircraft and almost all the air defences west of Suez. The Egyptians had retaliated against the Israeli attacks, but each retaliation seemed instead merely to invite an intensification of the Israeli response. It was with these thoughts in mind that Muhammad Anwar Al Sadat, Egypt's Vice President from 1969, went cap-in-hand to the Soviet Union to enlist Moscow's assistance for another round of reinforcement for Egypt's defences. Sadat scored and in February of 1970, a new influx of Soviet air defence equipment arrived along with Soviet advisors and both were put to use rebuilding the air defences which the Israelis had pulverised.

By March it was clear that Israel would have some serious new threats to contend with. The SA-2s had been replaced, but more worryingly, S-125/SA-3 Goa SAM systems had also arrived. Designed to operate with the SA-2, this missile was intended to cover the air defence gap at low level, with its 11 mile (18 km) range as opposed to the 27 mile (45 km) range of the SA-2. The missile had three accompanying radar systems; the P-15 Flat Face 155 mile (250 km) C-band target acquisition radar; the Low Blow 50 mile (80 km) I/D-band fire control/guidance radar and the PRV-11 Side Net 105,000 ft (32,000 m) height-finding radar. This was the missile's debut outside the USSR, and these defences were clustered around the Egyptian capital, Alexandria on the north Egyptian coast and around the Aswan Dam on the Nile.

But while the Egyptians enhanced their defences, so the Israeli attacks continued as part of a coordinated SEAD effort code-named *Prikha* (Blossom) which had begun in January 1970. The Phantoms were brought back to the fray and in February eight aircraft brought their M117 bombs to bear on SA-2 installations at Helwan, southern Cairo and Dahshur on the west bank of the Nile. These strikes were the first in a graduated series of SEAD attacks by the IDF/AF which saw Egyptian IADS targets being hit across coastal areas of the Red Sea but which brought a robust response from Egyptian SAMs, AAA and air defence fighters, reaching a climax on 30 June when two F-4Es were lost along with a third aircraft on 5 July. The all-out SEAD effort occurred as a new round of diplomatic measures was being prepared by the United States. The Israelis were clearly deter-mined to negotiate from a position of strength as US Secretary of State William Rogers embarked on an initiative to conclude a ceasefire between Israel, Egypt and Jordan, and the Israelis escalated their SEAD strikes accordingly.

One of the most intense duals between Israeli aircraft and Egyptian air defences occurred on 18 July after Phantoms went into action against five SA-2 batteries which were 31 miles (50 km) west of the Suez Canal. However, these exchanges also included tangles with the new SA-3s with one missile claiming an Israeli Phantom and another aircraft also being lost, possibly to either an SA-2 or SA-3. The Egyptians were thought to be using new frequencies for their radar which did not respond to the ALQ-101 jamming pods that the Israelis had obtained from the United States.

Moreover, as July drew to a close, the Egyptians again increased their air defences along the west bank of the Canal. Their rationale was to build an air defence curtain which would be impregnable to Israeli aircraft with AAA and SAMs taking care of the airspace at various altitudes. On the morning of 30 June after the Egyptians had bolstered their air defences in the area, they attacked a force of Israeli F-4Es, claiming two

Phantoms. This in turn brought a stiff response to the Egyptian air defences, although the missiles and radar were quickly repaired with the Egyptians bringing them back on line and able to inflict more damage. This tit-for-tat campaign continued with Israel putting a further seven SAM batteries out of action. On 3 August, the war was taken directly to the SA-3 batteries when a site near Ismailia on the west bank of the Suez was attacked with the loss of an F-4E in the process.

The SA-3 was not the only worry for the Israelis. A ceasefire finally brought an end to the War of Attrition on 7 August 1970 but this was not before Israeli pilots had encountered the 2K12 Kub/SA-6 (NATO codename Gainful) which had been supplied to the Egyptians by the Soviets. This system worked in conjunction with the 47 mile (75 km) range IS91 Straight Flush tracking/target illumination radar which allowed the system to acquire and track a target and guide the missile via a single radar and could be used in either a self-contained fashion, or at a regimental level, when linked together with the Spoon Rest, P-40 Long Track E-band 108 mile (175 km) range EW radar, Flat Face EW radar, Thin Skin or Side Net 148 mile (240 km) range E-band height-finding radar, or Score Board Identification Friend of Foe radar, allowing the Egyptians to link their SA-6s together to provide EW and air defence cover over a considerable area. What is more, the SA-6 could engage targets down to an altitude of 150 ft (46 m) which further reduced the heights at which Israeli warplanes could fly to prevent engagement by Egyptian SAM systems. The Egyptian ADF ensured that their air defences gave overlapping coverage in terms of area and altitude, while a favourite tactic of the air defenders was to fire a number of missiles in a salvo to make evasive action by the Israeli pilots more difficult.

The presence and strength of the Egyptian air defences led to discussions in the Israeli armed forces about an all-out ground offensive to wipe out the Egyptian IADS west of the Suez once and for all; however this raised the worrying possibility of Israeli combat with the Soviet advisers assisting the Egyptians. The commander of the Israeli Air Force called the Egyptian air defences a: 'Russian fist covered by an Egyptian glove'. The density of the Egyptian IADS *circa* 1971 was such that it was said to surpass even that which was defending Moscow, both in terms of sophistication and density. While Israeli attacks both with air and land forces had attempted to destroy these defences, it had only succeeded in damaging them. Not only were the air defences a hazard to Israeli fliers, they caused another problem as their presence meant that it would be difficult for the IDF/AF to provide adequate CAS to land units during any attempt to perform ground attacks in the region of the canal. Any Israeli aircraft choosing to fly west would now have to contend with SA-2, -3 and -6 systems along with the deadly, radar-guided ZSU-23-4 *Shikla* AAA system which had a 3 mile (5 km) vertical range and could bring its supersonic 0.9 in (23 mm) rounds to bear with its RPK-2 Gun Dish 13 mile (20 km) range J-band radar. As the region seemed to lurch uncontrollably towards another war, the IDF/AF may not have been able to predict when that conflict would begin, but they knew that when it did, they would have to run the gauntlet of these acute threats.

Yom Kippur
On the eve of the dramatic combined assault by Egypt, Syria, Jordan and Iraq, Egypt's air defences included 150 SAM batteries, sixty of which were positioned along the west bank of the Suez Canal. These SAM batteries were often protected by AAA pieces to provide a close-in defence against any air attack. In turn these defences were connected to a command and control system which included observers and search radar. The Egyptians had also established fake SAM sites which were camouflaged from the air and both the genuine and counterfeit sites were protected in concrete revetments and sand banks. Moreover, in addition to their AAA guns, the Egyptians had the 9K32/SA-7 (Strela) shoulder-launched MANPADS which used an Infra-Red (IR) guidance system, rendering the weapon invulnerable to interception by ARM or by anti-radar electronic countermeasures. High-temperature flares are the only real defence against the weapon and its existence can push pilots to higher altitudes to stay out of its 11,800 ft (3,600 m) range which forces the aircraft back into the range of medium and high-altitude SAM systems.

These Arab air defences were reinforced to the north of Israel by those constructed by the Syrians. The country had thirty-four assorted SA-2, -3 and -6 systems, most of which were located between the Golan Heights and the capital Damascus, along with strategic sites around the country. Syria also possessed an array of AAA weapons and SA-7 MANPADS which could accompany ground units as they advanced.

On 6 October 1973 at around 14.00 a force of Egyptian, Syrian and Iraqi aircraft began an audacious assault on several Israeli targets. Three Israeli airfields were attacked, while the Egyptians performed some SEAD raids against Israeli MIM-23 Hawk SAM and radar systems. This was in addition to the military command centres and artillery positions which the opening assault hit. That the operation was performed during a religious public holiday is well documented and the Israeli armed forces were not operating at their full readiness as they were struck by Operation *Badr*. The Israelis tried to take the war back to the Egyptians, but the air defence curtain on the west bank of the Suez made their lives extremely difficult and on 7 October six F-4Es were shot out of the sky, with another aircraft damaged. On one occasion an F-4E was being chased simultaneously by four SAMs. In total twenty-two Israeli aircraft were lost that day. Attempts to drive home attacks against Syrian air defences in the Golan were also hampered with bad weather, particularly heavy rain and many Israeli aircraft had to re-role themselves in flight from ground attack to air defence by dumping their ordnance to engage the incoming waves of Arab fighters.

That said, Israeli operations against Syrian air defences did get going on 8 October, when the IDF/AF began Operation Dugman. This was designed to press home attacks against the Syrian anti-aircraft missiles and was to use fifteen F-4Es. The problem was that both the SA-6s and the ZSU-23-4 systems were mobile and had been dispersed by the time that the Israeli aircraft arrived. To make matters worse, they kept their radar silent, knowing full well what the response from the Israeli aircraft would be in the form of an AGM-45 Shrike ARM. The operation, which intended to hit thirty-one targets, did eventually net three SAM batteries for the loss on one Phantom, with a further five SAM sites damaged. In the first three days of fighting alone, Israel had lost fifty aircraft, over 20 per cent of the IDF/AF front-line combat strength, mostly to the SA-6 and AAA.

For the IDF/AF, the problems revolved around the air defences that they were up against; notably the SA-6 and ZSU-23-4 which were hard to find and spoof. The latter did not use tracer bullets in the daytime so it was difficult for pilots to see the arc of fire. Also, despite the system's sophisticated radar it could be switched off, allowing the weapon to be 'blind fired' by the operators. The SA-6 radar used a continuous wave rather than more traditional pulsed signals. This was bad news for Israel's F-4E and A-4H RHAWS which were used to listening to pulsed-radar frequencies. The MANPADS caused additional headaches to the IDF/AF. More dangerous against low- and slow-moving aircraft such as C-130s, the weapon could also hit a fast jet that was coming in low to perform a dive-toss bombing. As the aircraft would pull up, the pilot would hit the afterburner to increase the separation between the aircraft and the bomb travelling towards its target so as to ensure that the jet was out of reach of the explosion when the ordnance found its mark. However, a suitably protected MANPADS operator could shoot a missile at the aircraft on the egress from the attack as the engine would be presenting a handsome, hot target for the SA-7 to follow.

That said, the Israelis did adapt to their situation. To foil radar-guided weapons, chaff launchers were placed behind airbrake doors and were used to present a more tempting target to an SA-6 missile. This would be used in combination with hard evasive manoeuvring which proved to be successful in spoofing the missile. The Israelis also began to hit the air defences from the ground, notably those which were in range of Israeli Army artillery. As well as having a destructive value, the use of artillery in the SEAD fight had a deterrent effect and SA-6 batteries which were seeing artillery shot fall near their location would shut down the system and head for safety. A third technique saw the Israelis jury-rigging their helicopters with electronic warfare equipment to jam enemy air defence radar. The upshot was that this joint approach began to work in the Israelis' favour. Unwittingly or otherwise, as they had done during the War of

Attrition with the use of commandos against Egyptian SAM sites, the Israelis had pioneered a truly joint approach to SEAD bringing whatever weaponry and forces which were at their disposal into the fight against the enemy's air defences. An approach which would be revisited almost two decades later by the US-led Coalition during Operation Desert Storm.

Other techniques used by the IDF/AF to foil air defences included the use of artillery for CAS wherever possible; and when aircraft were brought to the fray they would perform low-level attack profiles at high speed, only gaining altitude to deliver their weapons. Alternatively, a variety of aircraft could attack a single target from different directions to frustrate the defenders; a tactic that was also written into Soviet doctrine for frustrating air defence, and something that they made use of in the war which followed their invasion of Afghanistan in a bid to frustrate rebel *Mujahideen* anti-aircraft guns and MANPADS.

Meanwhile, observers on the ground, in helicopters or in other aircraft would watch the skies for approaching SAMs or enemy fighters to warn Israeli warplanes. Also, the IDF/AF brought their AGM-45 Shrikes into the fight which did force radar to disengage and manoeuvred their aircraft around the sky above the battle in an unpredictable and indirect fashion to make their behaviour less apparent to the air defenders on the ground.

During Yom Kippur, the Israelis applied a tactic which would be of tremendous utility nine years later when applied by the USAF during Operation Desert Storm, and later during Operations Deliberate Force and Allied Force in the Balkans which used Unmanned Aerial Vehicles (UAVs) for the SEAD effort. The IDF/AF already possessed BQM-34A Firebee UAVs which it had purchased from the United States to perform dangerous reconnaissance missions. These drones were placed into the fight where they were sacrificed to draw fire from the Egyptian IADS which were fooled into thinking that they were Israeli aircraft.

The SEAD effort took a back seat from 9 October as the IDF/AF took the war straight to the heart of the Syrian military machine. The headquarters of the air force in Damascus was attacked, following strikes in the morning against airfields in northern Egypt. That said, the Syrian air defences were far from benign and one of the attacking Israeli aircraft was hit by artillery as it returned home. In the afternoon, the IDF/AF pressed home attacks against four SAM sites around Port Said at the northern mouth of the Suez Canal. The Israelis retained the momentum of the attack until the 13 October when the defences around the city had been comprehensively decimated. However, fate intervened the following day. Israeli pilots were reporting notably less SAMs coming after them. The simple truth of the matter was that Egyptian and Syrian air defenders were running out of missiles. Suddenly a window of opportunity opened for the Israelis in which they could push attacks through the air defence gap to Syrian and Egyptian targets to hit the air defences and also to support their colleagues on the ground.

It was on the night of 15 October that Israeli ground units commanded by Generals Ariel Sharon and Abraham Adan drove into Egyptian territory. North of the Great Bitter Lake they hammered at the meeting point between the Egyptian Second and Third Armies, the latter of which had its supply lines cut and was encircled. In doing so they established a bridgehead on Egyptian territory. It was through this bridge-head that Israeli armour and troops would pour through to destroy, among other targets, Egyptian air defence sites, including three SAM batteries that had been making the lives of Israeli pilots a misery. Operations on the ground had a decisive effect in the air. The destruction below opened a gap in the once-impregnable Egyptian air defences and it was through this gap that Israeli aircraft could now fly to provide much needed CAS to their colleagues on the ground exploiting the breakthrough against spirited Egyptian counterattacks which sought to close the hole. At one point Israeli troops on the other side of the canal did become encircled, although the dogged determination of Israeli armour and paratroopers broke the Egyptian hold. Like other aspects of the SEAD campaign during the Yom Kippur War, it would be this tactic of creating gaps in an IADS which would be used by the Coalition at the start of Operation Desert Storm only on that occasion, as shall be illustrated; the piercing was done not by ground forces, but by helicopters.

By 18 October, the IDF/AF was well and truly increasing the tempo of the attacks on the Egyptian IADS. The attacks by

Sharon and Adan were so successful that Israel's Defence Minister Moshe Dayan was able to tell reporters in laconic style that; "I don't think this war is going to drag on". On the same day that the Israeli Defence Forces claimed ten SAM batteries destroyed, along with a number of SAM batteries captured intact. Although, with their air defences around Suez in tatters, the Egyptians had responded by sending fighters to intercept the Israeli strikes. However, these were engaged by their Israeli opposite numbers, but this did not stop Egyptian Su-7BMKs, MiG-17Fs and Dassault Mirage IIISDEs throwing everything that they'd got against the Israeli bridgehead. Even Aero L-29 Delfin jet trainers and Mil Mi-8 transport helicopters were thrown into the fray, one of which dropped a barrel of Napalm which almost hit Moshe Dayan during a visit to the front.

From the north to the south of the Suez Canal Israel unleashed an all-out effort against the Egyptian air defences, pressing aircraft, artillery and even tank fire into the battle. The SEAD effort was to last five days, targeting every air defence site between the Suez Canal and Port Said, from the north to the south. Not only were the Shrikes brought into play, but bombs and missiles laid waste to the air defences along with tank fire and artillery, while those radar sites which had survived the onslaught were blasted with electrons. The intensity was such that three days later, Egypt's Third Army had no air defences whatsoever, while the Second Army had lost the majority of its skyward protection. Unsurprisingly the air defence threat to Israeli aircraft diminished dramatically and IDF/AF aircraft could now begin providing heavy CAS to Israeli ground forces which were now pouring over the west bank of the Suez. The statistics spoke for themselves. In over 2,200 sorties mounted by the IDF/AF only four aircraft were lost. Prior to the effort against the Egyptian IADS, the Israelis had lost thirty-eight aircraft for 3,181 sorties. Four days after the bridgehead had been established, the Israelis had constructed an additional three crossing points and by the 19th were 62 miles (101 km) from Cairo; effectively holding a loaded gun at the Egyptian Government. A dramatic Israeli counter-attack in the north had also pushed the Syrian advance back to the pre-war border between the two countries and a similarly impressive drive took the Israeli Army within 25 miles (40 km) of Damascus.

On 22 October, negotiations between the USSR and the United States resulted in UN Resolution 338 demanding the termination of 'all military activity immediately, which would come into effect at 18.52 Israeli time after being unanimously passed by the UN Security Council. Although it would be ignored by both sides during isolated incidents which included the destruction of Israeli tanks by Egyptian forces on the night of the 22 October, and the encirclement of the Egyptian Third Army by the Israelis on the 23rd; the same day that the Syrians had accepted the ceasefire. Despite escalating international tension between the administration of President Richard Nixon in the United States and Soviet Communist Party General Secretary Leonid Brezhnev, an uneasy peace once again broke out across the Middle East. The Israelis had looked destruction in the eyes, but had secured a famous victory to which its SEAD operations contributed in no small measure.

The tally of losses for the Israelis from the combined air defences of the Arab forces included forty-one IDF/AF aircraft downed by SAMs and thirty-one shot down by AAA, while MANPADS only downed three, but damaged many others. Combinations of AAA and SA-7s were responsible for a further three aircraft lost. Arab air forces lost fifty-eight aircraft to their own air defences, which was reported to be due to a lack of IFF systems on their aircraft and trigger-happy air defenders. Air superiority over Israel itself had never been challenged by the combined Arab air forces and Israeli jets were able to down eighteen enemy aircraft for the loss of one of their own.

The SAM site tally was equally impressive. At the start of the conflict Syria had around thirty-one SAM systems in theatre, while the Egyptians had around seventy-three. Over half of the Egyptian SAM batteries were located along the Suez Canal between El Qantara, south of Port Said and the Gulf of Suez. These were now a memory along with the eight Syrian batteries that the IDF/AF also claimed. That said, a kill was claimed for 140 of the 1,300 SAMs launched, giving one hit for every nine missiles fired. Also helpful was the resupply effort mounted by the United States which got materiel into Israel. Operation

Nickel Grass established an air bridge between Israel and the United States taking tanks, ammunition and artillery into the country, and also additional Phantoms which were hurried from US stocks into theatre; the latter being especially important given the aircraft losses which the Israelis were suffering from the Arab SAMs.

For Israel's rivals in the region, there was perhaps a realisation that despite the audacity of the Yom Kippur attacks, fighting Israel toe-to-toe had become a dangerous business. On three occasions, shortly after Israel's creation in 1947, once again in 1967 and finally in 1973, the states surrounding Israel had put up a brave fight but had been driven to sue for peace. For Syria, the order of the day as the 1970s drew to a close was proxy warfare. Syria's President Hafez al-Assad, himself a former Gloster Meteor pilot and head of the *Al Quwwat Al Jawwiya Al Arabiya As'Souriya* ('Syrian Arab Air Force'/SAAF) decided in the wake of Yom Kippur that despite regaining some of the territory that Syria had lost to Israel in the 1967 war Syria would keep up the pressure on Israel.

Peace for Galilee
Israel's creation in 1947 had resulted in Lebanon absorbing a large influx of Palestinian refugees. By the mid-1970s these numbers had grown to around 300,000 and were mainly clustered around southern Lebanon along with the Palestinian Liberation Organisation (PLO), which performed regular artillery attacks from this part of the country against targets in northern Israel. This invariably brought Israeli retaliation and an undercurrent of violence existed between the Israelis and the PLO for much of the 1970s. Operations against Israeli targets abroad were performed, notably by the notorious terrorist Abu Nidal, who headed a militant Palestinian faction opposed to any cooperation with Israel. The Israeli government and military leadership effectively lumped the various and disparate Palestinian opposition groups together in the same basket, with Rafael Eitan, the Israeli Chief of Staff saying; 'Abu Nidal, abu shmidal', we need to screw the PLO.

As the 1980s unfolded, Lebanon had become a bitter battleground as Christians and Muslims locked horns in the country's civil war. Moreover, it had become a proxy conflict between Israel and Syria as they supported the Christian and Muslim factions respectively. IDF/AF aircraft engaged Syrian aircraft which were providing support to Palestinian factions. On 28 April, SAAF helicopters were airlifting Syrian troops providing assistance to a Palestinian force engaged with Christian militia cadres at Zahal on the Beirut-Damascus road. Israel's Prime Minister Menachem Begin ordered an F-16 strike against the Mi-8 helicopters as a demonstration of Israeli resolve and support for their Christian allies on the ground. This soon increased the pressure between Israel and Syria with the latter moving SA-6 systems into the Bekaa Valley in north-east Lebanon to deter further Israeli air strikes in this area. The Israeli Defence Force responded to this move by using UAVs to collect intelligence on the defences, some of which were downed by the missiles.

Begin's government had another issue to contend with. Northern Israel continued to experience regular artillery attack from PLO bases in Lebanon. In the nine years following the ceasefire in the Yom Kippur War, 103 Israeli lives were claimed in 1,548 attacks. To make matters worse, Shlomo Argov, the Israeli Ambassador to the UK, was left in a coma after a gun attack outside the Dorchester Hotel in London on 3 June 1982. The attack was the work of the Abu Nidal Organization militant Palestinian faction which had fallen out with the PLO in 1974 and rejected any peace deal over the Palestinian question with Israel. Israeli patience had been stretched to breaking point and the government moved to attack Palestinian militant targets in Lebanon. The aims of what became known as Operation Peace for Galilee were intended to halt the attacks on northern Israel by establishing a buffer zone from the Israeli-Lebanon border to the Beirut-Damascus highway which roughly bisects the country from west to east.

This would be done by invading southern Lebanon with ground units supported by attack helicopters and CAS aircraft. The shelling that the Israelis had suffered in the month preceding the ambassador's assassination attempt coupled with the act itself caused Begin to order air strikes against guerrilla bases in southern Lebanon, which in turn brought heavy artillery retaliation. On the eve of the war, Palestinian insurgents had around 15,000 regular troops and cadres reinforced with around 300 tanks, 150 Armoured Personnel Carriers (APCs), over 300 artillery pieces, a similar number of anti-tank weapons and in excess of 250 AAA pieces. The force dispositions for the Palestinians saw around 1,500 cadres south of the Litani river which runs east to west across southern Lebanon before meandering north-east, along with a concentration of 2,500 troops (the *Kastel* Brigade) positioned north of the Litani between Sidon, south of Beirut and Nabatieh in eastern Lebanon and up to 2,000 soldiers comprising the *Karameh* Brigade around Mount Hermon, also in eastern Lebanon. They were reinforced with 22,000 Syrian troops equipped with 352 tanks, 300 APCs, around the same number of artillery pieces, 450 combat aircraft, sixteen helicopters and an astonishing 125 SAM systems which could seriously threaten Israeli air operations in southern Lebanon. It was these forces that the Israelis would fight.

The 125 SAM systems that the Syrians had placed in the Bekaa Valley were of major concern to Israel, particularly as the Yom Kippur war was only nine years previous and memories of the threat that such weapons could pose were still fresh in Israeli minds. What was also of concern was that the Syrians could use their air defences as an umbrella under which they could perform a land attack into northern Israel and also protect their anti-Israeli Palestinian allies on the ground. Neither of these options was particularly palatable for the Israeli government.

The SAM systems which the Syrians had moved into the Bekaa Valley were networked in a similar fashion to the Egyptian IADS, which had redundancy allowing for certain parts of the IADS to be destroyed but for the system to continue functioning, and also included the dreaded ZSU-23-4. These systems were reinforced with MiG-21 and MiG-23 aircraft. On the eve of the war, the Syrians had moved a number of SAM systems into the valley including two SA-2, two SA-3, fifteen SA-6 and an undisclosed number of 9K33 Osa/SA-8 (NATO codename Gecko) SAM systems. The SA-8 has a Land Roll radar system which includes a 12 mile (20 km) range J-band tracking radar and an 18 mile (30 km) range H-band acquisition radar. As well as the 400 AAA pieces, these systems were backed up with

SA-7 and 9K31 Strela-1/SA-9 (Gaskin) vehicle-mounted IR SAMs which had a range of between 0.54 miles (0.86.5 km). Furthermore, the Syrians had an EW radar network which was positioned on the Chouf Mountains to the south-east of Beirut which allowed them to observe IDF/AF aircraft at medium altitudes. This rendered the element of surprise very difficult to achieve for the Israelis. Any attack on the Syrian IADS in Lebanon in support of operations on the ground to reduce the threat to CAS aircraft and helicopters supporting the army's drive into southern Lebanon would require some serious jamming before the SAM sites and the IADS could be taken out. To this end Boeing RC-707/720 converted airliners were used in the ELINT role to observe Syrian radar from stand-off ranges along with the IDF/AF's Grumman E-2C Hawkeye AWACs aircraft.

Since Yom Kippur, IDF/AF SEAD doctrine had adapted somewhat to take into account some of the lessons learned during that conflict. Particularly important was the need for airpower to work in a closely coordinated fashion with ground forces to prosecute the SEAD threat. During the Yom Kippur War, the IDF/AF's considerable Phantom force had been utilised on a much more *ad hoc* basis, attacking SAM sites as and when they were located. It was believed by some in the IDF/AF that this contributed to the losses suffered by the Phantom force. However, by 9 June, the IDF/AF had a detailed plan as to how they would attack the air defences which were arrayed against them.

While the IDF/AF had good stocks of ARMs, static sites which were not using their radar would be attacked with conventional ordnance; either free-fall bombs, laser-guided or otherwise, or stand-off air-to-surface missiles. The campaign to shut down the Syrian Bekaa Valley IADS radar early in the campaign was intended to render many of the air defence sites either blind, or in fear of activating their own radar which would cause them to be vulnerable to the ordnance discussed above.

So it was that the campaign was to be divided into three phases. The first of which would be a wide-scale deception of the Syrian IADS in the Bekaa Valley with UAVs being used along with electronic jamming. This would be followed by a second phase which would feature the actual destruction of the air defences by manned aircraft using ARMs and conventional ordnance while Syrian air defence fighters were lured into an ambush. Finally, the IDF/AF would keep a careful watch on the Valley to destroy any additional air defences that the Syrians might decide to move into the area after the initial attack. The Israelis might be incapable of performing a surprise attack due to the presence of the Syrian EW radar, but that did not stop the Israelis using the Syrians' radar against them. Like an agile cabaret magician, the Israelis would let the Syrians see what they wanted them to see, in this case a phantom force of attacking aircraft, to lure them into a false sense of security and then pull the rug from under them at the vital moment.

The ELINT effort, coupled with photographic reconnaissance had given the Israelis an excellent overview of how the Syrians had deployed their air defences and how these air defences used the electro-magnetic spectrum. The photo-reconnaissance effort was largely performed by IMI Mastiff and Scout UAVs which revealed that the Syrians had placed their SAM systems in static locations which would make them easier to hunt for the Israelis and harder to hide for the Syrians. The IDF/AF decided to use large packages of strike aircraft to smash the air defences and the IADS destruction would be the immediate task of the air war and all necessary forces would be committed to that effort. However, this would bring its own challenges, in particular regarding the timing of the attacks and the sequence in which the respective parts of the SEAD effort, those in the air and on the ground, would be brought into the fray.

Phase one of the operation was opened with the UAV attack. On this occasion, Samson UAVs were flown towards the air defences in the Bekaa Valley outfitted with radar reflectors to simulate the electronic behaviour of manned combat aircraft, with the sun behind them to mask them to the Syrian air defence operators. The Syrians took the bait as intended. They attacked the UAVs with a ferocious onslaught of missile and AAA fire believing it to be the opening stages of an Israeli attack. Meanwhile, the 707s were flying over the Mediterranean sending a torrent of noise to blind the Syrian radar. The idea behind the jamming was to create fake corridors of ingress over the Syrian air defences, forcing the Syrians to look at a particular area where they would devote the attentions of their ground based air defences thus encouraging their air defence fighters to engage a strike force that did not exist. Importantly, this would cause the Syrians to reveal themselves and allow the Israelis to see how their radar behaved. This had the added effect of masking the strike packages being assembled over Israel which would deliver phase two of the attack. It has also been reported that while the UAVs were working their magic, a commando raid by Israeli troops destroyed a key IADS command and control centre which further helped to disrupt the Syrian air defences.

Around fourteen minutes after the Samson UAVs began their work, twelve F-4E Phantoms launched a volley of AGM-78B/D Standard ARMs at the Syrian radar which had now revealed itself to the Israelis following the futile engagement of the Samsons. The missiles found their mark as the Syrians were radiating to find the drones. The immediate priority was to wipe out the radar element of the IADS. When this had created an acceptable environment by blinding the Syrian IADS, another wave of Phantoms roared in out of the summer sky to attack the SAM sites themselves with combinations of AGM-65 Maverick TV-guided air-to-ground missiles and Griffin laser-guided bombs. Other attacks came from A-4H Skyhawks and IAI Kfirs which used free-fall unguided bombs to smash what was left of the SAM sites after the guided weapons had performed their task. Syrian IADS installations were also attacked from the ground by surface-to-surface missiles. Within the first ten minutes, ten air defence sites in the Bekaa valley were destroyed. By 14.35, it was all over; with seventeen of Syria's twenty air defence targets in the Bekaa Valley destroyed by a combination of four attack-waves of ninety aircraft striking at medium level to remain out of the range of Syrian AAA and despatching hundreds of flares to fool IR-guided missiles. The only survivors of the onslaught were three SA-6 vehicles which had made the wise decision to keep their radar shut down during the opening attack. This was a profile they maintained throughout the Peace for Galilee operation, and by hiding under camouflage netting they managed to evade destruction for the duration of the campaign. What had taken the Syrians time and effort to build in the Bekaa Valley had been destroyed in less than twenty-four hours. The following day, 10 June, the IDF/AF claimed another two SAM sites which had survived the initial onslaught.

The devastation that the Israelis unleashed had several important effects on the wider campaign in Lebanon. The IDF/AFs' opening attacks against the Syrian air defences in Lebanon had sent an implicit message to Damascus that the Israelis could mete out similar punishment to Syria's home air defences if they chose. Moreover, the Israelis were persistent in ensuring that the Syrians did not try to reinforce their ruined air defences with new SAM systems by keeping a vigilant watch on the ground from the air. Also, with their umbrella in tatters, the will of the Syrian Army to fight the Israelis without their protective air defence screen was seriously degraded. This correspondingly gave Israeli aircraft providing CAS greater freedom of action on the battlefield by allowing the Israelis to seize the initiative of attack and to conduct the war against the Syrians and Palestinian guerrillas largely on their terms.

The Israeli Army began its ground operations to flush the Palestinian insurgents out of southern Lebanon and move them to a point 25 miles (40 km) back from the Israeli-Lebanon border. As fighting got underway on 10 June, Israeli warplanes shot twenty-eight Syrian aircraft out of the sky after the Syrian Air Force attempted to blunt an Israeli advance into the Bekaa Valley, while another advance moved towards the Lebanese capital. There was another Syrian counterattack on the 11 June which was directed at an Israeli effort to cut off the Bekaa Valley-Beirut road and again the IAF/DF exacted a heavy toll on the Syrian Air Force, this time claiming eighteen aircraft.

The SAAF (Syrian Arab Air Force) was also in no position to wrest air superiority from the Israelis over southern Lebanon. The opening Israeli attacks had also gone for the Syrian Ground Control Intercept (GCI) radar hitting it with both hard and soft kill electronic weapons to destroy and jam the communications links between the ground and the fighters. The Israelis used an ingenious tactic where they attacked the Ground Control Intercept centres after these had seen packages of Israeli aircraft. This lured the Syrians into a particular section of sky. The communications links between the GCIs and the aircraft were then jammed and the Syrian warplanes were ambushed by scores of their Israeli counterparts. Like the Soviets, the Syrians practised strong control of their fighter assets from the ground and with the means to identify aircraft for interception gone, the Syrian Air Force was not in a position to control their fighters adequately. MiGs that were airborne to meet any Israeli strike packages were said to be endlessly circling, awaiting directions from the ground *vis-à-vis* their targets which never came. Instead they were attacked by Israeli F-15 and F-16 aircraft which had been sheltering behind mountains in southern Lebanon and which were directed to their targets by the Hawkeyes. The IDF/AF bagged twenty-eight Syrian aircraft this way at the opening of the campaign which they would later add to their final combat tally of eighty-five.

As 11 June came to a close IDF/AF operations wound down. Twenty of the Syrians' SAM systems in the Bekaa Valley had been destroyed, along with major portions of their accompanying radar and command and control systems. Over eighty Syrian aircraft had been shot out of the sky while Palestinian forces and the Syrian Army on the ground had suffered heavy attacks from the Israelis. That said, on the 24 June, the Syrians attempted to strengthen their air defences once again by moving SA-6 systems into the Bekaa Valley and challenging Israeli aircraft in a dogfight which saw the destruction of two Syrian MiG-23s. However, the SA-6 move was largely a pointless exercise given that its appearance was soon detected by Israeli reconnaissance aircraft and a single SA-6 unit was destroyed on the same day, with other air defence systems which had been moved into the valley afterwards destroyed two days later. A month later, as the Israelis were increasing their pressure on Beirut against guerrilla bases in the city, the Syrians again tried their luck by driving four SA-8 systems into the Bekaa valley, but they were detected and three of the systems were destroyed by AGM-65s and laser-guided bombs. However, the one that got away was later able to down a Phantom on the same day as its arrival in theatre.

Israel's SEAD component of Operation Peace for Galilee arguably changed the face of air defence suppression forever.

SEAD was no longer the adjunct to an air campaign which was performed as it had been during the air battles of World War II, Korea, Vietnam, the Six Day War and Yom Kippur. Israel had set SEAD as the key objective at the outset of the air campaign. All other air operations would be performed after the SEAD effort had created a benign environment in which aircraft could operate without being at serious risk from attack. Moreover, once the initial assault had been inflicted on the Syrian IADS, the IDF/AF took strenuous steps to ensure that it did not recover an iota of strength by watching the battlefield closely to ensure that the Syrians did not bolster what was left of their defences, and hitting SAM systems when they did arrive in theatre.

The Israeli air force also ushered in the era of DEAD – Destruction of Enemy Air Defence. The aims of Israel's air defence suppression planners during the Peace for Galilee operations was not merely to suppress the Syrian IADS in the Bekaa Valley but to destroy it outright. This had two important effects. Firstly it meant that CAS aircraft and helicopters could roam over the battlefield with a diminished danger of being shot down, although the threat from AAA and MANPADS could still not be altogether discounted. Secondly, it reduced the SEAD burden on Israeli aircraft later in the campaign allowing fast jets to be deployed in other roles such as CAS while a smaller SEAD force maintained its vigilance. Destruction as well as SEAD sent a powerful message to Syrian air defenders about what they could expect if they kept their radar activated. Unwittingly, the Israelis constructed the template with which future SEAD campaigns involving the USAF would be performed. Operations in the Gulf and the Balkans during the 1990s all opened with a devastating attack on the enemy air defences that the United States forces and its Coalition partners had arrayed against them. Moreover, these attacks were aimed at the destruction and not just the suppression of these air defences. Like the Peace for Galilee operations they made heavy use of electronic jamming and deception. However, air defenders also learned from the Syrian example and, in the case of the operations in the Balkans, kept their air defence radar switched off which, as shall be explained in the following chapters, caused frustration for Coalition SEAD operations.

he German Würgburg radar were the victims of some of the earliest SEAD operations and were a much-prized rget for the Allies throughout World War Two. *(Philipe Wodka Gallien)*

front view of an F-4G from the 561st Fighter Squadron. Despite being the signature SEAD aircraft of the late old War, the Phantom continued to give illustrious service many years after the Berlin Wall collapsed. *(US DoD)*

An F-4G sits on the ramp at its Spangdahlem AFB home in Germany. These SEAD aircraft were deployed as part of the 52nd Fighter Wing, and despite providing air defence suppression in the event of a war with the Warsaw Pact and Soviet Union, their finest hour came in the deserts of Arabia. *(US DoD)*

An F-4G of the 37th Tactical Fighter Wing carries the other tool of the SEAD trade, notably the AGM-45 Shrike. *(US DoD)*

A USAF F-16 fires an AGM-65 Maverick during a test flight. The Maverick is a particularly potent general-purpose air-to-ground missile which can be used in the SEAD effort. *(Raytheon)*

The tools of the trade: the three US SEAD weapons from top to bottom: AGM-88 HARM, AGM-45 Shrike and AGM-65 Maverick. *(US DoD)*

In order to perform their mission, aircraft carrying the AGM-88 must also carry the Harm Targeting System. *(Raytheon)*

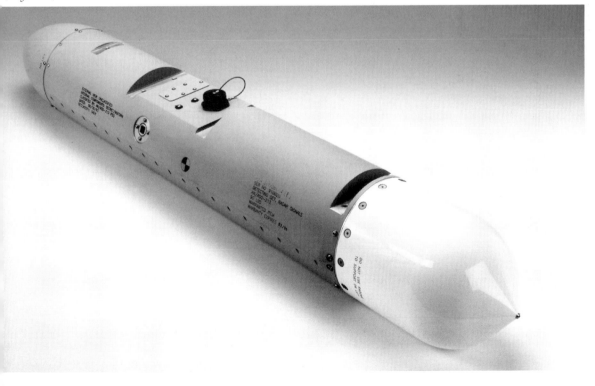

A fearsome sight: The Soviet SA-6 represented a low-cost but lethal mobile SAM system which could keep pace with advancing echelons of ground units and which proved to be a popular export to Soviet client states. *(US DoD)*

The Soviets designed SAMs to threaten every altitude. Low-level aircraft were to be engaged with SA-7 MANPADS systems. *(US DoD)*

Soviet SA-2 missiles seen here on their transport trailers. These missiles were a popular sight during the Red Square military parades through Moscow during the Cold War and were one of the most popular exports to Soviet client states. *(US DoD)*

In addition to their Fencers and Foxbats, the Soviet Air Force developed the TU-16 Badger bomber into an electronic warfare aircraft to attack NATO air defence radar. *(US DoD)*

The Soviet Air Force invested significantly in SEAD assets during the latter stages of the Cold War. Soviet doctrine envisaged aircraft like the Su-24 Fencer carrying anti-radar missiles backed up with significant electronic warfare support. *(US DoD)*

The SA-6 uses the Straight Flush fire control/short-range target acquisition radar which is carried on a separate tracked vehicle. *(Philipe Wodka Gallien)*

The Soviet SA-3 design was developed to work with the SA-2 system by engaging lower-level, manoeuvring aircraft. *(Philipe Wodka Gallien)*

The accompanying Land Roll radar of the Soviet SA-8 Gecko SAM system. The vehicle, like the missile's Transporter-Erector-Launcher, is amphibious allowing the anti-aircraft missile system to keep pace with an advancing Motorised Rifle Division. *(Philipe Wodka Gallien)*

The US Navy carried much of the SEAD burden during combat operations against Libya in 1986. Here, an F/A-18A Hornet from the VFA-131 fighter squadron waits on the deck of the USS Coral Sea armed with an AIM-9 air-to-air missiles and AGM-88 HARMs prior to a strike mission. *(US DoD)*

SEAD assets such as the F/A-18s were joined by EA-6Bs which provided electronic SEAD support. This aircraft is being prepared for a mission on the deck of the USS *Saratoga*. *(US DoD)*

A trio of French Air Force Mirage-IIIs carrying the MARTEL. Much of the SEAD burden is expected to be absorbed by the Dassault Rafale as this type enters service. (*Armée de l'Air*)

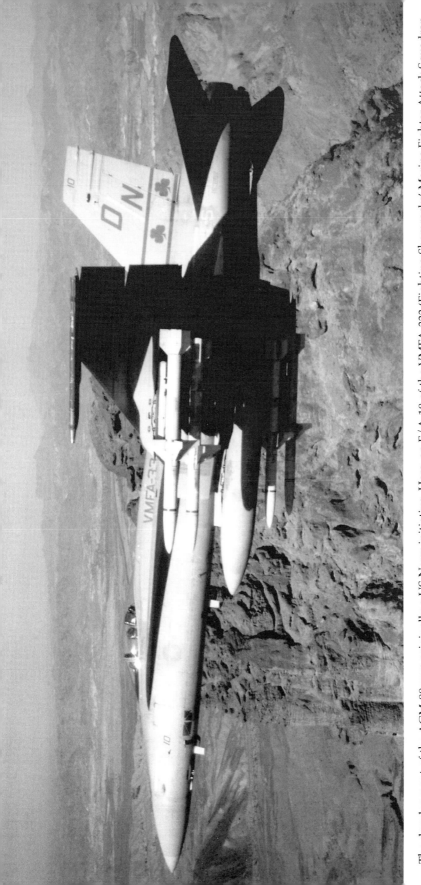

The development of the AGM-88 was originally a US Navy initiative. Here, an F/A-18 of the VMFA-333 'Fighting Shamrocks' Marine Fighter Attack Squadron flies with a pair of HARMs beneath each wing. (*Raytheon*)

Jam-packed onto the decks during Operation Eldorado Canyon, a US Navy F/A-18 is 'bombed-up' for a missio
with an AIM-9 and AGM-88. *(US DoD)*

During the 1982 Falklands crisis the Royal Air Force's Avro Vulcan bomber performed its final combat action
during the Black Buck raids. Among other tasks, the aircraft were used for SEAD attacks against Argentine rad
on the islands. *(US DoD)*

One of the biggest worries for the USAF and US Navy during Operation Eldorado Canyon was the SA-6 Gainful mobile SAM systems which Libya had procured from the Soviet Union. *(US DoD)*

French Air Force SEAD efforts were greatly aided by the C-160 Gabriel conversion of the Transall freighter which can gather data on the enemy's electronic order of battle. *(Philipe Wodka Gallien)*

A French Air Force Jaguar armed with the AS-37 MARTEL anti-radar missile. This weapon was particularly effective during operations against Libya in Chad. *(Yves le Mao)*

A pair of MARTEL missiles fitted onto each hardpoint of this French Air Force Jaguar. (*Yves le Mao*)

A pair of F-4Gs perform a SEAD mission in the twilight during Operation Desert Storm. (US DoD)

An F-4G from the 37th Tactical Fighter Wing waits on the ramp ready for a SEAD mission during Operation Desert Storm. (US DoD)

The 'WW' tail code leaves no doubt regarding this Phantom's mission. This aircraft is deployed form the 35th TFW during Operation Desert Storm. (US DoD)

During the effort code-named 'Operation Desert Shield', US-led forces deployed to the Gulf in preparation for war with Saddam Hussein. Here, a 35th TFW F-4G Wild Weasel receives fuel from a KC-135 tanker during a training sortie. (US DoD)

SEAD assets were among the most heavily tasked airframes during Desert Storm: Phantoms are readied for another mission over Iraq following the start of combat operations to liberate Kuwait. (US DoD)

One of the first actions during Operation Desert Storm was a SEAD raid against key air defence targets in and around Baghdad. They were led by F-117A Nighthawks which proved their worth as valuable air defence suppression platforms. *(US DoD)*

Another key lesson from the Israelis SEAD effort was that they improvised and used what they had available for the task. When targets did not need to be attacked with ARMs because they were not radiating they were hit with conventional ordnance; ARMs could instead be used when the radar was in operation. This had the added effect of helping the Israelis to conserve their ARM stocks, although that said ARMs were used in large numbers at the beginning of the operation as a kind of insurance policy allowing the Israelis to score positive kills on those radar sites which were still active trying to get a fix on the UAVs.

However, there are issues which should be remembered as regards Israeli operations over the Bekaa Valley. The Israelis had the luxury of time to conduct a full and thorough reconnaissance effort regarding Syria's air defences. Peace for Galilee was not a 'come-as-you-are' war in the sense of the Anglo-Argentine Falklands Crisis of the same year where a sudden provocative action by one nation catches another unaware. If the Syrians had moved their air defences into Lebanon and then followed this with a rapid assault into Israel, the IDF/AF might soon have had a multi-aspect fight on its hands, having to divide air power between the SEAD effort and supporting ground units attempting to repulse the invasion; something which it had to do during the Yom Kippur conflict. However, with hindsight, Syria's war aims were not to invade Israel but to protect their allies on the ground and also their own forces which were attempting to turn back the Israeli ground invasion of Lebanon. That said, with time to prepare the Israelis could map a robust SEAD campaign. Again, looking to modern examples, both Saddam Hussein and Slobodan Milosevic arguably made serious errors by allowing the US-led Coalition to amass forces close to their borders and to build a comprehensive map of their air defences. This is perhaps one of the reasons why many strategists in the West are now concerned about so-called 'anti-access' strategies which seek to use weapons such as cruise missiles to deny the United States and its allies territory to amass forces in preparation for either a campaign of air strikes or combined air-land operations.

There is also the argument that the Israelis were able to benefit greatly from the environment in which they were prosecuting the SEAD operation. The skies that their aircraft were operating in were not the hazy and cloud covered affairs of Central Europe in which NATO would have been expected to press home their SEAD effort against the Soviet Union and Warsaw Pact forces, but were instead relatively clear which greatly assisted visual reconnaissance. Moreover, the landscape was bereft of Germany's forest and woodland which would have given the Soviets plenty of locations to hide their air defences. The Bekaa Valley was fertile, known as the 'Breadbasket of the Empire' by the Romans, but it was also noticeably more arid than northern Europe. As history will show, desert favours the SEAD hunter, while the forests and rolling countryside of large parts of Europe favour the air defender.

That said, the Israelis had rewritten the rule book. It is a foolish planner who takes all the tactics of a campaign and seeks to transpose them onto another. Specific tactics apply to specific challenges and these challenges are often unique given that no two military campaigns are ever the same. Yet it is a skilled planner who looks to history for tactics that they can 'pick and mix' and adapt for the task that they face. Israeli operations in the Bekaa Valley gave SEAD planners a new set of tools that they could draw on and adapt for their campaigns.

What is more, the Israeli armed forces had taken a clear path as their SEAD doctrine evolved. Initially, SEAD had been performed alongside the opening strikes on enemy airfields as was done during the Six Day War. During Yom Kippur, SEAD was performed in more of a 'freelance' capacity as the Israelis were forced to divide their airpower between air defence, CAS and SEAD. This campaign also showed the important role that ground forces had in the SEAD fight after bridgeheads were established on the western side of the Suez Canal and a gap subsequently opened in the Egyptian air defence curtain. The intervening years had allowed the Israelis to maintain their pressure on the Egyptian SEAD system and also to keep it persistently under threat. When the time rolled around for Peace for Galilee, the Israelis had over a decade of experience combating Soviet SAM designs of a more diverse range than those that had been witnessed by the United States in Vietnam. They knew the strengths and weaknesses of their adversary's equipment and command and control networks, and they also got inside the decision-making cycles of their enemies. Ten years later as a coalition of nations drew a line in the sand and prepared to fight one of the most well-defended regimes in history, the lessons that the Israelis had learned and the techniques that they had devised would be adapted for use in a post-World War II air campaign the likes of which the world had never seen; but before that line was drawn, the last few years of the Cold War would be played out in continental Europe.

CHAPTER FOUR

Cold War SEAD

As America was withdrawing from the Vietnam quagmire, the thoughts of the USAF once again focused on the threat to Western Europe from the Soviet Union and Warsaw Pact nations of Poland, East Germany, Czechoslovakia, Bulgaria, Hungary and Romania. The Soviet Air Force (VVS - *Voenno-Vozdushnye Sil)* had watched the Vietnam War with interest and had taken note of the importance that the US Air Force and Navy had attached to air defence suppression.

Needless to say, both the Soviets and NATO had robust air defences protecting their respective parts of the Central Front, arrayed on either side of the Inner German Border (IGB), between the East and West segments of the country. The Soviets expected these air defences to form rings of steel around troops deployed in the field and key static targets such as tactical nuclear weapons storage facilities. If the VVS was to inflict serious damage on NATO from the air, then it had to keep NATO air defences suppressed or preferably destroy them. Therefore, the High Command took the SEAD mission as seriously as their NATO counterparts. Their SEAD doctrine was not overtly dissimilar to that of the USAF and the US Navy. The VVS favoured a layered approach to SEAD using electronic warfare, dedicated anti-radar weaponry and specialist aircraft to press the soft and hard kills home.

The Soviets did not separate SEAD missions from their other air operations in the event of a shooting war between East and West over Germany. For the VVS, the SEAD task was indivisible from other air operations. It was part and parcel of the same thing. For Soviet CAS and air interdiction to operate over the battlefield a robust SEAD effort would be required. The imperatives were to build routes into and out of enemy airspace for the strike aircraft, to maintain these routes as the battle developed and to prosecute new attacks against air defences as the targets emerged. Their doctrine also focused on performing attacks against known NATO air defence targets as opposed to prosecuting targets of opportunity in a similar fashion to their American counterparts in the Vietnam War. This may have been a reflection of the Soviet desire to control air operations tightly and place less of a premium on developing individual pilot initiative.

From 1959 Soviet doctrine had placed a strong emphasis on the nuclear battle. Any war on the Central Front was expected to focus on the early use of tactical and operational-level nuclear ballistic missiles against so-called 'battlefield' targets: supply depots, tank parks and troop concentrations being three examples. The air force would then 'clean up'; attacking battlefield targets which had not been obliterated during the initial atomic onslaught. The SEAD effort at the start of the campaign would have focused on a series of high-altitude nuclear airbursts which were intended to trigger the electro-magnetic pulse to destroy the circuitry in NATO air defence radar and communications. Aircraft which were entering enemy airspace would fly over areas of nuclear devastation, which would be cleansed of air defence, to press home their attacks on other targets around the battlefield.

The VVS lacked a specific squadron or wing which was tasked with SEAD. In essence, SEAD assets were parcelled out across the air forces that would fight the air campaign over Germany. The Soviets had their air power organised into so-called Task Groups which were usually of a squadron strength and within these task groups, there would be up to four aircraft which were outfitted either with ARMs or with conventional free-fall munitions to attack air defence targets such as SAM sites or radar which were positioned along the planned Soviet routes of ingress over the NATO area. It was expected that in the event of an attack being ordered against a specific tactical target, the SEAD aircraft from each task group would proceed ahead of the main strike force to sanitize a corridor to the target with either ARMs or with conventional ordnance. Such targets were expected to be airfields, corps headquarters, reserve/second echelon areas and military-industrial targets such as munitions factories. The SEAD aircraft would be tasked with smashing the air defences arrayed around such installations.

At the crux of Soviet air force thinking was the plan to begin any campaign against NATO with air strikes deep into Alliance territory to attack targets such as nuclear weapons storage facilities and NATO airfields - a reason why aircraft such as the USAF A-10A Thunderbolt and the RAF's Harrier GR3 aircraft could operate from roads. The Soviet military command was especially concerned with preventing tactical nuclear weapons from being dispersed into the field and therefore placed a high premium in attacking these facilities before this could happen.

When planning how they would perform these attacks against the air and nuclear targets, the Soviets realised that NATO's air defences would have to be smashed. To this end, Soviet air-war planners were said to have built models of NATO air defences which they envisaged as having a pyramid structure. The Alliances' air surveillance and EW radar was located at the top of the pyramid. Below these were the initial and final target acquisitions radar and then the guidance radar for individual weapons systems.

The VVS placed the attack of the air surveillance and EW radar at a premium and would concern itself with these systems at the start of a campaign. The idea was to blast these systems with countermeasures. With the radar at the top of the pyramid destroyed, delays would be sown into the system as radar further down the chain would not have information on which to base their targeting decisions because they would not know what to look for until it was well within their own field of view, which would consequently give the air defence AAA and SAMs less time to act.

The Soviets also placed a premium on attacking the critical CoGs in the air defence pyramid. This takes us back into the realms of the Manoeuvrist approach to SEAD, but the VVS clearly realised that if it could paralyse key junctions in the system where information was to be passed to other radar or where attack decisions would be made, then they would have to face less of a threat once their aircraft were performing attacks on battlefield targets. Interestingly, the Soviets placed a high premium on using electronic countermeasures to perform this mission. The Soviets would also engage the radar and defences at the bottom of the pyramid, but they had made a shrewd calculation that these systems were the most numerous, mobile and ultimately the most difficult to engage. They would still present a serious threat, but with the NATO IADS decapitated, they would work in a less coordinated and adroit fashion. These systems at the bottom tier could be dealt with using organic aircraft countermeasures and ARMs as and when required by a strike force.

Soviet Arms
The VVS were not overly keen to 'get in close' in a similar fashion to how their American counterparts had confronted air defences in Vietnam. Instead, they focused on stand-off SEAD and their weapons designs are testament to this. For example, the Kh-28 (NATO codement AS-9 Kyle) anti-radar missile had a range of 75 miles (110 km), compared to the 10 miles (16 km) of the AGM-45 Shrike. Moreover, the VVS also placed a premium on using their considerable signals intelligence aircraft such as the Tu-16PP (NATO codename Badger-H), Tu-22KD (Blinder-C) and Yak-28PP (Brewer-E) for the SEAD battle, tasking them with collecting as much intelligence as possible on the electronic behaviour of NATO's air defences. By doing this, they could paint a comprehensive picture of the electronic order of battle they faced across the Iron Curtain and the most appropriate measures for dealing with it.

Prior to any air operation by the Soviet air force across the NATO area, Signals Intelligence (SIGINT) units on the ground, along with those in the air, would listen hard for electronic emissions emanating from NATO's air defence system. The results of this intelligence trawl would then be forwarded to the command centre planning the air operation to help plot the electronic order of battle so that the VVS could plan its routes into and out of NATO airspace. The SIGINT effort would not be performed in isolation, it would be joined by an intensive effort from photo-reconnaissance aircraft which would also look for radar and SAM sites from the Soviet side of the IGB. The most intensive photo and SIGINT collection efforts would be directed to those areas where the VVS would established their air corridors. The idea was to perform a two-tiered SEAD effort. Electronic jamming would be used intensively against known radar when the time for the attack came, meanwhile aircraft carrying hard-kill SEAD weaponry would be assigned to those targets of opportunity not originally mapped as part of the electronic order of battle.

The first large-scale strike by Warsaw Pact aircraft into NATO areas, namely West Germany, would see a huge electronic jamming effort to saturate NATO's air defences with as much white noise as possible. The VVS was expected to prioritise NATO air defence threats based on the danger that they could pose to the Soviet/WARPAC (Warsaw Pact) air offensive. Some targets could be rendered useless by jamming alone, but the VVS recognised that this would not be the case for all air defence targets and that a hard kill would be necessary for some, presumably those close enough to inflict losses on the VVS/WARPAC aircraft using corridors of entrance and exit over NATO territory. The hard kill technology developed by the Soviets which is examined in greater detail below reflected this. Soviet SEAD doctrine called for the most dangerous and robust NATO defences to be smashed with a deliberate onslaught of both jamming and missile attack.

The VVS was also expected to place Mil Mi-8MV (NATO reporting name Hip-J) helicopters in the SEAD fight. These aircraft were outfitted with powerful jamming systems which had a stand-off range of 62 miles (100 km). This could allow the helicopters to operate at some distance from the targeted radar emitter. They would work in conjunction with fixed-wing aircraft armed with free-fall bombs. The helicopters could provide the radar jamming while the planes flew towards the radar at low-level, dropping their ordnance on the SAM site. Traditionally, Soviet military doctrine is seen as stressing mass, just look at the numbers of ground units arrayed against NATO during the Cold War (five Soviet armies in East Germany alone). However, Soviet SEAD doctrine seemed decidedly Manoeuvirst in some ways.

The SEAD effort was focused on puncturing a single hole through a weak point of NATO SAM and air defence coverage. It was through these weak points that the attack corridors would be established for waves of Soviet/WARPAC aircraft to follow their jamming and SEAD hard kill escorts over the Forward Edge of the Battle Area (FEBA) to their battlefield and their tactical targets. These aircraft would also be accompanied by photo-reconnaissance planes which could perform Battle-Damage Assessment (BDA) of the air defences which had been attacked to ascertain whether there was any need for a second attack.

The kinetic SEAD attack would work by providing 'top cover' to attacking VVS/WARPAC aircraft which would race towards their targets at below 328 ft (100 m). The ARM shooters would meanwhile fly at between 1,640–13,123 ft (500–4,000 m), if they were attacking a Hawk site, which they would do at a range of up to 31 miles (50 km) from the missiles. If they were engaging an MIM-14 Nike Hercules SAM battery, they could do this from around 75 miles (120 km) away from the target at an altitude between 6,561–19,685 ft (2,000–6,000 m). Badger-H aircraft were able to fly over enemy air space with the opening attack packages to sow chaff to further extend the length, breadth and integrity of the air corridor as the NATO air defences were rolled back. VVS/WARPAC aircraft expected to experience their most intense concentrations of NATO air defences near the frontlines where numerous MIM-23 Hawk SAM batteries were expected to be located, intertwined with the Nike Hercules batteries.

Air Defences were also expected in depth as the NATO FEBA stretched back towards the rear, it was through these defences that the gap in the NATO IADS would be pushed. The shorter range systems such as Gepard, Roland, Rapier and Vulcan SAMs used by the German, French, British and American forces would be engaged by Soviet/WARPAC artillery. These systems would not be attacked using ARMs and attack aircraft would instead avoid them, unless of course they were arrayed to protect another target. In this case, it was expected that such targets would be attacked by aircraft armed with free-fall bombs. Soviet doctrine clearly did not place a high premium on hitting the shorter-range systems with ARMs which would instead be reserved for the longer range air defence systems.

All in all, Soviet air-war planners expected their sanitized ingress and egress corridors to be up to 31 miles (50 km) wide and up to 124 miles (200 km) in depth which again mirrors the

characteristics of the chaff corridor which was sown prior to the
Czechoslovakia invasion. Both operational and tactical aviation
were expected to use the same ingress and egress corridors which
would take them to waypoints from which they would pursue
separate routes to and from their targets. In essence, the corridors
were designed to get them some way over the most dangerous
NATO air defences. Strike groups were expected to fly through
the corridors at low level in tandem with each group of strike
packages separated by around six miles (10 km) at five-minute
intervals. VVS/WARPAC planners were also thought to have
drafted carefully precise ingress and egress times for the packages, which may have also been designed to reduce the risk of
fratricide from CAPS which would know where a certain package
of aircraft was expected to be at a certain time.

An example of an attack profile for a Hawk battery would have
seen a total of eight aircraft, organised into two flights of four
aircraft, attack the battery. Two of the aircraft would be outfitted
with anti-radiation missiles and would approach the target at low
level. They would climb to allow their acquisition and designation system to paint the radar before the missiles were fired,
these would then fly towards the radar giving the operators a
choice of either disengagement in an attempt to break the
missile's lock, or destruction. They would approach the target
from up to three different headings with groups of two aircraft
each making a single pass. It was envisaged that the Soviets
would establish at least one corridor over each front as
Soviet/WARPAC ground units went into action. In total, NATO
expected around six corridors to be created over the IGB and the
West German border with Czechoslovakia.

This was not all idle supposition. It is true that the Soviets did
not have a level of SEAD experience equivalent to the Americans
in Vietnam, but that said, they did perform isolated examples that
NATO analysts were able to exploit in order to gain an insight
into how the Soviets might prosecute a defence suppression
effort. On 20 August 1968, Soviet forces launched a land and air
invasion of Czechoslovakia in response to a period of
Czechoslovak liberalisation of the press, politics and the
economy. Mindful of the ability of Czechoslovakian radar to
detect the incoming force of Soviet aircraft, the VVS sewed a chaff

corridor which was 230 miles (370 km) in length alongside an intense electronic jamming effort which lasted for around six hours. This operation betrayed the ability of the Soviets not only to sow a chaff corridor but also maintain it. The chaff corridor had two distinct attributes in that not only did it screen attacking aircraft but it also shielded those aircraft performing jamming operations.

In the event of a corridor being punched through NATO's air defences the stand-off jamming effort would continue using Antonov An-12C/D (Cub) aircraft which would coordinate their radar jamming in conjunction with jamming by ground units of NATO air defence communications nets. It was the Cubs that were primarily tasked with jamming NATO's EW radar and fighter Ground Control Intercept systems. As well as jamming the radar electronically, these Cubs could also sow chaff corridors. The idea was to prevent NATO radar from seeing the VVS/WARPAC strike packages which were being assembled behind the Soviet frontlines. These aircraft were initially intended to be stationed well back from the Soviet FEBA, but presumably they could be moved further into West Germany as the air defences on the NATO side of the front line were depleted and as Soviet forces pushed through NATO forward echelons.

In terms of SEAD hard kill, the Soviets would not just use their ARMs. The importance that they placed on the anti-SAM operation is reflected in the fact that a number of different weapons systems could be applied to this end. That 'God of War', as Stalin had termed artillery, could be turned to the SEAD task with tactical rockets and missiles being applied to the fight, in particular hitting time-critical air defence targets as they became available especially if they were just too dense to be attacked by SEAD aircraft. Some commentators have even argued that the Soviets would have attacked NATO air defences with as much artillery as possible before a VVS/WARPAC air assault got underway and it is certainly not inconceivable that Soviet air war planners would want to deplete as much NATO air defence as possible before sending their aircraft into harms' way. It was thought that the Soviet 9M714U *Totshka* SS-21 (NATO reporting name Scarab) surface-to-surface missiles could have been applied to the SEAD fight in this fashion with the weapon being outfitted with an anti-radar guidance system to attack Hawk radar. Its conventional 9N123F 264 lb (120 kg) high explosive fragmentation warhead which would have been used to attack Hawk SAM batteries.

Bearcraft

Soviet design bureaux did turn their impressive talents to developing SEAD versions of aircraft which were put into production. The first attempt to develop a comprehensive SEAD platform was the Yak-28N which appeared on the drawing boards between 1964–65. This aircraft represents the only Soviet attempt to build a 'pure' SEAD aircraft, in a similar fashion to the USAF's F-4G Phantom-II Advanced Wild Weasel. The airframe for the Yak-28N was to be the Yak-28I which had been designed as a tactical bomber. That aircraft had been fitted with an *Initsyatyva* targeting radar which was traded for a radar detection and target acquisition system. This system was to be connected to a pair of Kh-28 ARMs. The detection and acquisition system would listen to the spectrum for the enemy radar and the Kyles would be sent in for the kill. The aircraft was developed as a prototype and by 1972 had completed testing, yet the project was abandoned because the Yak-28 design was not considered up to scratch as a modern attack aircraft. That is not to say that the aircraft was abandoned completely. Instead the Yak-28PP (NATO codename Brewer-E) was developed for waging electronic warfare using equipment which had previously been fitted on the Tupolev Tu-16PP (NATO codename Badger-J) electronic warfare aircraft. The employment for the Yak-28PP called for a formation of three aircraft, each of which would jam a separate part of the electronic spectrum to cover as many radar threats as possible. The aircraft would operate in such a way as to establish a jamming corridor through enemy air space which a strike package of aircraft could follow.

Other Soviet SEAD aircraft would continue the early efforts of the Yak-28N. The Mikoyan-Gurevich design bureau would build the MiG-25BM (NATO reporting name Foxbat-F) aircraft which was to be used for the SEAD mission, despite the fact that this was not its principal role. The BM was designed from 1976 ostensibly as a high speed tactical nuclear bomber and sixty were built between 1982 and 1985, however a third of these were re-roled as MiG-25RB reconnaisance aircraft outfitted with a target acquisition system. The rolling of the BM for the SEAD fight focused on the fact that the aircraft could operate well into the heavens at an altitude of 68,900 ft (21,000 m). Interestingly, in a departure from normal Soviet SEAD doctrine, the BMs were expected to operate independently of other aircraft and to roam above the battlefield in groups looking for air defence targets to engage. One attack profile called for the aircraft to use tactical nuclear weapons to perform a high-altitude area attacks against concentrations of SAMs or other large air defence targets. Needless to say, such attacks did not place a heavy emphasis on accuracy, but instead relied on explosive mass to vaporise the target. The MiG-25BMs were allocated to the 98th Reconnaissance Wing was based at Monchegorsk, near Murmansk, north-west Russia.

The VVS did develop another SEAD aircraft, notably the Su-24M (NATO codename Fencer-D). The aircraft was able to carry Kh-31T and Kh-58U anti-radar missiles which could use data collected by a 'Fantasmagoria' pod which would monitor the spectrum for enemy radar in a similar way to the HARM Targeting System (HTS) on the F-16CJ Wild Weasel.

The VVS did contemplate deploying Fencers to Afghanistan during their intervention in the country between 1979–1989. This was not so much because of the threat from the Mujahideen rebels operating FIM-92A Stinger missiles but because of Soviet aircraft operating over Afghanistan being illuminated on a regular basis by Pakistani air defence radar when the aircraft were performing raids into Pakistan air space to attack Mujahideen supply and infiltration/exfiltration routes. During the attacks, usually performed by Tu-16 Badger bombers, it was proposed that an accompanying Su-24M join the formation armed with Kh-58s to attack the Pakistani radar if necessary. However, this idea was never more than just that. It was realised by the Air Force command that there was a risk that the Kh-58s may decide to home-in on Afghan Air Traffic Control radar at Khost and Kandahar airfields and that attacking and destroying a Pakistani air search radar could cause an international outcry and cause a dangerous escalation in the conflict if the south Asian country decided to become overtly involved. As it was, Soviet aircraft would perform raids into Pakistan unescorted by SEAD assets.

Missiles

The first dedicated Soviet ARM was the Kh-28. The missile was envisaged as a tactical weapon and work began on the system in January 1963 by the OKB-2-155 Raduga design bureau. It has been alleged that one of the reasons for the development of the missile may have been a growing lack of confidence that the Soviet military command had in the ability of their tactical nuclear weapons to destroy all their major targets at the beginning of a campaign; targets which would include NATO's air defence infrastructure. The development of the missile was part of an effort to develop the so-called K-28 *Protivradiolokatsyonny* or 'anti-radar' complex of systems which was to include the Kh-28 missile along with the Yak-28N.

Ten years after development of the missile began it entered service with the VVS. The supersonic missile was propelled to its target by an R-253-300 rocket motor. The missile's range was up to 124 miles (200 km) to target NATO's Nike Hercules systems from a stand-off range. In turn, the missile's APR-28 targeting system was optimised to listen for the radar which accompanied the Nike Hercules system. The missile was also calibrated to search for the British Thunderbird SAM system. The Kh-28 would enjoy a twenty-year life span, finally leaving production in 1983. The Kh-28 was undoubtedly a great first step for Soviet anti-radiation missiles. That said, it did have its shortcomings. Weighing in at 1,576 lb (715 kg), the missile was not exactly light which resulted in the Su-17M being able to take only a single missile aloft which was connected to the aircraft's Myetyel radar detection and acquisition system.

The MiG-27 (NATO codename Flogger D) could not carry any of the Kh-28s at all, given that it was simply too heavy and large to attach to underwing hardpoints on the aircraft. It was these weight issues which led to the development of the Kh-27 (NATO codename AS-10 Karen). The missile was part of two anti-radar programmes which were launched in 1972, the other being the Kh-24 system. It is noteworthy that the Soviets did not seem to develop a single ARM system which was rolled out across various aircraft types for SEAD missions as did the Americans with the Shrike, Standard and the later HARM systems. Instead, they developed specific ARMs for specific airframes. For example, the Kh-27 was developed for the MiG-27 while the Kh-24 was developed for the Sukhoi Su-24.

Developed by the OKB Zvezda design bureau, the construction of the Kh-27 owed its lineage to the Kh-23/AS-7 (NATO code-mane Kerry). The latter was a guided missile which had been developed for the MiG-23 (NATO codename Flogger). Three years after its development began the Kh-27 began trials in 1975 before entering service in 1977. The missile did not see a huge production run as it would be replaced by the Kh-25MP. That said, the weapon was deployed with the MiG-27D/K/M and also the Su-17M3, with each aircraft carrying two missiles along with their *Vyuga* targeting pod.

Soviet ARMs underwent a minor design revolution with the advent of the Kh-25M. The missile used a modular design concept which allowed guidance systems and tail assemblies to be inter-changed on a common missile core. The Kh-24/-27 missiles became the common core around which the Kh-25M system was developed. The missile could use three different guidance systems which included a laser system, radio command and, in the case of SEAD, an anti-radar system. The different missile configurations were designated Kh-28ML/MP and MR accord-ingly. By using the modular concept, the Kh-25 gave the Soviets a SEAD system which could be deployed on a whole host of aircraft given that the Kh-25 could be fitted to the Su-17M3/M4 as well as the MiG-27M/K and D. In terms of SEAD, the radio-command guidance system for the MR allowed the missile to attack the AN/MPQ-33/-39 and -34 radar for the Hawk systems and the AN/MPQ-46/-48 system for the I-Hawk. An aircraft carrying the missile could also be outfitted with SPS-141/-142 and -143 jamming systems which gave the host aircraft a fully self-contained SEAD capability, with the radar targeting and acquisition system, the missile to kill that radar and the counter-measures to provide protection during the attack.

Soviet Su-24M Fencer-D aircraft were outfitted with the Kh-58 (NATO codename AS-11 Kilter) anti-radar missiles as their stan-dard ARM. These weapons were slaved to the L-086A

'Fantasmagoria-A' or L-086B 'Fantasmagoria-B' target acquisition and designated system. The Fencer was able to carry two of
these missiles, and they entered service in 1982. The Kh-58 maintained the stand-off tradition, being launched at ranges of up to
99 miles (160 km) when fired at an altitude of 49,212 ft (15,000 m).
This allowed the missile to engage the I-Hawk and MIM-104
Patriot system, which entered service in 1984, from beyond the
SAM's range. The missile was designed to attack the target from
with a steep dive, by performing a climb after the missile was
launched. This was to attack the radar from the 'dead zone' which
covers the airspace directly above a search radar which the
system cannot observe due to the position of its dish. The Kh-58
was able to intercept radar such as the AN/TPS-43/-44 EW
systems. The missile's seeker system was also calibrated to recognise the AN/MPQ-53 search, target detection, tracking and
identification radar of the Patriot SAM system.

The missile received further improvement as the Kh-58U
variant entered service. The Kh-58U had substantial range
improvement, allowing it to be launched an astonishing 155 miles
(250 km) from the targeted radar. Other improvements to the
weapon gave the Soviets new tactical options. The Kh-58U seeker
system allowed the missile to be fired and then to lock onto a
target after launch. This would allow the host aircraft, in this case
the MiG-25BM, which was its principal carrier to fire the weapon
pre-emptively as it worked to clear a corridor of air defences.

Soviet design bureaux were quick to take lessons from their
rivals. When the AGM-88 HARM entered service in 1983, it
became clear that speed was also a potent weapon in the SEAD
fight. The HARM was, after all, capable of reaching speeds of
1,416 mph (2,280 km/h). In the SEAD fight, speed is life. The
faster an ARM, the less time the doomed radar operators would
have to react by moving their SAM site for example or by
switching off the radar in an attempt to break the missile's lock.
The OKB Zvezda design bureau decided to combine its expertise
in long-range missiles with a high-speed design. The result was
the Kh-31 (AS-17 Krypton) series. This yielded two missile
designs; the Kh-31A anti-ship variant and the Kh-31P anti-
radar missile. A boosted rocket motor and four ramjets could take
the missile to Mach 3.6 while its weight of 1,499 lb (600 kg) made

it noticeably lighter than the Kh-58 system. With the target radar illuminated, the missile's Circular Error of Probability was in the region of up to 22 ft (7 m), but if the radar was deactivated, the missile could still score a hit up to 98 ft (30 m) away. Added to this was the missile's range of 68 miles (110 km).

Development of the Kh-31P began in the early 1980s, and following trials concluded in 1990, the missile entered service the following year as the Cold War drew to a close. It is perhaps ironic that the Soviets' most potent SEAD asset entered service as its intended purpose evaporated, although that is a fact of military life that can arguably be applied to an array of other military systems. The missile found its way onto the Su-34M and it was also trialled with the MiG-29, Su-25, Su-34, Su-35 and Yak-141, although it would enter service on the Su-24M. The ensuing economic implosion that Russia suffered in the wake of the Soviet Union's disintegration had severe effects on the Russian air force budget and it was thought that only a handful of the missiles ever entered service, with enough to equip a solitary unit of Su-24M. Weapons designers took the weapon forward in the mid-1990s by designing the Kh-31PD which had an increased range of 93 miles (150 km), although none of these missiles ever entered service.

The Soviets knew full well that NATO aircraft could pose as much of a threat to their own fielded forces as the Soviets could to the Western alliance. Typically, a Motorised Rifle Division (MRD) would possess around 100 SA-7 MANPADS spread across infantry and tank companies. These would be supplemented by two batteries each containing four ZSU-23-4 systems and four SA-9 self-propelled SAM launchers. In addition, the unit would also have twenty SA-6 launchers carrying sixty missiles in total, or twenty SA-8 launchers carrying eighty missiles. The Soviets had ten MRDs deployed throughout their five armies in East Germany, and this does not include the air defence tally for their tank divisions.

What is more, much of this air defence was mobile and could move with the ground units as they drove through the Fulda Gap on the IGB in West Germany. The USAF had experienced Soviet air defences in Vietnam and clearly had accumulated much experience in dealing with systems such as SA-2s. However, the Soviet units in East Germany featured air defences which neither the United States, nor their allies, had encountered *en masse*. What is more, there would be a massive array of air defences to contend with. If war had ever been unleashed across the IGB, many of the SEAD tactics would have been learnt on the hoof which could have led to significant losses for NATO SEAD aircraft. It was with this in mind that following its withdrawal from Vietnam, the USAF began to look afresh at the Central Front battlefield and what SEAD assets it could bring to the fight. The Soviets had spent the 1970s and 80s reinforcing their SEAD and air defence capabilities; it was time for the West to reply in kind.

The Phantom Menace

As the war in South East Asia wound down in the mid-1970s, the USAF looked to beef-up its SEAD capabilities in Europe. NATO received a squadron of F-4G Advanced Wild Weasels from 1979 and they were deployed as part of the 52nd TFW at Spangdahlem AFB, West Germany. The Wild Weasel unit was designated as the 81st TFS and was tasked with not only getting used to operating over West Germany and Europe in general, but also operating with NATO air forces which had a distinct and often disparate array of aircraft.

The Phantoms of the 81st heralded a change for the Wild Weasel community. The trusty F-105G had been the mission stalwart since 1967 and it was now being put out to pasture. The final F-105G Wild Weasel mission was flown on the 25 May 1983 by the Georgia Air National Guard. The Thud was a well-loved aircraft and the transition to the F-4G Wild Weasel had been difficult at times. The F-105G was felt by some flyers to enjoy more agility at low altitude compared to the new kid on the block. Some members of the community felt that the USAF should commission a new dedicated Wild Weasel airframe and not simply use a modification of an existing aircraft. There were also concerns as to whether the Phantoms could keep abreast of the new generations of F-15 and F-16 aircraft that the USAF and allied air forces throughout NATO were introducing into service from the mid-1970s. However, a choice had to be made on what could replace the F-105G given that production of the aircraft ended in 1964, thus making the replacement of the aircraft lost through attrition impossible. The great hope for the USAF was the F-4C

Phantom-II which was to be rolled out as a multi-role aircraft across the USAF following the Navy's successful experiences with the plane from 1963.

The first attempt at developing the Phantom into a SEAD platform had been conducted using the F-4C. A number of F-4C Wild Weasel airframes were converted into the F-4C Wild Weasel IV and they were delivered from August 1968. The F-4C aircraft were upgraded, being outfitted with the AN/ALR-53 Countermeasures Receiver. This system was notably more accurate and lower maintenance than the ER-142 system which it replaced. Other modifications include the Charlie's APR-25/26 RHAWS being replaced by the AN/ALR-46 RWR which was also installed on the F-105G from 1973. Despite these upgrades the air force planned to phase out the Charlies as the F-4G Advanced Wild Weasel was developed.

In order to get from the F-4C to the F-4G Advanced Wild Weasel, the USAF experimented with two F-4D aircraft. The initiative was primarily to provide the Phantom with the ability to fire the AGM-78 Standard Anti-Radiation Missile. To make this a reality, the aircraft were outfitted with an AN/APS-107 and ER-142 RWR; the latter of which was already in service on the US Navy's A-6B aircraft. However, the AN/APS-107E system was fitted to F-4D aircraft as the 1970s drew to a close, although this was not used for aircraft operating in the SEAD role. What these two Delta aircraft did that was so important to the Advanced Wild Weasel programme was to ensure that the Standard missile was compatible with the aerodynamic characteristics of the Phantom and the aircraft's RWRs. Interestingly, the original plan called for the F-4D to form the basis of the Advanced Wild Weasel programme, but this was abandoned by the air force top brass in favour of using the F-4E airframe as the basis for the aircraft after the latter became available from 1965.

The F-4G had several features which betrayed its identity: its F-4E shape being the most obvious. Secondly, the aircraft had a chin pod which dispensed with the M61A 0.78 in (20 mm) cannon while a large fairing was visible on the aircraft's vertical fin. Each of these additions housed one of the IBM AN/ALR-74 RWRs. Each side of the nose was adorned with six low-band stub antennae with another two also mounted on the vertical tail.

There was an additional two-blade antenna beneath the chin fairing which would receive radar signals in the mid and high bands, along with additional low band antennae positioned below the chin fairing and on the aircraft's spine. In total, the aircraft contained fifty-two antennae which were linked to the AN/APR-38 RHAWS.

The Advanced Wild Weasel was designed with precisely the mobile Soviet SAM threat in mind. Under the bonnet, the secret of the F-4G was the AN/APR-38 which was designed to process a larger quantity of information that had been the case with the AN/ALR-31 system on the F-105G during the Vietnam War. The F-4G later received an upgrade which removed the AN/APR-38 system in favour of the AN/APR-47 RHAWS. For the backseaters the rear cockpit was unlike anything ever seen by a Wild Weasel Bear. The office featured three large scopes which included the large Plan Position Indicator. To the left a Panoramic and Analysis display and the Homing and Attack display on the right-hand side. Other controls included the missile programmer panel and a recorder control panel. The rear cockpit also included the aircraft's flight controls although the backseater has no forward vision to fly the aircraft. Moreover, although the F-4G had its internal cannon deleted, the aircraft was able to carry air-to-air missiles in the form of AIM-7 Sparrow and AIM-9 Sidewinder weapons to improve its self defence against other aircraft, along with a phalanx of air-to-ground weapons which also included AGM-65 Mavericks, it was the AGM-88 HARM anti-radar weapons which would be its most sought-after characteristics in the event of a war with the Soviets.

It is worth spending a moment to dwell on the AN/APR-38 to appreciate fully what this system brought to the SEAD party. At the time, it was the most sophisticated attack system of its kind in service anywhere. The AN/APR-38 took data from a number of sources including the aircraft's position in the air and its flight characteristics, its weapons load-out and their fire control systems. This would present a picture of any threat faced by the aircraft and the aircraft's position as regards that threat. This would in turn prioritise the threats which were around the aircraft and highlight the ordnance available to eliminate them. The capabilities of the system allowed the Bear to monitor up to fifteen different threats using the Plan Position Indicator. What is more, the APR-38 was also able to tell the EWO *what* kind of threat they were facing, while also telling them the range of the emitting radar from the F-4G and its bearing from the aircraft. Taking all of these factors into account, the system would then recommend attack profiles based on the ARM missiles on board the aircraft, along with the maximum and minimum ranges for employing those weapons and the limit of the azimuth from which they could be fired. There was an added function built into the system which would allow the EWO to override the recommendations of the AN/APR-38 if they had been ordered to attack more pressing targets.

The ARMs which could be carried by the F-4G included the AGM-45C Shrike which was gradually phased out to make way for the AGM-88 HARM. The AGM-78D Standard ARM was also available and had the capacity to be fired by the Phantom 'off-boresight'; that is when the aircraft is pointing away from the hostile radar. The Standard also went some way to addressing the favourite North Vietnamese tactic of switching off their radar if they thought that a Weasel or one of its missiles was homing in on them. Sure, they could throw the switch but what they could not control was the fact that the missile would remember where the radar was located and unless the radar operators were highly skilled at packing up their radar and getting away from their location in double-quick time, they would almost certainly be giving their lives for their country. The ultimate incarnation of the Standard would be the D-2 variant which was produced from 1973 and would stay on the production line until 1976. This version had a 223 lb (101 kg) blast-fragmentation warhead, along with active optical fusing. The production run would lead to a total of 700 D-2 variants being produced. Like the Shrike, Standard was eventually replaced by the HARM.

On the F-4G the AGM-88 missile would take its targeting information from the APR-38 system and had three times the range of the ten miles (16 km) of the AGM-45A Shrike which was good news for the F-4G crew and their survival.

Not dependent on radar signals for homing, the AGM-65 Maverick nevertheless found a niche as an anti-radar missile. The weapon was guided by television which had a disadvantage of needing clear weather to keep watch on its target which meant that cloudy or dusty skies could make it unusable. Of course, the other side of this coin was that once sited by a Maverick, there was little point in the radar operator switching off their signal as it would make no difference. Some way was found around the visibility issue by developing the AGM-65D version which used IR to allow the missile to be used in low-visibility conditions. To protect the aircraft, the F-4G also had the AN/ALQ-119V-17 and AN/ALQ-131 countermeasures systems to enhance its self-protection.

The significant increase in the capabilities of the F-4G led to a commensurate rise in the training syllabus to get the crews ready to operate with the aircraft. Before pilots could enrol for F-4G Advanced Wild Weasel training they had to have 500 hours experience in tactical aircraft. Meanwhile, the EWOs were creamed off from the electronic warfare school at Mather AFB, California after they had completed a twenty-five week course. Training was performed at the 39th Tactical Fighter Training Squadron which was in turn part of the 37th Tactical Fighter Wing located at George AFB. California. Before they were let loose flying against the Soviet Air Defence Radar simulator at Nellis AFB the would-be Weaselers learned the characteristics and employment options for anti-radiation missiles along with tactics for the Wild Weasel mission.

Once they had completed their eight week course, these crews were sent to the one of a number of Wild Weasel units. These could include either the 561st or the 562nd TFS which were themselves housed at George AFB, of the 81st TFS at Spangdahlem in West Germany. Alternatively the 90th TFS which was located at Clark AFB in the Philippines was also an option. It is worth noting that each F-4G could be teamed with a pair of F-4Es. This was intended to widen defence suppression coverage by having the F-4G act as a command and control platform which could hand-off air defence targets for the Echoes to attack. Thus the F-4G also made its name as a force multiplier and allowed the air force to increase the size of its SEAD assets in Germany without buying any additional aircraft. During the Cold War the practice time for the F-4Gs was rigorous, with the aircraft performing up to fifteen sorties each month which equated to a similar number of hours flight time, while in addition to this, the crews would also participate in the annual Red Flag multinational training exercises at Nellis AFB each year respectively.

The first time that the F-4G was in a real life SEAD situation was on 26 August 1981. A Lockheed SR-71A Blackbird reconnaissance aircraft had left Kadena AFB, Japan for a flight over the North Korean borders. Unbeknownst to the Blackbird pilot, the North Koreans had established a SAM site at Choc Ta Rie which fired on the aircraft, fortunately, the Guideline missed the Blackbird by two miles, although it was enough to cause the SR-71As to be escorted with defensive assets from the 90th TFS operating from Clark AFB, Philippines. The F-4Gs would fly near the so-called Demilitarized Zone (DMZ) which separated the Communist north from the Republic of Korea in the south. On these occasions the North Koreans desisted from warming up their radar and sending some SAMs aloft; a wise move given the destruction that they would have invited.

Even as they were entering service on the Central Front the F-4Gs still had detractors which were concerned at the aircraft's ability to perform the SEAD mission without sustaining massive losses. One concern focused on the weather over the IGB which could feature a cloud base at between 5,000–10,000 ft (1,524–3,048 m) for much of the year; forcing the Weasels to get down in the weeds to prosecute their SEAD mission. It was feared that this would put them squarely in the grip of Soviet short-range air defences such as the ZSU-23-4 mobile AAA system which were known to be particularly numerous near the Forward Edge of Battle Area, (FEBA). There were concerns in some quarters that unless the F-4Gs initially concerned themselves with these devastating threats they would be shot out of the skies like pheasants. However, the F-4Gs were not designed so much with the AAA threat in mind, therefore recommendations were made that two-seat versions of the A-10A should have been designed and tricked-up with a RHAWS to allow them to engage the short-range threats with their sledgehammer armament while the F-4Gs raced ahead to hit the SAMs further back. One of the attractions of the Warthog was that it was designed from the outset to fly at low level and cut Soviet armour, vehicles and troop positions to pieces, a similar treatment which it could visit on a Soviet AAA piece. Needless to say, for one reason or another, the idea never saw the light of day and the overarching responsibility for the SEAD fight remained with the Phantoms.

However, throughout the 1970s and 1980s, the USAF did not place all of its SEAD capabilities in one F-4G basket. The force looked at the SEAD mission from a holistic perspective and thought hard about what other platforms could offer to the fight. The Yom Kippur war of 1973 had been a wake-up call for the USAF and they were greatly fearful of a similar, sudden strike by the Soviets in Europe. A wholesale renewal of the force's electronic warfare capabilities was seen as just as important to the introduction of impressive platforms such as the F-4G. At the heart of the EW renewal was the Pave Strike initiative which was intended to find a replacement for the EB-66s which had worked so hard in Vietnam.

A solution was found in the form of the EF-111A. The F-111 tactical bomber was already a key element of NATO and US air power in Europe as a potent, high-speed swing-wing nuclear bomber. The EF-111A used the F-111A airframe and was outfitted with the AN/ALQ-99E radar jamming system. This equipment was already in service with the US Navy's EA-6B Prowler EW/SEAD aircraft and as the F-111A had a weapons bay, these jamming systems could be conveniently tucked away in the aircraft's belly. The bomb-aiming part of the F-111A's AN/AVQ-26 Pave Track electro-optical targeting system was discarded with the latter retained. They were also moved onto the aircraft's central panel where they could be accessed by either the pilot or the 'Whizzo', given that the Aardvark had a side-by-side cockpit. Instead the Whizzos would have the controls for the AN/ALQ-99E system located in front of them.

In terms of missiles, the seminal HARM would be fielded during the latter part of the Cold War, although the missile could trace its routes back to the late 1960s when the US Navy began to think about its own ARM. The scientists at the Naval Air Warfare Center at China Lake, California turned their brains to the AGM-88 HARM development. The design brief was to build a missile that would be quick off the rail, have an adequate size warhead to achieve a first hit, first kill. Flexible targeting, either pre-emptive or target of opportunity functions for example, had to be included and it had to be easily maintained in the field. One of the problems they had to confront was how to make the seeker distinguish between the emissions coming from the target and those reflected back from the ground when the emissions collided with terrain. This was to ensure that the missile would go for the radar as opposed to a patch of Earth. Flight testing of the missile began in 1975, although it would not be until 1981 that the seeker challenges were addressed, by then, the experiments with the missile were giving it a 75 per cent accuracy rate.

In combination with the missile, the AN/AWG-25 HARM control system was also developed which included that CP-1269 Command Launch Computer and C-10035 Control Indicator, it was the latter system which contained the missile's library of known radar emissions which could be updated regularly as new air search radar operating bands were detected. HARM could be employed in several fashions; these included being fired in a volley which was used for the pre-emptive attack of radar whose frequencies were already in the missile's memory and known to be operating in a particular area in which the HARM-carrying aircraft was operating. The missile could also be fired in Target of Opportunity (TOO) mode which, as the name suggests, could be used to attack radar targets as and when they became available and were highlighted by the aircraft's RWR. This could be done by the missile operator entering new targeting details into the AWG-25 system when the details of new threats had been briefed to the pilots before they took off on their mission.

And so it was that the HARM went through several incarnations with the first being the AGM-88A. This weapon carried a potent 145 lb (66 kg) blast-fragmentation warhead. The missile made its operational debut in 1986 during the Gulf of Sidra incident with Libya and was usually fired in a pre-emptive fashion to keep the air defences' heads down. Moreover, the Electronically Erasable/Programmable, Read-Only Memory (EEPROM) incorporated into the missile allowed it to be re-programmed on base with new radar threat details as they became available.

The AGM-88B became available from 1987 and was factory-fitted with the EEPROM system. Changes were also evident in the missile's computer software which allowed the missile to perform targeting for pre-emptive attack, along with its usual Self-Protection function against unexpected threats, and TOO mode for targets that the HARM flagged itself, while taking into account the latest information on the enemy's electronic order of battle, or could also be programmed in-flight to allow more flexible targeting. It was the Block-III version of the AGM-88B which worked especially hard during the SEAD operation in Desert Storm. In one interesting twist, the US Navy opted out of Block III, this was because the changes to the weapon required it being powered-up prior to a sortie if the missile was to be updated with new radar target information. The Navy was uneasy about having a live weapon powered-up below the decks of an aircraft carrier given the danger that this could pose to the ship if an uncontrolled explosion caused other weapons in the vicinity to 'cook-off'.

The first time that the HARM saw combat was when it was deployed by US Navy A-7E Corsair-II aircraft from the USS *America* and USS *Coral Sea* during Operation Eldorado Canyon against Libya. The missile was rolled out across the US Navy, equipping F/A-18A/B Hornets and EA-6B Block 82 Prowlers, with the first sea cruise of the weapon occurring in 1987 with the VAQ-131 Lancers and their EA-6B aircraft.

The weapon could be employed using a 'loft' manoeuvre by the pilots: sharply pulling their aircraft up and then the weapon releasing automatically once it was in-range of the target. Similarly, the missile could be fired without the aircraft pulling up, once the missile was in range and at the optimum angle to the target. After firing, the missile would climb and then dive down towards the target. Typically, Hornets would be catapulted with two missiles on the aircraft with a similar number being carried on the EA-6B.

It is perhaps a matter of irony, or that the Navy was in charge of the missile's development, but the F-4G received the AGM-88 after the Navy. As part of the Performance Update Program, the Advanced Wild Weasel received the AGM-88 as part of Phase I of the project which began in October 1982. The AN/APR-38 was modified and re-designated as the AN/APR-47 RAWS. The AN/APR-47 was a quantum leap over the previous system; it could flag up to thirty hostile radars within range of the aircraft on the PPI; with a threat flagged, the APR-47 would transmit the information on the threat, including the radar type, operating frequencies and pulse intervals. What was really clever about the system was that the APR-47 could also send information on secondary threats in the vicinity of the primary target giving the missile the option to engage other targets if for one reason or another, the primary radar went off the air.

However, as HARM was being rolled out across the US Navy and USAF, the DoD still had significant stocks of the Standard ARM which had been made largely obsolete. However, the Pentagon found homes for the surplus weapons sending some to Israel and South Korea with each receiving around 300 missiles. In the case of Israel, these missiles would be used over the Bekaa Valley to smash Syrian air defences. While the HARM was designed with the lessons of Vietnam and the reality of the Cold War in mind, this weapon would earn its many spurs in the post Cold War world. From Baghdad to Bosnia it would make the lives of radar operators thoroughly miserable, either turning them into ex-radar operators or turning them into nervous wrecks, terrified that opening their electronic eyes would invite a 'HARMful' response.

CHAPTER FIVE

Non Cold-War SEAD Operations 1965–1987

India and Pakistan would clash once again in 1965, as they had done in 1947, over the disputed northern and predominately Muslim, region of Kashmir. In the wake of infiltration by Muslim militants from Pakistan into the province in 1947, shortly after the British granted independence to Pakistan and India, the local leader Maharaja Hari Singh acceded the state of Jammu and Kashmir to the Indian Union in exchange for an Indian military deployment to repulse the infiltration. His actions, and India's continued administration of Jammu and Kashmir, has become a bone of contention between the two countries with Pakistan claiming the province as one of its own because of its Muslim demography and India holding onto its part of the state claiming its religious characteristics as an integral part of India's secular demographic composition.

Tensions between the government of Pakistan's leader Mohammad Ayub Khan and India's Prime Minister Lal Bahadur Shastri reached a peak in 1965 after Kashmir's full integration into India. Talks over the province's future through the auspices of the UN broke down in 1963 and two years later, Indian troops moved into a disputed border region between the two countries known as the Rann of Kutch in north-west India, where they took over a Pakistani police outpost. The police post was later recaptured by

Pakistani troops but the tensions between the two countries escalated to intolerable levels.

A month after the police outpost was once again in Pakistan's hands. In May 1965 Khan's government ordered guerrillas, which had been armed and trained in Pakistan, to infiltrate into Kashmir with the intention of causing unrest and a subsequent uprising against the Indian administration of the state. The insurgents received support from the Pakistani army as they went about their task in the form of artillery fire. Shortly afterwards the Pakistani Army then attempted to trap Indian troops located in the Chhamb salient in Kashmir. The result was a ferocious seventeen-day conflict between the two countries.

Air operations during the war were mostly focused on bombing raids along with air-to-air combat and reconnaissance missions with neither side achieving air superiority during the fighting. However, the conflict did feature a notable example of air defence suppression by India against a Pakistan radar station.

The *Bharatiya Vayu Sena* (Indian Air Force/IAF) No.16 squadron had been deployed to Bareilly AFB, north-eastern India in September 1965 and was equipped with English Electric Canberra B(I) Mk.58 bombers. The unit was tasked with attacking several targets in West Pakistan (the country was at the time divided into two 'wings' with East Pakistan attaining independence as Bangladesh in 1971, and West Pakistan subsequently becoming the modern day state of Pakistan). No.16 Squadron was enhanced with aircraft from No.5 Squadron which was also flying the Canberra. The target list for the two units from Bareily included the West Pakistan airfields of Chak Jhumra, Akwal, and Sargodha in northern Pakistan. Yet by far its most dangerous mission was to be the attack on the EW radar station at Badin in the south-west of the country.

Badin was located in Sindh in the south-east of Pakistan's western wing. The installation was located in a flat, lush part of the country and was operated by No.408 Squadron of the *Pakistan Fiza'ya* (Pakistan Air Force PAF). The installation was extremely important to the PAF. It contained not only an Air Defence Ground Environment search radar which allowed it to look at the air space to the east, a function it shared with the PAF radar station atop the 4,992 ft (1,521 m) Sakesar Peak which covered approaches to the north-east of the western wing; it was also a Sector Operations Centre, plotting inbound contacts and directing air defence fighters accordingly. At the heart of the system was the FPS-6 height-finder radar which had a 217 mile (350 km) range. The radar was constructed by General Electric and had been handed over from the United States as part of the military assistance that Pakistan received as a member of the US-led South-East Asian Treaty Organisation. The range of the radar gave it a good view of the IAF airfields at Bhuj, Jamnagar, Uttarlai and Jaisalmer; all near the western Indo-Pakistani border. In turn, the facility was also within easy reach of the No.32 Fighter Ground Attack Wing at Masroor AFB in southern Pakistan.

At the time, the IAF lacked ARMs which might have gone some way to assist the attack on the radar station and electronic jamming was also unavailable. Indian pilots would rely on their aircraft; training and tactical ingenuity to blind Pakistan's southern EW radar and to run the gauntlet of AAA defences and air defence fighters that they were sure would be there to meet them as they attacked the radar station. However, the IAF did have some up-to-date photo-reconnaissance of their target after a Canberra PR.Mk.57 of No.106 Squadron was flown over the facility. What the Indian pilots saw were two radomes which were atop a pair of 80 ft (24 m) high towers. The attack was to hit the eastern tower because intelligence operatives had deemed that this housed the radar's azimuth antenna which would determine an aircraft's point in the sky. The priority would be to destroy this target. Interestingly, it has been reported that the IAF's assessment was wrong in this regard and that the azimuth antenna was actually located in the other tower.

In the briefing room at Bareilly, it was decided that a single Canberra should lead the attack equipped with a Boulton Paul 0.79 in (20 mm) four-gun pack located in the weapons bay, and 2.67 in (68 mm) rockets. Behind the solitary Canberra would be another four aircraft equipped with dumb bombs along with a single Canberra acting as a decoy. This aircraft would climb to 10,000 ft (3,048 m) at a distance of 80 miles (128 km) from the target to draw any PAF fighters which may attempt to intercept the strike. The strike would commence from Agra AFB. The advantage was that this took the strike package slightly closer to their target, but still placed them in excess of 621 miles (1,000 km) from the radar station. Low-level ingress was a prerequisite and once in the vicinity of the target the lead Canberra would launch its rockets at the towers to mark the target while the four following aircraft would climb to bomb the radar station.

The lead aircraft approached the target skimming the surface at 30 ft (9 m) flying in to the radar station from the south. The lead aircraft fired the rockets at the dome and then turned towards the east to head for home. The eastern tower was destroyed by the nineteen rockets fired by the lead Canberra. The opening Canberra attack had left the target covered with smoke, and flak started to burst around the skies as the AAA defences woke up.

The strike package got underway with the first of the four bombers arriving at the radar site after the target had been marked. The aircraft were intended to fly in at two minute intervals staying at low-level before the pilot pulled up on the yoke and the aircraft climbed to 7,000 ft (2,133 m). The first two aircraft in the formation were armed with two 4,000 lb (1,814 kg) bombs, with the remaining pair of Canberras carrying six 1,000 lb (453 kg) weapons. However, the first two bombs landed some distance from their target. This was largely blamed on the fact that the ballistic flight profiles of the weapon were unknown. The second aircraft which arrived two minutes later had more luck while the last two scored direct hits. The radar station was wiped off the map, claiming the lives of two PAF members.

Despite the attack, the PAF did upgrade the radar at Badin. This time installing the FPX-89/100 radar system, although this system was later decommissioned, its task instead being absorbed by the Westinghouse TPS-43G air-search radar which had a range in the region of 279 miles (450 km). The PAF also sought to frustrate future targeting by building fake radar sites, but this did not stop Badin and Sakesar being attacked during the 1971 Indo-Pakistan war.

1971

The strategic backdrop to the 1971 Indo-Pakistan war was focused on the eastern wing of Pakistan. Popular resentment in the eastern wing had grown regarding its rule from Islamabad in the western wing. An independence movement in the east began to flourish led by the *Mukhti Bahini* guerrilla force. The eastern wing declared independence in March 1971 which brought an immediate armed response from Pakistani army units that were deployed in the eastern wing and additional troops which were airlifted from West Pakistan.

India became involved in the conflict after the country began to absorb huge numbers of Bengali refugees fleeing the fighting from the eastern wing, and following an air-to-air skirmish in late-November in which the IAF claimed two PAF F-86 Sabres. The PAF launched twenty-eight sorties against IAF airfields at Amritsar, Ambala, Agra, Awantipur, Bikaner, Halwara, Jodhpur, Jaisalmer, Pathankot, Srinagar and Uttarlai on 3 December 1971 which brought a response in kind from the IAF after Prime Minister Indira Gandhi declared war on the same day.

To the south-east of the action, the USAF and Navy were embroiled in SEAD strikes of their own against the considerable air defences of the North Vietnamese. Meanwhile, across one of the world's most fractious borders between two of its bitterest rivals, the earth would reverberate once more with the sound of explosions as India not only supported Bangladesh's birth pangs, but audaciously undertook a two-front war against West Pakistan.

The air campaign in this conflict was noteworthy for suppression operations being performed by each belligerent. Such missions were focused on the EW radar operated by either side. On the same day that the PAF performed its pre-emptive strikes intending to destroy a significant part of the IAF on the ground, *a la* IDF/AF during the Six Day War, the PAF also performed SEAD missions against India's EW radar. At 17.35 local time, a pair of Lockheed F-104As struck the IAF radar station at Fardikot in north-west India. While PAF attacks on the other targets may have had arguably a more lacklustre performance, the strike by two F-104A Starfighters on the P-35 'Bar Lock Early Warning Radar – a system which could look up to 217 miles (300 km) into Pakistani airspace – damaged the system, as did an attack on a radar at Amritsar, close to the Indo-Pakistan western border. The damage to the system kept it off the air for an hour, before it was repaired. These strikes were part of the PAF's Operation *Chengiz Khan*; intended as a pre-emptive strike against India's forward air bases and EW radar, but they were largely inconclusive. The PAF had intended to re-create Israel's dash by keeping the IAF from getting airborne, although it had opened the next round of conflict with surprise and drama.

During the 1971 war, the PAF used Martin RB-57D/F bombers, which they had acquired from the United States, for attacking Indian radar. Principally, they would direct strikes on the facilities by maintaining an altitude of around 71,000 ft (21,640 m), while one or two additional RB-57s would keep tabs on the Indian EW radar's behaviour and jam it accordingly. However, generally speaking, the conflict did not witness an all-out SEAD effort of the kind that Israel would perform during the Yom Kippur war, or was performing at the same time against Egypt's dogged attempts to strengthen its air defences on the west bank of the Suez canal.

Angola
As the 1970s unwound in Africa, the southern segment of the continent was plunged deeper into deadly conflict, with South Africa embroiled in major counter-insurgency campaigns. These included action against the South West Africa People's Organisation (SWAPO) in Namibia, in south-west Africa and Angola, situated to Namibia's north. The implosion of the Portuguese Empire in the 1970s gave SWAPO another country to operate from in the form of Angola from 1974. Namibia was under South African rule despite the UN not recognising Pretoria's sovereignty over the country, given that it had been awarded via the League of Nations following World War I as Namibia had been a German colony.

SWAPO's use of Angolan territory brought the South African Defence Force (SADF) into the country to fight what has become known as the Bush War. The tempo of violence in the scrub land increased from the mid 1970s, and the South African response increased therein. Not only did the combat become increasingly intense, so did the supplies of weapons which SWAPO received from its Soviet sponsors, including SA-3 SAMs. The latter necessitated a response from the SADF.

Brigadier-General RS 'Dick' Lord was in command of the *Suid Afrikaanse Lugmag* (South African Air Force/SoAAF) operations during the conflict. He describes how the air operations increased, and the gradual move towards SEAD operations: 'Up until 1978, the cross-border insurgency was contained by our ground troops supported tactically by Alouette III gunships. These helicopters were initially mounted with 0.3 in (7.62 mm) machineguns fired by the flight engineer out of the left-hand side of the cockpit. Later, the single-barrelled gun was replaced by a four-barrelled version giving a very high rate of fire, but still firing solid shot. This in turn was replaced by a single 0.7 in (20 mm) cannon, giving the helicopter a great stand-off range (and) a higher single-shot capability'.

Operation Reindeer commenced on 4 May 1978 and was South Africa's first major offensive in Angola mounted against SWAPO targets, notably bases at Chetequera and Dombondola 155 miles (250 km) inside Angolan territory which saw Canberra BIII Mk.12 and Blackburn Buccaneer S.50 aircraft perform air-to-ground attacks while C-160 Transalls and C-130B/F transports were used to perform para-drops. Brigadier Lord notes that; 'this action significantly altered the nature of the war. From then onwards, SWAPO camps were situated under the protective umbrella provided by the air defence systems deployed by the Angolan Defence Force. This meant that if we were to get at them we had to enter Angolan Air Defence Zones'. This was not a palatable prospect as the Angolans had enhanced their air defences with Soviet assistance, creating the style of air defence network that had been the bane of Israeli and American pilot's lives. Brigadier Lord again: 'At this stage the Angolans had a radar line extending from Lubango in south-western Angola to Menongue in the south-east with P-35 radar. Their bases were defended by SA-2 and SA-3 missile sites and a range of AAA including 0.5 in (12.7 mm), 0.6 in (14.5 mm), 0.8 in (20 mm) and ZSU-23-4 mobile AAA systems and 2.2 in (57 mm) batteries guided by SQN-9 FireCan fire-director radar. All SWAPO units carried shoulder-launched SA-7 Strela missiles'.

Brigadier Lord notes that these systems received further re-inforcement in the early 1980s: 'After 1983, the Russians pumped in extraordinary amounts of sophisticated weaponry and used 50,000 Cubans as surrogates to fight alongside the Angolans. This weaponry included additional radar systems allowing them to extend their radar line southwards in typical saw-tooth fashion. MiG-23s with forward-firing air-to-air missiles were flown by Cuban pilots. The AAA scenario was reinforced with the arrival of the deadly tank-mounted ZSU-23-4 Shilka system guided by the Gun Dish radar which really was a threat. The SAM shield was bolstered by the addition of track-mounted SA-6 and SA-8s and wheeled SA-9 systems. To our surprise all of these sophisticated systems could "Bundu-Bash"; bouncing through African bush is tough on any electronic system but this Russian equipment stood up to the severe test'.

Operation Protea occurred on 23 August 1981. The objective was to hit SWAPO facilities at Xangongo and Ongiva, southern Angola, but was also designed to attack Angolan air defences which were providing a SAM umbrella to SWAPO forces on the ground. SEAD brought its own tough challenges for the SAAF. While their colleagues in the USAF, USN and IDF/AF had radar-hunting ARMs to throw into the fight, international isolation and arms embargoes because of South Africa's apartheid regime and the ongoing Bush War, made it impossible for the air force to outfit itself with Standards, Shrikes or HARMs. Instead, conventional air-to-ground weaponry became the tools of the trade: 'We never had the sophistication of ARMs. We often initiated our air strikes against enemy radar installations by Buccaneer-launched AS-30 air-to-ground missiles'.

1982

In April 1982, the UK Ministry of Defence (MoD) planned several air raids in response to the Argentine invasion of the Falkland Islands. Code-named Operation Black Buck, the RAF bombed the runway at Port Stanley airfield to prevent its use by the fast jets of the *Fuerza Aérea Argentina* (Argentine Air Force) which could increase their sortie rate and reduce their response times when attacking Royal Navy shipping to the east of the islands, in comparison to the long and fuel-hungry sorties that the air force's Dassault Mirage IIIEA/DA, Mirage 5PA and Douglas A-4C/P Skyhawks and the *Comando de le Aviacion Naval* Argentina (Argentine Naval Aviation) Dassault Super Etendards were having to perform from the Argentine mainland.

Towards the end of May after a successful attack on the runway early that month, the British high command changed its strategy. The Vulcans would no longer target Port Stanley airfield, but would instead attack Argentine radar installations throughout the islands. These systems included a Westinghouse AN/TPS-43F long-range EW radar with a range in the region of 200 miles (322 km) and a Cardion AN/TPS-44 surveillance radar. The strikes would use two AGM-45 Shrike air-to-ground missiles, which were fixed onto two underwing hardpoints on an Avro Vulcan B.2 bomber. The Shrikes were covertly supplied from the United States and originally it was thought that the Vulcans could use Hawker Siddeley/Matra AS.37 Martel ARMs, but the RAF settled on using the Shrikes once they became available. This left extra space in the aircraft's weapons bay for two auxiliary tanks which could accommodate an additional 15,428 lb (7,000 kg) of fuel. This also reduced to four the number of fuel transfers required for the outward portion of the flight from Ascension Island, while the number of refuelling sorties on the return flight would be reduced to two. The first Shrike mission, codenamed Black Buck 5, left the runway at Wideawake Airfield, Ascension Island, on the evening of 30 May. The Vulcan performed five re-fuellings from accompanying Handley Page Victor K.Mk.II tankers, before diving to 300 ft (90 m) at a speed of 345 miles-per-hour (555 km/h) to stay below the radar as the aircraft approached the islands. Around 20 miles (32 km) away from the Falklands the bomber climbed to 16,000 ft (4,876 m) to locate the radar. Forty minutes later the Vulcan had found the AN/TPS-43 system and fired its two AGM-45s. These landed 10 m (32 ft) away from the radar which was sufficient to cause minor damage to the set and to encourage the Argentine operators to stay off the air. This allowed a subsequent Harrier attack to be pressed home on Port Stanley airfield with the minimum of opposition.

A second Shrike mission, Black Buck 6 was flown on 2 June. The Vulcan would this time deploy four missiles, and would be accompanied by a simultaneous Harrier strike against additional Argentine radar installations. These systems included a SkyGuard radar and Super Oerlikon AAA units. However, the Argentines had been quick learners and elected to keep their radar switched off. The aircraft then descended to 16,000 ft to tempt the Argentine unit to attack. The radar obliged and illuminated the Vulcan and the bomber responded by firing two Shrikes which destroyed the radar and killed four Argentine radar operators. The weather conspired to make the Harrier strike impossible, and more trouble was in store for the Vulcan crew. The refuelling probe of XM597, the bomber being used for the sortie, broke off on contact with the hose of a Victor as the Vulcan refuelled for its flight back home. The Vulcan did not have sufficient fuel to return to Wideawake. Although the crew had been briefed to ditch in the Atlantic in the event of an irrevocable technical problem with their aircraft, they climbed to 43,000 ft (13,106 m) to get the most economical flight profile for the aircraft and headed for Brazil to find an airfield for an emergency landing.

It became apparent to Squadron Leader Neil McDougall, who was commanding the Vulcan, that the nearest suitable runway was at Rio de Janeiro International Airport, Brazil. At altitude, the aircraft was depressurised and the Vulcan crew disposed of their top-secret mission documents, throwing them through the cockpit door, while one of the Shrikes was jettisoned into the Atlantic, a technical problem caused another of the missiles to cling stubbornly to the aircraft's wings. McDougall then took the aircraft down to 20,000 ft (6,096 m) and successfully evaded a pair of *Força Aérea Brasileira* (Brazilian Air Force) F-5E/F fighters which were attempting to intercept the aircraft.

McDougall was anxious not to alert the Brazilian authorities to the fact that a British military aircraft was seeking permission to land. When asked to identify the aircraft he replied, 'we're from Huddersfield' to bemused Brazilian Air Traffic Controllers.

The aircraft made a perfect landing at Rio with precious little fuel in the tanks. Both the crew and the aircraft were immediately interned by the Brazilian authorities and housed in the military compound of Galeao airport. The Brazilians also removed the remaining Shrike missile from the aircraft for display in a local museum.

The crew were treated well, and were eventually allowed to leave Brazil with their aircraft, on the proviso that it would not be used again for the duration of the conflict. One rumour states that the Vulcan was parked in the same area where the Pope would make his photo call during the forthcoming Papal visit. It seems that the Brazilian authorities believed that it would be far less embarrassing to allow the Vulcan to leave, lest this erstwhile nuclear bomber appear as the backdrop to the official pictures of the Papal visit!

The crew of the aircraft included Flight Officer Chris Lackman, co-pilot; Flight Lieutenant Brain Gardner; air-to-air refuelling pilot; Flight Lieutenant Rod Trevaskus, Air Electronics Officer; Flight Lieutenant Barry Smith, Navigation Plotter; Flight Lieutenant Dave Castle, Radar Navigator and Squadron Leader Neil McDougall who was awarded the Distinguished Flying Cross.

Lebanon 1983

As the British and Argentines were locked in combat over the Falkland Islands, tensions in the Middle East continued to escalate. Israel was not the only country feeling the heat from the fire of Lebanon's civil war. The United States sent a peacekeeping force which included French, British and Italian troops to supervise the PLO withdrawal from the country following a truce between the former and the Israelis which would see both sides withdrawing from Lebanon.

F-14 Tomcats which were performing aerial reconnaissance to keep tabs on the situation on the ground were fired upon by Syrian AAA positions. The repeated attacks against US aircraft tried the patience of President Ronald Reagan. The result was that the President ordered the US Navy to perform a series of strikes against artillery positions and SAM systems which were located at Hammana to the south of the Beirut-Damascus highway and Falouga, Mghite and Jabal al Knaisse to the east of the Lebanese capital.

The Grumman A-6Es of the VA-85 Black Falcons would be catapulted from the USS *John F. Kennedy* with sixteen Intruders taking to the skies. These aircraft would be joined by the Intruders from the VA-176 Thunderbolts which were armed with Mk.82 free-fall bombs. These two squadrons were in turn accompanied by twelve Vought A-7E Corsairs of the VA-15 Valions and the VA-87 Golden Warriors squadron; both carrying Mk.82 Rockeye cluster weapons.

As night turned to morning on 3 December, the flight decks of the carriers were a maelstrom of activity as aircraft were armed, fuelled and elevated to the flight decks ready to be flown off the carrier into a Mediterranean morning. From 05.45 the aircraft were catapulted from the decks. The first strike package, Alpha, was earmarked to be over its targets at 08.00 at an altitude of 20,000 ft (6,100 m).

The strikes were not cost-free and the US Navy lost two aircraft; the first being an A-6E which was downed by an SA-7 that hit the aircraft as it was preparing to attack an SA-9 site located at Hammana. One of the A-6E crew, Lieutenant Mark A. Lange, was killed in the attack, but his weapons systems officer Bombardier/Navigator Robert Goodman did survive, although he was captured. Efforts to locate and rescue Goodman immediately swung into action and an A-7E pressed home attacks on Druze militia gun emplacements in order to suppress fire which might interfere with the rescue, but this aircraft was hit by a missile causing Commander Ed Andrews to eject, although he was later rescued by a US Navy SH-3H Sea King.

The losses suffered by the US Navy during this operation prompted some major soul searching. A pilot had been killed and two aircraft had been lost. The air defences that the Navy had faced that day were robust and able to inflict serious damage. Several lessons were taken on board by the US Navy aviation community. The first was that SEAD aircraft would from now on accompany all daylight strikes and the SEAD support would always include AGM-88s and wherever possible packages would approach the target area at night to minimise visual detection of the aircraft as much as possible. These lessons would become hugely important as the United States prepared for action in the western Mediterranean against the regime of Libya's flamboyant and enigmatic Colonel Muammar al-Gaddafi.

Libya
The *Armêe de l'Air* (French Air Force –AdlA) had been active in the Sahara for a number of years since the days of Beau Geste in the 1920s to the 1980s when President Francois Mitterrand's government ordered troops from the French Foreign Legion and AdlA warplanes to support the regime of President Goukouni

Oueddi in the troubled state of Chad. Chad had been a French colony before achieving independence in 1960; however the French had maintained a military presence in the country since 1968 to fight the *Islamic Front de Libération National de Tchad*, before withdrawing in 1975. The French were invited back in 1978 after Libya occupied a stretch of land known as the 'Aouzou Strip' on the northern Chad-Libyan border which Colonel Gaddaffi had annexed in 1973.

Chad then descended into civil war as the government split with the formation of the *Forces Armée du Nord* (FAN) under the leadership of Hissene Habré while his former government partner Oueddi invited Libyan armed forces into the country to aid his attacks against FAN facilities in Chad and neighbouring Sudan. Undeterred by the attacks, Habré's FAN gradually won control of large portions of the country with the east and centre under his belt and eventually the capital N'Djamena. The Libyan force withdrew from the country and Oueddi moved north to establish the *Armée de Liberation Nationale* with Libyan support. The French re-intervened in the country in 1983 and established a 'Red Line' along the 15th Parallel stretching from Torodoum in west central Chad to Oum Chalouba in the east near the Sudanese border. This became the *de-facto* border between the north and south parts of the country controlled by Oueddei and Habré respectively. French forces withdrew once more in autumn 1984 and then, following an invasion of Habré's area by Oueddie, returned and began an offensive against the Libyan forces supporting the ex-President.

The conflict saw some significant SEAD raids performed by the AdlA against Libyan air defences. In December 1985, C-160s were moving 1,400 Legionnaires into N'Djamena while a force of twelve Jaguar-A ground attack aircraft, eight Mirage F.1C-200s, two C-135FR tankers and a solitary Breguet Atlantique left their base at Bangui airfield in the Central African Republic (CAR) with the intention of delivering a major strike against Ouaddi Doum AFB, Northern Chad. The attack was to be performed with the Jaguars dropping their DBAP-100 anti-runway bombs. Eleven Jaguars participated in the raid after one aircraft had to return home because of technical problems.

The raid achieved that all-important element of surprise as four of the Jaguars in the strike package dropped 551 lb (250 kg) bombs on the air defences surrounding the base, while the remaining seven aircraft in the force rolled in to destroy the base and its runways. The damage was such that the airfield remained closed for several days.

Colonel Pierre Alain Antoine was heavily involved with AdlA SEAD operations throughout his career with the service: 'I got my wings on 10 June 1970 and my first aircraft was the F-100D Super Sabre. You have two different kinds of fighter pilots; the F-100 drivers and the others! This aircraft was very difficult for a young pilot. I stayed in the F-100 Operational Training Unit only six months. After that, I was transferred on the Mirage-3E at the 3rd TFW in Nancy and the mission of this Wing was SEAD. In the French Air Force we had eight squadrons of Mirage-IIIE in four Wings at that time, with two squadrons in Dijon for air defence, two squadrons in Colmar for air defence, two fighter-bomber squadrons in Nancy and two squadrons in Luxueil of fighter-bombers'.

French Air Force SEAD really came of age in the early 1970s with the arrival of the Martel missile: 'In 1972, the two fighter-bomber squadrons in Luxeuil were dedicated for nuclear purposes and the 3rd TFW at Nancy was equipped with the AS-37 Martel (Missile Anti Radar TELevision). The missile was used by the 3rd TFW and also by the Breguet Atlantique of the French Navy. At that time, the 3rd TFW was operated with two squadrons of Mirage-IIIE'.

Col. Antoine recalls that: 'We had two different kinds of mission with the Martel. If you know the frequency of the radar and the area where you think that the radar is located you match the missile's warhead with the radar frequency and when you arrive in the radar area, the missile locks on to the radar frequency and follows that. With the second mission, you know that exact point and the frequency band. You can launch the missile at high altitude at supersonic speed or at low altitude. At low altitude you must fire the missile at between 8–18 nautical miles (14–33 km) from the target. The missile is launched with one booster and three seconds after the launch, the missile climbs at 60 degrees and this manoeuvre is the reason that you cannot fire below 8 nautical miles because the manoeuvre takes a minimum of 8 nautical miles. For example if you fired at 6 nautical miles (9 km), the missile would climb 60 degrees and then dive at 80 degrees, but the target will be behind the missile by two nautical miles'.

In 1972, the first AdlA squadron became operational with the Martel. A technical squadron was also established in Nancy to teach the mission and the missile to the pilots. Col. Antione remembers that:

> During the same time, the intelligence officers began to teach everybody in the squadron the electronic warfare order of battle of all of the Soviet radar systems. We had special SIGINT aircraft to build, step-by-step, our electronic order of battle. This was performed using the C-160 Gabriel and the Douglas DC-8 Sarique.
>
> The Martel training round had a recorder built into the missile instead of the warhead to record all the radar frequencies. Very often we were able to fly into the air defence identification zone along the Iron Curtain. We had the authorisation to fly in-bound into the Iron Curtain and then turn away at 10 nautical miles (18 km) and record the frequencies, but when the Russians understood that they were being recorded they would switch off the radar.
>
> The Jaguar would be the SEAD platform of choice for the AdlA in Chad. The Jaguar squadron was operational for Cold War SEAD missions and also for operations in Africa. All 160 French single-seat Jaguars could carry the Martel. During this time (the mid-1980s), we were going to Africa for between two and four months, every six months to launch the Martel against the Ouaddi Doum Libyan air base in the north of Chad. For more than ten years we had a minimum of twelve Jaguars in Africa. Four in Dakar, Senegal, four in Libreville in the Gabon and a batch of four in N'Djamena in Chad or four in Bangui. At one point in the mid 1980s we had twenty-four Jaguars in Central Africa and Chad, and also the Mirage F1 for the air defence mission and escort plus a lot of transport aircraft including the Transall along with the Breguet Atlantiques as an airborne command post and also some Navy Atlantiques dedicated

to the SIGINT, COMINT and ELINT missions. It was a huge force deployed in Africa against the Libyans.

For the Martel missions we were based at Bangui which was 512 nautical miles (948 km) south of N'Djamena. Bangui is in the middle of a forest and the weather was very hot and wet, and the altitude of the airfield was 1,500 ft (457 m). To take off, with the Jaguar carrying the two drop tanks, the Martels and the ECM pods, was very difficult as it was not the most powerful fighter in the world.

While we were in Chad, the Martels were modernised. The first version of the missile had three different seekers for the Sierra, Lima and Charlie frequency bands. At the beginning, the missile was designed to be fired against the SA-2 and the SA-3 batteries with the new seeker called ADAM Auto-Director AMelioré. we had the possibility of firing against the SA-6 and SA-8. This new generation of missile was only operational with the French Air Force and not with the French Navy. They did not buy the new seeker for the Martel and continued with the older generation because their targets were typically the radar carried by a destroyer or a frigate and the first generation of Martel covered the frequencies of the naval radar.

We planned a lot of missions against Libyan radar in Chad and the Libyan base in the north of the country which was protected by Flat Face radar, Spoon Rest and three batteries of SA-2s with Straight Flush. The first mission against the radar was expected to be flown in December 1996, but we were awaiting the green light from the French government. In January 1987 we fired the missile.

The mission was briefed and prepared with one aircraft carrying a missile specially dedicated for the Flat Face with another three other Jaguars carrying missiles with seekers configured for the Straight Flush radar On the 5 January the four ships took off from Bangui with the number two Jaguar carrying a Flat Face-configured missile, but this aircraft had a problem with the missile. The other three aircraft took off and landed in N'Djamena. Three hours later they were joined with the second aircraft carrying a new missile. In the morning, the French Air Force launched two Mirage F1Cs as a diversion for the raid. The Breguet Atlantique revealed that the Flat Face was switched on and the radar was destroyed by the Martel. For the Libyans it was the beginning of the end. After that, the Chadian forces attacked the airfield and all the Libyan garrison became prisoners.

Then something strange happened.

Once the airfield had been overrun we took two of the Flat Face radars and also two SA-6 launchers. I was in N'Djamena and listened to the arrival of an aircraft. I saw a C-5A Galaxy of the US Air Force landing in at the airport. I spoke to the crew and I discovered the mission of this aircraft. They were to pick up one SA-2 and one Flat Face for the Americans and the two others for the French. The C-5As made two flights – one to Nellis AFB and a second one to Mont-de-Marsan in south-western France

At these two locations, the radar and the launchers were extensively studied. Fast-forward to 2000, and Col. Antoine was attending a function in Las Vegas.

In 2000 I was at a convention of the Association of Old Crows (an electronic warfare association) in Las Vegas and we paid a visit to Nellis AFB. We visited part of the base where there is a museum of old Soviet equipment and during the visit I was speaking to a USAF General and a Colonel, and I saw the SA-6. I asked them where it was from and the General said, 'I cannot answer this question, I told him "Sir, I can give you the true story of the radar. I was on the C-5A when you were loading this SA-6!"'

However, one year after the French action the USAF and USN prepared to strike targets in Libya. Washington had grown increasingly irate at Gaddaffi's apparent support for terrorist organisations which were attacking US targets in Europe. Moreover, the Libyan navy insisted on pressing its claims to a disputed stretch of water. Gaddaffi had established what he referred to as the so-called 'Line of Death' located north of the Gulf of Sidra which would invite armed retaliation if US Naval vessels moved into the area during Freedom of Navigation exercises which the US Navy was performing in recognition of the standard international practice of territorial waters being recognised up to 12 miles (22.2 km) from a country's coast.

As the collective blood of the Reagan administration boiled at what it saw to be continued provocation by Gaddafi, the Libyan leader acquired air defences from the Soviet Union and strengthened those which were already protecting Libya. From 1985, as the French strikes on Ouaddi Doum AFB were occurring, the Colonel had scoured the catalogues to purchase new air defences. The browsing led to the acquisition of S-200VE (SA-5 Gammon) SAM systems, which included the 5N62 Square Pair H-band 168 mile (270 km) fire control radar, which were operational by March 1986; however at that time the deployment consisted of only a single battalion (six single-rail launchers) of missiles. The Libyan deployment of the system was somewhat unorthodox compared to standard Soviet doctrine which recommended such missiles being deployed in a group of battalions which would be protected by SA-3 systems which could cover lower altitudes, while the SA-5s would cover medium to high altitudes.

The US Navy's Carrier Task Force 60 did eventually steam south on 24 March 1986 to perform Operation Attain Document which was planned as a provocative action intended to assert freedom of navigation rights over the Gulf of Sidra. Operations got moving on the morning of 24 March 1986 as two F-14As from the VF-102 Diamondbacks fighter squadron shot off the flight deck of the USS *America* into a cool Mediterranean spring morning. By lunchtime, the US Navy had begun to tangle with the Libyans. A pair of MiG-25PDs from the 1025th FS of the *al-Quwwat al-Jawwiya al-Arabiya al-Libiya* (Libyan Air Force) tried to intercept the same number of Tomcats from the VF-33 Starfighters FS which had also launched from the USS *America*. The Foxbats took the wise decision of giving the Tomcats the benefit of the doubt and headed for home. However, the F-14s came under attack from the SA-5 battery when flying 24 miles (40 km) from the Libyan coast. Instant SEAD, in the form of EA-6B Prowler support, was ordered by the felines but not before they had been attacked once more by the battery. Fortunately all the aircraft trapped without sustaining any hits. The action brought a response from a Libyan air defence battery at Sirte which fired SA-3 SAMs at US Navy aircraft flying combat air patrols to protect the ships below from Libyan air attack. Fortunately, for the F/A-18s from the USS *Coral Sea* which were performing CAPs, the SA-3s were fired at the extreme of their range and had run out of steam by the time the were near the Hornets, which they missed by a considerable margin. As the provocation escalated, Libyan MiG-25s wheeled above the Gulf of Sidra only to be intercepted by the US Navy causing them to head for home. The day rounded off with the Libyans firing SA-2 missiles at US aircraft and following these launches with an SA-5 firing ten minutes later. In total the estimated number of SAM firings against US Navy aircraft that day may have included around twelve such attacks. While the actions were continuing in the air, the Libyans had sent *Nanuchka* patrol boats into the Gulf of Sidra to challenge the US Navy's presence. However, this resulted in attacks on the patrol boats from US Navy A-6Es carrying Mk.20 Rockeye cluster bombs. A Libyan patrol boat was also destroyed near Misratah with AGM-84 Harpoon anti-ship missiles. The Navy had provided the bait and the Libyans seemed more than happy to swallow it.

The US Navy did, however, have a treat in store for the Libyan air defences. Determined not to be targeted by the battery again, on the night of 24/25 March, A-7E Corsair-IIs from the VA-83 Rampagers Strike FS were launched from the USS *Saratoga* carrying AGM-88A HARMs. These missiles smashed the Square Pair SA-5 fire control radar. However, the Libyans moved a second radar to the site the following day, which was rather a wasted effort as this too was destroyed by the HARMs.

While Gaddafi's interpretation of international waters was annoying for the United States, its support for international terrorism was making both Washington and London incandescent with fury. Gaddafi's suspected involvement with a list of crimes was amassing with depressing velocity. British policewoman Yvonne Fletcher fell on 17 April 1984 to bullets fired from the Libyan Embassy in St. James Square, London. The Colonel had also been implicated in the trafficking of Semtex plastic explosives to the Provisional Irish Republican Army in Northern

Ireland, as well as the death of Leon Klinghoffer, an elderly wheelchair-bound passenger, during the hijack of the *Achille Lauro* cruise liner in October 1985. The Libyan leader's involvement with terrorism escalated on 27 December 1985 when thirteen people were killed and seventy-five injured after the Abu Nidal terrorist group attacked the El Al Israeli airlines and Trans World Airlines ticket counters at Rome's Leonardo da Vinci airport. The icing on Gaddafi's cake of terror was completed at 01.40 on 5 April 1986 when 2 kg (4.4 lb) of plastic explosive packed with shrapnel tore through the La Belle nightclub in West Berlin taking the lives of American serviceman Sergeant Kenneth Ford and Nermin Hannay. Sergeant James Goins later succumbed to his injuries, while a further 230 of the disco's occupants were hurt. However, the Libyan leader had been sloppy and US intelligence was able to intercept cables which were sent to the Libyan Embassy in East Berlin showering praise for the successful attack.

The Reagan administration was determined to show the Libyan leader that his conduct was at odds with international norms of behaviour and his sponsorship of terrorism would not be tolerated, while also attacking directly at the heart of Libya's political apparatus to prevent its continual support of terrorism.

Planning for the raid began on 7 April and a list of five distinct targets drawn up by the National Security Council, which received endorsement from the Chairman of the Joint Chiefs of Staff, Admiral William J. Crowe, and Defence Secretary Casper W. Weinberger. These targets, which were to include 'purported terrorist installations comprising command and control systems and training, logistics, intelligence and communications facilities, were then approved by President Reagan and 'Operation Eldorado Canyon', the bombing of Libya, could begin.

The planning for the operation had focused on destroying the Libyan government's ability to perform terrorist acts and terrorist training facilities. Pentagon planners eschewed a daytime series of air-strikes following the experience of Lebanon, and Navy and Air Force operations would be performed at night. Bomb delivery would be from low-level before popping up over the target. Both of these measures were designed to make the Libyan air defender's life as difficult as possible and it was a pre-requisite that Eldorado Canyon was to feature some serious SEAD.

The air defences with which the US Navy and USAF would dual with included the trusty but deadly ZSU-23-4 along with L/70 1.6 in (40 mm) AAA guns; the latter of Swedish origin. These guns were arrayed to provide low-level point defence along Libya's coast. The defence of the country's air space was parcelled along three regional defence sectors covering the capital Tripoli on the western Mediterranean coast, Benghazi on the east of the Gulf of Sidra, and Tobruk on the extreme eastern coast near the Egyptian border. In terms of missiles, the Libyans could throw French Crotale SAMs into the skies and were also in possession of a pair of SA-2 brigades (three SAM battalions of one battery each), three SA-3 brigades (three missile batteries each) and up to four SA-6 and SA-8 brigades connected to numerous air search radar. By the time Eldorado Canyon was ready for kick-off the Libyans had also acquired a brigade's worth of SA-5 which were mainly clustered around Sirte on the western side of the Gulf of Sidra. The air search radar was reinforced with an *ad hoc* collection of French, British and German naval surface-search systems which were re-roled for the air search function. As the SEAD plan was drafted it was these latter systems which gave the planners some problems regarding how to jam equipment not usually encountered in the air battle. For the Libyans, it was all-well-and-good having air defence technology sourced from a number of suppliers, but a side-effect of this was that it was nigh-on impossible to make, for example, German radar systems, compatible with Russian SAM systems.

The SAMs were deployed to defend missile engagement zones which corresponded with the air defence sector. Tripoli itself had two brigades of SAMs deployed on the eastern and western sides of the city. Benghazi was defended by a single regiment of SA-6 systems along with SA-2 and SA-3 systems spread across either side of the city. Libyan air defenders faced a major problem in that Tripoli, Benghazi and Tobruk were all coastal cities which precluded the emplacement of air defences along the coast. Instead, it was thought that the Libyans would establish CAPs of Dassault Mirage F1ED and F5D fighters to cover this gap. Yet for reasons known only to the Libyan Air Force, it moved its air defence fighters to the south, which could have been to protect targets in the desert from attack by the French Air Force. All that the LAF could call on in the northern sector was a squadron-sized detachment of 12 MiG-23ML (NATO codename Fishbed) jets based at Benina AFB.

The eyes of the missiles included up to two P-14/5N84A Tall King 372 mile (600 km) range EW radar, while P-12 Spoon Rest and P-18 Spoon Rest-D systems were pressed into the surveillance and target acquisition role for the individual SAM brigades. Low altitude detection was provided by P-15/19 Flat Face-B systems along with P-35 and P-37 systems which were positioned near air bases for fighter interception control, not that this would be a big consideration for the Libyans given the dispersal of their fighter aircraft. Tripoli was surrounded by the Crotale system, although this French SAM was not linked into the wider Libyan air defence network presumably because of data compatibility issues. However, the Libyans had overlapped some of their radar coverage and, while deployments of SAMs to coastal areas was difficult, because of a lack of available sites, they had tried to orientate their SAMs to fire towards the sea.

The Soviets, who had the credit for designing much of Libya's IADS had taken a few lessons from the Israeli operations over the Bekaa Valley which they sought to incorporate into Libya's IADS. First and foremost, the structure had to be constructed in an especially dense fashion so that the destruction or jamming of a single radar would not leave a gap through which attack aircraft could ingress. Allied to this was the need for the radar to be capable of operating across a range of frequencies so that the jamming of a select frequency would not lead to the comprehensive breakdown of radar operating on the same frequency. Also linked into the frequency issue was the need to ensure that the Libyan system use a variety of different electronic waveforms which would in turn confuse aircraft gathering information on the IADS electronic order of battle. Finally, the all-important redundancy was built in by using hardened communications landlines and several radio links. The logic was that even if an adversary managed to smash the radio communications, then the landlines could be used and vice-versa.

That said the Libyans had not bargained for the use of computer technology by the USAF and Navy to plan the raid. Satellite reconnaissance revealed the position of Libya's SAMs and this information was used to plan the ingress to the targets and egress routes to enable the aircraft to steer clear of the SAMs and AAA. Computer programmes also helped a great deal in determining the numbers of aircraft and the type of weaponry which would be required to make the missions a success. In terms of the overall operation, the planners did not have to draft a prolonged SEAD campaign. The SEAD had to be good enough to get the pilots and their aircraft safely to and from their targets for the attack but there was no need to engage in a prolonged campaign to destroy the Libyan IADS. Thus the SAM and radar sites were not the primary targets of the operations, merely threats which had to be neutralised for a finite period. This meant that the electronic jamming of the Libyan radar would become especially important.

To this end, the 42nd Electronic Combat Squadron was earmarked to provide five EF-111A Ravens to the armada of eighteen F-111Fs from the 48th TFW which would perform the attacks, and twenty F-111Es from the 20th TFW which was the reserve force. Two of the Ravens would act as spares while the other three would accompany the tactical bombers that would fly from RAF Lakenheath (48th TFW) and RAF Upper Heyford (20th TFW) in Suffolk and Oxfordshire, England. The package of aircraft left the UK in the early-morning gloom on 15 April. After take-off they flew around Spain and through the Straits of Gibraltar, approaching Libya from the west. Below them the US Navy prepared to launch a wave of aircraft in support of the strikes on Tripoli and Benghazi.

Libya's preparations, or lack of them, prior to the raid was puzzling. Gaddafi and his cohorts had plenty of reason to believe that Libya could be attacked given the bellicose noises emanating from Washington, yet they still inexplicably relented from placing their air defences on a state of high alert. Some radars were switched off, which may have been a sensible precaution given the AGM-88 HARMs that the Navy had at its disposal. However, two of the P-14 EW radars were active which would seem to suggest that an IADS-wide radar shutdown had not been a Libyan plan because all the radars would have been switched off. No officers were present at the SAM batteries, leaving them in the command of Non-Commissioned Officers who may have been reluctant to take decisions without their superiors present. Making matters even more bizarre was the fact that one of the P-14 radars was switched off at 22.30 on the evening before the attacks, leaving a single P-14 operational at Benghazi, which was eventually subject to intense jamming. The radar operators do not seem to have performed any measures to render the jamming ineffective and one report said that instead Libyan soldiers manning the radar awoke their officers at home with telephone calls alerting them to the jamming.

As night became morning, the Al Jumahiriya Barracks at Benghazi absorbed an attack by a sextet of A-6Es from the VA-34 Blue Blasters attack squadron which dropped Mk.82 Snakeye bombs onto the facility. Benina airfield, outside the city, which was home to the Fishbed squadron, was smashed by A-6Es of the VA-55 Warhorses attack squadron which attacked with a mix of Mk.82 and Mk.20 Rockeye cluster bombs. To the west the Aardvarks went to work on Tripoli International Airport and the Al-Aziziyah barracks while also pressing home a strike on what was believed to be the Libyan leader's tent and along with the Murat Sidi Bilal terrorist training facility.

The SEAD component worked extremely well. The EF-111As blasted radar networks around Tripoli and Benghazi with noise, although, as noted above, the jury is still out on the extent that the radar network was operational. The Ravens maintained stand-off orbits to keep the air defences down, while the VAQ-135 Black Ravens Navy Tactical Electronic Warfare Squadron and VMAQ-2 Playboys Marines Electronic Attack Squadron which used their EA-6Bs alongside the Ravens in the provision of stand-off jamming. Kinetic kill was provided by the Navy with six F/A-18As of the VFA-132 Privateers Navy Strike FS and the VMFA-323 Death Rattlers Marine FS catapulted from the USS *Coral Sea*. They were joined by six A-7Es from the VA-46 Clansmen and the VA-72 Blue Hawks Navy Attack Squadrons. These units were tasked with pre-emptively firing off AGM-88s and AGM-45 Shrikes to keep the radar down. There were Libyan attempts to down aircraft as the strike packages moved in, but the jamming and pre-emptive HARM effort seemed to do the job, and while it didn't stop the missile launches it caused the Libyans to fire their weapons ballistically, that is without guidance, in the hope of scoring a lucky strike.

The famous SA-5 battery at Sirte did try to have a pop at the Navy aircraft, but only switched on its radar after the aircraft left the target area and then chose not to fire its missiles. The use of ARMs possibly coupled to Libyan air defence eccentricities, had served to keep the radar off the air and had allowed the Navy to eschew direct and highly dangerous attacks on the air defence batteries. That said, the Navy did not have the magic AN/APR-38 RHAWS used on the Air Force's F-4G which reduced the pilot's ability to listen out for hostile emitters and instead caused them to launch their ARMs in the general vicinity of a radar site, whether or not the system was on the air. One report summarised Naval SEAD logic with the ARMs thus: 'The Navy concept is straightforward; if a radar comes on the air, one of the missiles will guide toward it. If the sites under attack practice emission control and shut down their radar, the missiles have still accomplished their purpose of suppressing the radar by keeping it off the air. As we have seen earlier, the space-based vision of the USAF allowed it to determine where the Libyans' radar was located.

The HARM tally for the raid included around thirty AGM-88s fired over 20 minutes which smashed into the fire control radars of two SA-2 batteries, a single SA-3 battery and two SA-5 batteries rendering the SAMs pretty much useless. One SA-2 battery was said to have attempted two unguided attacks of departing US aircraft at ranges of 16 miles (25 km) and 22 miles (35 km). The P-35 radar located at Benina was also attacked and destroyed, the lack of GCI radar was said to have prompted a MiG-23 pilot to refuse to take off. However, one report disputes this, arguing that 'it is more probable that the majority of the pilots were at home and that the duty section had no orders to take off.

Around Tripoli, none of the air defence radar was said to be active before the jamming effort began; the defences included a Volex radar for the Crotale system, along with P-19 and P-15 radar systems. It is thought that the SAM batteries tasked with defending Tripoli emerged from the strike operational and intact. The raid did see SAMs being fired and it is claimed that the Libyans shot off at least twelve; fired either singularly, or in salvos of two. A Soviet report claimed that the air defence effort of the Libyans was chaotic but that it forced one package of F-111Fs to desist from an attack. We know that the Remit and Karma sections of the Aardvarks attacked their respective Al-Aziziyah barracks and Murat Sidi Bilal targets, along with the Puffy and Lilac sections attacking Tripoli's airport, but it is not clear whether another group of F-111Fs had to abort their attack although we do know that USAF Major Fernando L. Ribas-Dominicci and Captain Paul F. Lorence were both killed when their aircraft crashed into the Gulf of Sidra.

The choice of jamming rather than flying F-4G Phantom-IIs from their base in Spangdahlem, Germany for the USAF element of the operation made sense. This would have added an extra refuelling and logistical burden to the operation, so for Eldorado Canyon the USAF relied on the Ravens and the SEAD support provided by the Navy and Marine Corps. All in all this was a fine example of joint SEAD in action, a concept which had been pioneered during Vietnam and would be further refined in the skies above Iraq and the former Yugoslavia over the following decade.

Jamming was a sensible SEAD measure for the Eldorado Canyon operation. The Aardvarks taking the attack to the targets only had to remain insulated from the prying eyes of Libyan air defences for a short time while they ingressed and egressed. Moreover, the aircraft would come in at high speed and low level. Simple physics come into play here. The curvature of the earth will block a radar's line of sight and this allows an attacking aircraft to ingress and egress below the radar. If an aircraft approaches the target at 80 m (200 ft) it will only be seen when it is about 25 miles (46 km) from the radar. Presuming that the aircraft is travelling at considerable speed, this will give the radar operators no more than a few minutes to spot the aircraft, perform friend or foe identification and allocate a SAM battery to engage the aircraft. That is presuming that there are no HARMs in the area which may home-in on the radar as it starts radiating. Finally, many of Gaddafi's radars, particularly the Soviet systems were older generation models and the type that F-111s and their 'Sparkvark' siblings expected to encounter over the skies of Central Europe. The result was that these aircraft had electronic countermeasure systems configured precisely for these machines. Things were a little different for the EA-6s. While they could carry the superb HARM and their AN/ALQ-99 Tactical Jamming System they were a little more ponderous than their supersonic speed-freak F-111 counterparts. This served to keep them in a stand-off role although the Prowlers did work closely with the EF-111s in performing stand-off jamming of the air defences around Benghazi and performing similar missions for the largely air force component of the operation around Tripoli.

Furthermore, the operation was designed to perform a wholesale jamming of the Libyan IADS in its entirety rather than using the destructive suppression which the Israelis had utilised over Bekaa Valley. Also, unlike the Bekaa Valley operations neither the US Navy nor USAF used target drones or UAVs to create a distraction. Again, this may have been because the strike packages were going after selected targets and would only be over Libya for a short period of time, while the Israelis had to ensure that as much of the Syrian IADS was destroyed at the start of a campaign to prevent it posing a threat to its pilots for what the Israeli military leadership had envisioned as a prolonged campaign.

SEAD operations statistics for Eldorado Canyon

Target	Aircraft used	Weapons used
Tripoli air defence network	Six A-7E	8 AGM-45 Shrike 16 AGM-88 HARM
Benghazi air defence network	Six F/A-18s	4 AGM-45 Shrike 20 AGM-88 HARM

Some reports talk of the Libyan IADS being a complete shambles, gripped by mass confusion as the strikes began. As we have noted above, anti-aircraft fire was brought to bear on the aircraft in the form of SAM launches *after* the aircraft had attacked and were turning towards the Mediterranean. Secondly, the air defences also seem to have been completely out-foxed by the jamming effort and by the number of HARMs that were fired at them. It was claimed that the latter helped to create a climate of terror amongst the air defenders, some of whom fled their post, while the confusion which had infected the IADS caused the commanding officers to delay giving orders.

Despite the presence of western equipment in Libya's air defence network, the much larger presence of Soviet equipment caused the Libyans to place a high reliance on Soviet doctrine. Close command was something that characterised Soviet command and control methodology and this tended to discourage individual decision-making. Without available information and data on what was happening around them Libyan air defenders might well have been very cautious about acting without orders from their superiors. Unwittingly, those operating the Libyan IADS may have actually aided the American SEAD effort by paralysing their own decision-making structure in the absence of data upon which to act; data which was supposed to be coming from radar which was being saturated with torrents of white noise from the jamming effort overhead.

To make matters worse, the Libyan IADS was not always overlapping and despite Soviet efforts to the contrary when designing the system there were gaps present in the air defence network. One such gap was said to exist around Tripoli which allowed F-111Fs to fly inbound to their targets at around 197 ft (60 m). Apparently, Soviet engineers advising the Libyans on the IADS had flagged the gap but their observations were ignored. There were also said to be calibration issues in how the radar was tuned in some areas and it seems that some of the Libyan air defenders did not fully comprehend their systems' abilities, choosing to perform an engagement with their SAMs when the chances of hitting an American aircraft were low. One example of this was Libyan missiles attacking American aircraft as they exited the combat area.

Finally, the Libyans should have performed some SIGINT to listen to the airwaves for anything strange or unusual which might indicate that an attack was imminent. However, this could have been more difficult. The US operation was performed in conditions of superb communications discipline. Those call signs which were used by the strike force of F-111Fs were said to be typical of those used by American aircraft during peacetime exercises. Incidentally, the commander of the Soviet 1st Signals Intelligence Regiment of the *Protivo-Vozdushnaya Oborana* (Anti Air Defence) force lost his job after his unit failed to collect any long-range SIGINT on the operation. This paradoxically also indicates that it might have been relatively easy for the USAF and US Navy to mask their intentions well before performing air attacks across the Iron Curtain in the event of a hot war. Suffice to say that the jamming operation during Eldorado Canyon was so comprehensive that not a single Aardvark was said to have been acquired by tracking radar and no enemy fighters were seen in the sky. However, we do know that a single aircraft was lost and whether this was the result of a lucky ballistic SAM shot, AAA fire or a guided attack is unknown.

One very interesting element of the campaign as relates to SEAD was the primacy that both US forces had placed on jamming. Electronic countermeasures had always been important to the SEAD fight, but now the jamming operation was the primary means of SEAD, with the ARMs continuing to play a vital role in their stand-off capacity. Again, this was where Eldorado Canyon set a precedent for US forces in the future in terms of how they would perform SEAD. Jamming at the start of a campaign was a primary objective. This makes sense in a number of ways. As jamming can sometimes be performed in a stand-off capacity, this allows radars to be disrupted without placing ARM-equipped warplanes in danger. This works to save pilots' lives and also to conserve stocks of ARMs. Instead kinetic kills can be used on those difficult radars which are either out of range or are not responding to the jamming. The bottom line for SEAD in this operation and subsequent ones involving US forces was that if jamming could be used to shut down the radar, then this should be a priority before ARMs are brought into play.

Gaddafi had spent a lot of cash on air defences, but was not left with much to show for his shopping spree. The IADS he had developed were comprehensive, but the Americans and the French were one step ahead of the game. Moreover, the Americans could add yet more experience of Soviet SAM systems to their SEAD report books. Vietnam, Lebanon and now Libya. They would need every lesson from history just four years after Eldorado Canyon as they prepared to enter mortal combat with the world's most potent air defence system outside the Soviet Union. Iraqi strongman Saddam Hussein, a paranoid soul at the best of times, had gone to great lengths to employ state terrorism, divide and rule tactics, corruption and lies to consolidate his grip on power, even body doubles were used to keep his enemies off balance. The former Tikriti cigarette seller was also concerned that he could be attacked from the sky and his bodyguards in this regard would be SAMs, AAA and fighters. The US-led Coalition which would confront him after he invaded Kuwait in 1990 would have to punch, cajole and fool his skyward bodyguards into cowering submission.

CHAPTER SIX

Desert Storm SEAD

Saddam Hussein had spent the 1980s building up the most formidable air defence network in the world outside the Soviet Union. The Iran-Iraq war which the two countries waged between 1980-1988 saw air attacks by each belligerent and in a determined effort to blunt the effectiveness of Iran's attacks the Iraqi president had browsed the international arms bazaar and purchased off-the-shelf Soviet and French air defence weaponry, command and control systems, radar and know-how. Once imported, this technology was knitted together into a robust air defence umbrella.

The defence of his private kingdom was under the control of Iraqi Air Force Air Defence Command (IAFADC). Echoing Soviet doctrine, air defence fighters were part of the force, along with Iraqi Air Force personnel who staffed the EW radar and intercept reporting and control centres. The SAMs and AAA units that defended key politico-military targets, henceforth termed 'strategic', were also under the IAFADC's jurisdiction. Air defence units that were deployed in the field continued to remain under the operational control of the Iraqi Army.

The Russian equipment bought by the Iraqis included a collection of SA-2, SA-3, SA-6, SA-7, SA-8, SA-9, SA-13 and SA-14 SAMs, along with MIM-23B I-Hawk SAMs captured following the Kuwaiti invasion in August 1990. These were joined by the French Roland SAM system, all of which were deployed to protect strategic assets. These were reinforced with ZSU-23-4 and ZSU-57-2 self-propelled AAA pieces plus 0.57 in (14.5 mm) and 0.9 in (23 mm) anti-aircraft guns. The Army had SA-7, SA-8, SA-14, SA-9, SA-13 and 9K310 Igla-1/SA-16 (Gimlet) SAM

146

systems along with ZSU-23-4 AAA pieces which could be
deployed in the field. At the time of the Kuwaiti invasion, Iraq's
newest systems were the Roland, Gainful and ZSU-23-4 systems,
but that said, all of these defences represented a serious threat to
any aviator wanting to try their chances in Iraqi skies.

Estimates ranged between 9,000–10,000 in terms of available
AAA pieces, and up to a staggering 16,000 SAMs. In terms of air
defence fighters, the Iraqi air force could put Dassault Mirage F1s,
MiG-29 Fulcrum and MiG-25 Foxbat warplanes into the air. But
the hardware was not the only important part of the system. The
command and control technology which knitted the weaponry
and aircraft together allowed the IADS to be used in a responsive
and coordinated fashion during an air attack. The C2 structure
featured a French designed-and-built C2 system called KARI
(the French name for Iraq reversed). One analysis described the
system as being arguably the finest air defence technology available on the international market in 1991. However, previous
experience did not bode well for the Iraqi IADS system. Certainly,
it was robust and sophisticated, but without skilled personnel in
control, the system was little more than redundant wires and
weapons. During the Iran-Iraq war, the fire discipline of the Iraqi
air defenders had been noted as lax at best and non-existent at
worst. Trigger-happy operators would loose-off missiles and
AAA at anything that happened to be in the sky, friendly or not.
One report spoke of 75 per cent of Iraqi aircraft losses being the
result of friendly fire when Army air defences were deployed to
the field. Moreover, the Iraqi air force was said to have a similar
disdain for combat identification and recognition as it fought the
war in the skies with its Iranian enemies.

Saddam's invasion of Kuwait on 2 August 1990 received robust
condemnation from the international community. The United
States pledged to defend Saudi Arabia against any attempt by
Saddam to expand his territorial aggrandisement further. USAF
F-15C/D Eagles from the 1st TFW were sent to Saudi Arabia to
protect the Kingdom to this end, and their arrival heralded the
start of a massive military build-up in the country as the United
States, under the leadership of President George H W Bush,
assembled a Coalition of nations (including the United Kingdom,
Canada, France, Italy, Kuwait, Saudi Arabia, Bahrain, Qatar, The

United Arab Emirates, Australia and New Zealand) to comprise the UN-mandated military force that would eject Iraq from Kuwait.

As the military build-up in the desert rolled on under the code-name Operation Desert Shield, the thoughts of the military planners, led by US Army General Norman Schwarzkopf, turned to how the war would be fought and within this, how Iraq's potent air defences would be neutralised. This effort would follow many strands. The US DoD's Joint Electronic Warfare Center began to publish information on the composition of the Iraqi IADS. These reports were updated and disseminated to the air war planners as new information came to light from the intelligence effort. The goal of this effort was to find the system's Achilles' Heel; those critical points that, when attacked, would force the IADS to operate below par, or even better, not at all. Looking back to the definitions, Coalition planners arguably adopted a Manoeuvrist approach, but we shall also see that as the campaign evolved, a host of different approaches would be taken for the suppression and destruction of Iraq's air defences. In military jargon, this identification process of flagging these critical points was known as Critical Node Analysis.

Key to the process was gathering as much data on the electronic behaviour of the Iraqi IADS as possible. How did its radar operate? What frequencies did they use? How was information transmitted around the IADS? What route did this information take? What was the disposition of radar across Iraq? Computer technology provided SEAD planners with another indispensable tool. Computers could build models of the IADS based on the electronic data which was being gathered. This allowed a detailed understanding to be built of how the IADS would respond to a number of SEAD methods. Here, the Coalition was able to learn what might work and also what might not.

By September 1990 Lieutenant General Charles 'Chuck' Horner (himself a former Vietnam Wild Weasel pilot), Commander, US Central Command Air Forces (CENTAF), who would lead the Desert Storm air war, and his colleagues, who included Brigadier General 'Buster' Glosson CENTAF Director of Campaign Plans, and Lt. Gen. Larry 'Poobah' Henry, a former Wild Weasel Bear, who would be in charge of the SEAD effort, devised how the air war would be fought. It was to be split into four phases. Phase I would gain air superiority over Iraq and Kuwait to smash Iraq's Weapons of Mass Destruction (WMD) capabilities; namely its chemical, biological and nuclear weapons production facilities and its SS-1 Scud-B surface-to-surface missiles and accompanying infrastructure. Phase II would be the SEAD effort while phase III would see the destruction of Iraq's political and military command and control systems while finally, phase IV would focus on the support of the ground war to liberate Kuwait. Yet by November 1990, it became clear that, given the number of aircraft which were now in theatre, all phases could be run simultaneously to enhance their effect.

As 1990's Christmas turned to New Year, it was becoming clear that war in the Persian Gulf was increasingly likely, despite a last-minute flurry of diplomatic initiatives aimed at averting conflict. Saddam Hussein was in no mood to compromise and neither was the international community. Having failed to withdraw from Kuwait by mid-January as the UN had demanded, war was now certain.

Far away from Saddam and his entourage as dusk fell over the desert, a formation of helicopters took off from their base. They consisted of nine AH-64A Apache attack helicopters from the US Army's 101st Airborne Division and they were joined by three MH-53J PAVE LOW helicopters form the 20th Special Operation Squadron. The force was tooled-up with AGM-114 Hellfire missiles, rockets and cannon rounds. The object of this force, known as Task Force Normandy, was 435 miles (700 km) inside Iraq and for this reason the Apaches were also outfitted with an external 230 gallon (1,046 litre) fuel tank.

In the dead of night, somewhere near the Iraq-Saudi border, a couple of hours after the deadline elapsed this package of helicopters was hugging the desert as they raced to their objectives. At 02.38 local time the Apaches delivered their deadly cargo. From between 1.5–3 nautical miles (3–6 km) from their targets the Apache pilots used IR night-vision equipment to despatch the Hellfire missiles into the electrical generators at the two radar sites they were attacking which were home to P-15M(2) Squat Eye trailer-mounted low altitude C-band target acquisition radar, Flat

Face C-band truck-mounted low altitude target acquisition radar and Spoon Rest A-band 171 mile (275 km) range EW and target acquisition radar. Seconds later more Hellfires and M260 Hydra 2.75 in (70 mm) rockets slammed into the radar tearing them to pieces, along with around 4,000 1.18 in (30 mm) cannon rounds from the helicopters' devastating M230 Chain Gun. Where there had once been a radar station, there remained tortured sculptures of ash and metal. Helicopters were chosen for the mission because it was vital that the targets were visually identified as destroyed. Task Force Normandy had delivered the first attack of Operation Desert Storm, they turned their tails and headed for home.

The helicopter attack was part of a finely coordinated effort to build an ingress route into southern Iraq. With the radar stations destroyed, air defence operators watching this part of Iraq's airspace would have seen their screens go blank, they may have also received a very short emergency warning from one of the stations that it was under attack shortly before it was destroyed, but this would be the first, and only, clue that something was wrong. That said these same operators did not have much time to think, although an order was still transmitted for AAA pieces arrayed around Baghdad to begin spraying the skies with tracer.

At little over an hour-and-a-half before Task Force Normandy destroyed the radar site, a force of F-117A Nighthawk stealth fighter-bombers from the 37th TFW left their base at Khamis Mushait in southern Saudi Arabia and quietly flew towards the Iraq-Saudi border. By the time that Task Force Normandy was finishing off the radar stations, the F-117As were minutes away from their targets in West Baghdad.

Twenty minutes after the radar had been destroyed hell was unleashed on Iraq's air defence command. The contemplation of the southern Iraq's radar destruction by the staff of Iraq's air defences was swiftly followed by death for those in one of Iraq's air defence command and control centres, located in the west of Baghdad as GBU-10s dropped by the F-117s slammed into the Nukhayb IADS command and control centre. The Nighthawks were tasked with hitting thirty-four targets in the vicinity of Baghdad that evening connected with the IADS. The Nighthawks, from the 415th TFS hauled 2,000 lb (907 kg) GBU-10 and 500 lb (226 kg) GBU-12s with each aircraft carrying a weapons load of 4,000 lb (1,814 kg).

However, the Coalition had another ace up their sleeve as well as the famous black jets which could deliver their killer blow. As part of Operation Senior Surprise, B-52G Stratofortresses from the 596th Bomb Squadron assisted the opening salvos of the attacks with stand-off attacks using AGM-86C Conventional ALCMs. These were a close cousin of the Air Force's AGM-86B nuclear-tipped cruise missiles, but their kiloton-capable warhead had been replaced by conventional explosives which slammed into, among other things, an electrical transmission station depriving the air defence command and control centres in Baghdad of power.

The Iraqis did not realise this at the time, but the Coalition was taking apart their air defences from the inside out. The months of hard work getting into the Iraqi IADS decision-making cycle had allowed the air war planners to flag exactly where the CoGs were. Here was the Manoeuvrist approach in action. Iraq's electricity grid had been flagged, and one of the weak points was the power supply for the air defences.

What is interesting to note is that the Desert Storm SEAD effort was clearly an all arms battle. This was a campaign which had learned the lessons of Vietnam and had moved away from SEAD being the provision of dedicated aircraft and weapons (the Wild Weasels, Prowlers, EB-66s, Shrikes and Standards). The intervening years gave the USAF technological advances in the world of computing and also in the world of electronic eavesdropping which had allowed SEAD planners to gain a hitherto unheard of advantage in understanding their adversary's defences. Crucially, those same intervening years had also furnished the US military with new weapons which could be applied, devastatingly as we have seen, to the SEAD fight; Apache gunships and Nighthawks being but two examples. Moreover, from 1981, the USAF had developed a powerful 'triad' of SEAD assets. The F-4Gs carrying their AGM-88s were reinforced by the electronic warfare capabilities of the EF-111s and the communications-jamming attributes of the EC-130Hs.

The equipment was only half of the equation. From 1981, the air force had hosted the annual Green Flag exercise which closely focused on the abilities and tactics which could be used in electronic combat. These exercises were held at Nellis Air Force base in Nevada. Meanwhile a similar exercise called Cope Thunder was held from 1976 for the Pacific Air Forces of the USAF which would provide similar training. Finally, in Europe the POLYGONE EW range had been created over the border between France and Germany which allowed the USAF forces in Europe to improve their electronic warfare skills. The net result of this was that before Desert Storm began, USAF crews and personnel who would perform the SEAD mission had over ten years of training to familiarise themselves with using electrons to reinforce SEAD. Essentially, what this allowed the Coalition to do was to move the SEAD fight into the realm of the 'total force' concept by which any and all assets at the Coalition's disposal, irrespective of service, could be applied to the SEAD fight. The examples were all around; the helicopter gunships hitting the radar stations and the use of target drones as a feint being just two. Even the US Army's M270 Multiple Launch Rocket System was brought into the fight to bring its 'steel rain' to bear on Iraqi air defences on the battlefield.

The SEAD campaign in Desert Storm followed two distinct trends with the campaign borrowing both from the Bekaa Valley and the Eldorado Canyon operations. SEAD sorties were supplied in support of raids heading for specific targets, while the air and land forces in the theatre were also applied to the attack of the Iraqi IADS. The comparison is stark, with the Libya operation lasting a total of eleven minutes while the Bekaa Valley missions saw continuous SEAD for the duration of the campaign. Similarly, James R. Bungress in his *Setting the Context: Suppression of Enemy Air Defenses and Joint War Fighting in an Uncertain World* report notes that; 'the destruction of the Iraqi strategic IADS and command and control net was a function of air superiority, strategic bombardment and SEAD all at the same time. Most importantly, the destruction of the Iraqi air defence network was not seen as an isolated element of the campaign. All forces could be brought to bear on the entire Iraqi IADS. Furthermore, the attacks on the key nodes in the Iraqi IADS occurred at the start of the campaign when the CoGs were hit to allow Coalition aircraft to gain entry into the Iraqi airspace to perform other attacks

uring Operation Desert Storm, the F-111F aircraft from the 48th Tactical Fighter Wing, RAF Lakenheath,
gland were joined by EF-111 Ravens. The aircraft performed two very different but essential tasks; the former
ting Iraqi tanks, the latter jamming Iraqi air defences. *(US DoD)*

her USAF electronic attack assets in theatre during Operation Desert Storm included the EC-130H Compass
ll communications jamming aircraft of the 66th Electronic Combat Wing. *(US DoD)*

Many US SEAD aircraft types were nearing the end of their service lives during Operation Desert Storm; one such aircraft was the US Navy's A-7E Corsair which is seen here armed with AGM-88s during an Operation Desert Storm SEAD mission. (*US DoD*)

HIGH SPEED BOOM

Mission accomplished without a shot being fired: a clutch of Corsairs from the VA-72 attack squadron, still carrying their AGM-88s and AIM-9s return to the USS *John F. Kennedy* after a SEAD mission during Operation Desert Storm. *(US DoD)*

An F-14 Tomcat performs a test of the Tactical Air Launched Decoy. These small and non-descript objects are invaluable for sowing utter confusion into air defence networks. *(US DoD)*

The Flying Telegraph Pole; the SA-2 Guideline was the scourge of pilots in Vietnam, Iraq and also the Balkans. This example is a captured Iraqi weapon. *(US DoD)*

SEAD victim: The charred wreck of an Iraqi SA-6 truck after it had been attacked as part of the air defence suppression effort during Operation Desert Storm. *(US DoD)*

Enemy air defences can be attacked with a variety of weapons including dedicated anti-radar missiles. Since the end of the Cold War, cruise missiles such as the BGM-109 Tomahawk Land Attack Missile have been pressed into this role. *(Raytheon)*

ALARM bell: A Panavia Tornado armed with ALARM anti-radar missiles. This weapon saw its combat debut during Operation Desert Storm. *(MBDA)*

The US Navy deployed its EA-6B Prowlers during Operation Deny Flight. The rear display shows the Electronic Countermeasures Officer the location of suspected air defence radar. *(US DoD)*

An F-16CJ from the 169th Fighter Wing is prepared for an Operation Northern Watch mission as an AGM-88 is loaded onto its hardpoint. *(US DoD)*

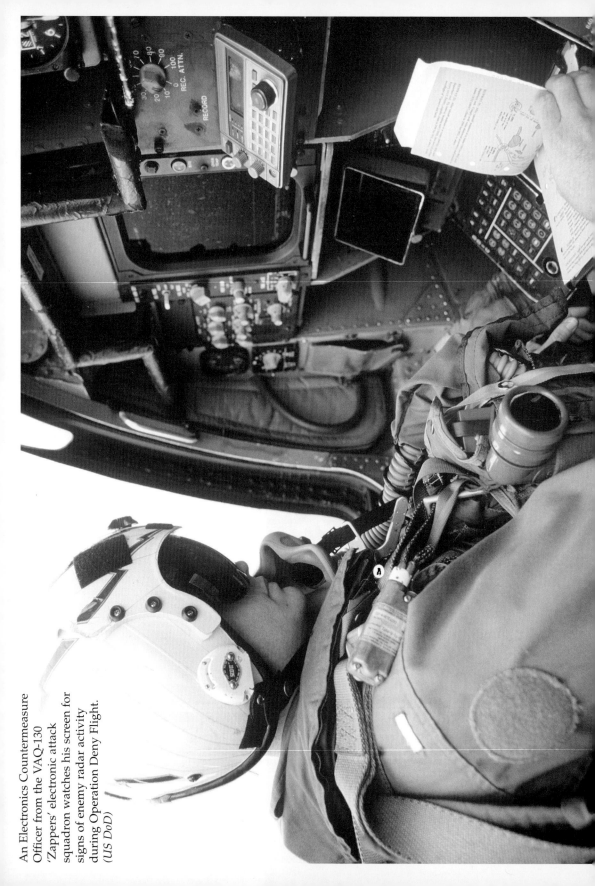

An Electronics Countermeasure Officer from the VAQ-130 'Zappers' electronic attack squadron watches his screen for signs of enemy radar activity during Operation Deny Flight. (US DoD)

F-16CJs from the 77th Fighter Squadron prepare for an escort mission during Operation Allied Force from Aviano AFB in northern Italy. (US DoD)

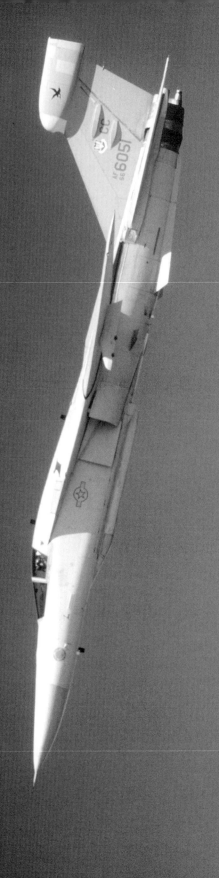

An EF-111 Raven of the 429th Electronic Combat Squadron deployed to the Balkans as part of Operation Deny Flight. Along with the F-16CJs, these aircraft were also based at Aviano AFB. (*US DoD*)

Several countries contributed SEAD assets during Operation Allied Force. One nation to do so was Germany which sent its Panavia Tornado ECR aircraft to support the SEAD effort. This aircraft carries both AIM-9 AAMs and AGM-88s. (*US DoD*)

With the retirement of the F-4G, the F-16CJ became the primary SEAD aircraft for the USAF. The aircraft was combined with the AGM-88 and would become a potent Wild Weasel combination in its own right. *(Raytheon)*

During Operation Enduring Freedom, the B-2A Spirit was the scourge of the Taliban's rudimentary air defences. This aircraft is from the 325th Bomb Squadron. *(US DoD)*

SAF F-16CJs deployed to southwest Asia as part of the 363rd Expeditionary Fighter Squadron. Ground crew move the safety pins on the aircraft's weapons prior to a combat mission during Operation Iraqi Freedom. *(US oD)*

Tooled-up and ready to go, AGM-88s and AIM-120 air-to-air missiles have been loaded onto this F-16CJ ready for a night mission during Operation Iraqi Freedom. *(US DoD)*

A trio of missiles on this F-16CJ from the 157th Expeditionary Fighter Squadron. From left to right they include an AGM-88 HARM, AIM-9 and AIM-120 AAMs. *(US DoD)*

An F-16CJ from the 77th Expeditionary Fighter Squadron maintains vigilance on the ground below during an Operation Northern Watch sortie. *(US DoD)*

Following the cessation of hostilities in 1991, EF-111s from the 42nd Electronic Combat Squadron stayed in theatre to provide electronic SEAD as part of Operation Provide Comfort. *(US DoD)*

An EA-6B Prowler un-sticks from the runway at Incirlik AFB during an Operation Northern Watch SEAD mission. The aircraft is from the VAQ-133 electronic attack squadron. *(US DoD)*

Playing a vital role in building the Iraqi air defence's electronic order of battle were the RC-130V/W Rivet Joint aircraft. *(US DoD)*

n RC-130V/W from the 55th Wing at Offut AFB, ebraska patrols the airspace above Iraq during a ission to enforce the no-fly zones. *(US DoD)*

Future SEAD planners and pilots will have to counter new air defence threats such as the Russian S-300 SAM system. *(Philipe Wodka Gallien)*

From Prowler to Growler: Boeing is developing the F/A-18E/F Hornet into the E/A-18G Growler to replace the EA-6B to provide the US Navy's electronic warfare and SEAD requirements. *(Boeing)*

The shape of SEAD to come? The pan-European nEUROn initiative could provide a UCAV design which removes the pilot from the cockpit for the SEAD mission. *(Dassault)*

The BQM-74 Chukar provided one of the earliest airframes which allowed the concept of the pilotless SEAD platform concept to be developed. These drones played a vital role in Scathe Mean operations during the Persian Gulf War. *(US DoD)*

which would decapitate the Iraqi air defences and serve to cut the air defences in the field from their commanders in Baghdad.

That did not stop the mobile air defences in the Kuwaiti Theatre of Operations from remaining a threat, but it did mean that they were more haphazard in their decision making and firing without their communications links to their superiors in Baghdad. Moreover, this served to make them easier targets for SEAD aircraft which were tasked with hitting the battlefield air defences. Television viewers the world over who were glued to their screens watched dramatic footage of amber plumes igniting the skies as laser-guided bombs found their targets. As the flashes left viewers eyes blinking they could also see streams of tracers spraying into the Baghdad night. Certainly, the combination of tracer and munitions made for a macabre firework display, and any television viewer would be further forgiven for thinking that the Coalition aircraft had awoken a hydra in the form of the air defences which would begin claiming scalps. This is not to say skies over the Iraqi capital were not a highly dangerous place, but like Gloucester in Shakespeare's *King Lear*, blinded and bereft of site and guidance, the fire was acutely inaccurate and amounted to little more than a Canute-esque attempt to repulse the focused waves of destruction smashing against Iraq's air defences. The wildly inaccurate AAA fire which was often hosed through the skies continued to provide a clear threat to Coalition aviators flying over the battlefield and to this end, sorties had to be planned carefully and *ad hoc* SEAD had to be organised to prevent battlefield preparation missions from falling prey to the Iraqi Army's mobile air defences.

Iraqi radar operators did change their behaviour once they became aware of the threat that the AGM-88 HARM missiles could pose to them. That said it did not stop them from continuing to threaten Coalition aircraft. Instead of using their tracking radar, Iraqi SAM operators could fire their missiles and then activate the tracking radar for a short time in the vain hope of scoring a 'lucky hit' against a Coalition aircraft.

Scathe Mean
As explained in Chapter One, the Manoeuvrist approach often requires some kind of feint and in the opening hours of Desert

Storm, this was applied. Under a cloak of tight secrecy, 'Poobah's Party' was assembled. This was a group of individuals who would execute Project Scathe Mean. The lessons of the Israeli campaign over the Bekaa Valley in 1982 had not been lost on those who would be responsible for Scathe Mean. They would plan a similar treat for the Iraqi air defenders.

Project Scathe Mean was designed to seduce the Iraqis into using their air defences. The plan focused around the BQM-74C Chukar drone. The drone was ostensibly used for target practice but in Desert Storm it was used to simulate aircraft and cruise missiles flying over Baghdad.

As conflict neared, Poobah's Party was reassembled into the 4468th Tactical Reconnaissance Group. Staff were drawn from units such as the 501st Tactical Missile Wing ground launched cruise missile units which had been disbanded at the end of the Cold War. There was an impressive sense of practicality as the unit obtained the necessary equipment for its task. Trucks were purchased along with tool kits from Sears and other materiel bought from army surplus stores. The unit was also outfitted with 44 BQM-74Cs spread across two teams each of which had six target launchers. By 15 October, the unit had arrived at its basing near the Iraqi border in Saudi Arabia. One team was to cover Baghdad and other strategic targets in the vicinity of the Iraqi capital, while the other was tasked with covering Iraq's second city of Basrah and also Kuwait City.

The drones would fly for around 310 miles (500 km) at speeds of 390 mph (630 km/h). They would orbit over their target area and wait to be illuminated by Iraqi air defence radar. When they were, the radar would by default show itself to an AGM-88-equipped aircraft within range which would blast the radar off the face of the Earth. The decoys had two impacts on the Iraqi IADS. First of all, they forced the radar into showing itself, but secondly, the saturation of decoys in the air was also intended to overwhelm Iraqi air defences and also confuse the air defenders as to the sheer numbers of aircraft above them.

Exploiting the Breakthrough
Air defence radar in Western Iraq was now a memory, while a significant portion of the Iraqi IADS command, control and

communications system was now either non-existent or badly damaged. As Iraqi air defenders tried to understand what was happening and to make sense of the chaos suddenly visited on them; from where and how they did not know. The radar attacks had opened a western ingress route and the Nighthawk attack had destroyed Iraq's western air defences. Through the gap came a follow-on package of EF-111A Raven aircraft which could set up orbits in the now relatively-benign airspace of western Iraq and start blasting Iraq's surviving air defences with noise.

Meanwhile, a swarm of aircraft was preparing to continue the bombardment. The targets were not just air defence installations; F-15E Strike Eagles for example began to use their famed LANTIRN (Low Altitude Navigation and Targeting Infrared for Night) targeting pods to attack other air defence targets. These targets included the Al Taqaddum Ground Control Intercept centre which was sited to the south-west of the city and also the Al Kark communication tower located on the west bank of the Tigris River, along with the Baghdad International Telephone Exchange. This was an important building as Iraq's communications links for its IADS were thought to run contiguous with the same lines used by the civilian telephone service. No doubt destroying that building was also intended to deprive the Iraqi IADS of a major node in their air defence communications system. Finally, in the Taji suburb of Baghdad an air force bunker was also attacked. However, the Strike Eagles did not just attack the IADS targets they also began to hunt down Scud missiles. Aircraft that were attacking the phase one targets could draw on SEAD support from AGM-88 HARM equipped A-7 Corsair-II and F/A-18 Hornets, along with an electronic suppression force which included EF-111A Raven, US Navy EA-6B Prowlers and EC-130H Compass Call aircraft., the latter being tasked with blasting those IADS targets not hit by the hard kill weapons with electrons to stop them functioning effectively.

The totality of the attacks was such that a major portion of Iraq's once feared IADS had been rendered useless in one night of carefully planned and coordinated attacks. The months of preparation for what amount to a few hours of strikes paid off handsomely. The dire predictions of Allied aircraft losses had failed to materialise. General Schwarzkopf, always quick with a pithy comment, said that the night's attacks had 'plucked out the eyes' of Iraq's air defences.

After the Nighthawks had unleashed their deadly cargoes, the Chukar decoys went to work. In total the 4468th Tactical Reconnaissance Group launched thirty-seven of the drones in groups of three in precisely spaced timings. The first group were intercepted by Iraqi fighters which no doubt believed them to be an incoming strike group of aircraft, while the others headed towards their target areas. The drones were also fitted with radar reflectors that were designed to emit a similar radar signature to the strike aircraft which were in the Iraqi skies that night.

The US Navy also played its part in the deception. A-6E aircraft launched AN/ADM-141A Tactical Air Launched Decoys which could glide for 80 miles (129 km) after they were launched from their carrier aircraft. The decoys were also outfitted with emitters which would mimic the radio frequency characteristics of US combat aircraft to lure the Iraqi IADS to engage these decoys rather than the strike aircraft. The decoys were constructed by Brunswick Defence and during the first three days of the air war, a total of 137 were launched. In one incident during the opening US Navy SEAD strikes twenty-five TALDs were launched by A-6E aircraft. Curiously, with characteristic bluster after the first day's air strikes, the Iraqis claimed the scalps of numerous Allied aircraft which, known or otherwise to Baghdad, were decoys.

The air campaign moved through January into February as preparations for the land campaign increased, and SEAD continued to be an indispensable part of the air campaign. There is no doubt that the Coalition's opening strikes had punched the Iraqi IADS hard, but there was no way that Horner and his staff were going to be complacent. Dedicated SEAD support was provided to nearly all strikes that went into theatre. AGM-88s carried by A-7s, F/A-18s and electronic jamming support from USAF EF-111A Ravens, EA-6B Prowlers and EC-130H Compass Call were used in tandem to make the SEAD coverage as comprehensive as possible. It was the EF-111As and the EA-6Bs which were particularly focused on Iraqi SAM guidance radar while the Compass Calls were primarily tasked with disrupting the IADS communications networks. It is interesting to note that the Iraqis did have secure radio communications, although these were first and second generation systems. The result was that they made themselves more vulnerable to interception as the Compass Calls could listen in to their frequencies and then initiate jamming. Communications jamming had another useful side effect. The Iraqi air defenders relied on the radio network to provide them with targeting information so as to avoid activating their search radar. With no radio communications available, they were forced into activating their radar to search for targets. One anecdote told of a commander of an Iraqi air defence battery who revealed in a captured diary that he had not had any communications from his superiors for the last three weeks of the war.

The backbone of the USAF's SEAD effort, along with the Compass Calls and Ravens, was the F-4G Wild Weasel II. These aircraft were equipped with HARMs and also the AN/APR-47 RHAWS. This equipment would listen for enemy radar across a large area. Information on enemy radar emitters would then be displayed for the Bear to prioritise the most dangerous threats and then to loose-off a HARM for the attack. The missiles could be fired responsively, but they were also fired pre-emptively as a package neared its target area with the intention of keeping the Iraqi radar off the air. The F-4G served Iraqi air defences a total of 268 HARMs in the first 36 hours of battle. It is important to note here that the Navy and the Air Force performed SEAD slightly differently. The Navy tended to use their SEAD assets in support of a specific mission against a specific target. The air force, however, would operate their Phantoms in more of a freelance capacity. They could also escort strike packages, or alternatively they could prowl the skies hunting for radar and SAM sites and then attack them when found. The Navy would also use HARM as a way of keeping the Iraqi radar down while the radar and SAMs were attacked by non-specialist SEAD ordnance such as free-fall bombs. Moreover, as the air war continued the SEAD mission also encompassed the 'roll-back' of air defences which were present in southern Iraq and Kuwait where the land war would be fought to prevent these air defences interfering with Coalition CAS aircraft when the time came.

Moreover, the F-117As were not only used during the opening of the campaign. Their unique capability made them the platform *par excellence* for keeping the air defences subdued. One example is noteworthy in illustrating how the aircraft could operate with other assets in attacking heavily defended targets. North of Baghdad was where the Taji military logistics facility was based. The area housed a network of supply depots and maintenance facilities. Horner and his staff had earmarked the target to be turned to dust by a pride of B-52s, but there was just one slight problem. The Iraqis, fully realising the value of their logistics facility, had ring-fenced the site with a phalanx of SA-2, SA-3 and SA-6 SAMs to defend it from every direction. However, once again Saddam had wasted his efforts. The Iraqis may have thought that prickly missile defences such as these would make the lucrative target unappealing for the Coalition, yet they were proved wrong as the bombs from sixteen Nighthawks turned the missiles into a scrap yard, shortly before the Stratofortresses meted out similar treatment to the rest of the facility. The Nighthawk was not designed primarily as a SEAD platform, any more than the Stratofortress was expected to have a long life after the Soviet Union and its subsequent original *raison d'etre* imploded yet both were working with supreme competence in new and evolving roles.

Alarm

The RAF fielded its own dedicated SEAD asset in the Iraqi theatre for the first time. The BAE Systems' Air-Launched Anti-Radiation Missiles (ALARM) was still in developmental stages when the war kicked off, but that did not stop some missiles being sent to theatre where they would be used in a combat environment. The ALARM would be fired from its carrier aircraft, in this case a Panavia Tornado GR.Mk1 to an altitude of around 70,000 ft (21,336 m) where it could watch the ground below and listen for a radar emission which it then matched with an internal memory of signals as it floated down to earth, on its ten minute journey, suspended from a parachute. With a radar located the parachute would be jettisoned and the missile would dive towards its target. Emitter information was gathered in theatre by No.51 Sqn. Nimrod R1 aircraft. These aircraft had performed eavesdropping missions from 1990 to develop a comprehensive order of battle of Iraqi air defences around the airfields which would be the

Tornado's targets. The available missile stocks were allocated to the No.20 Sqn. at Laarbruch, Germany and the units' accompanying GR.1 aircraft. The crews of the squadron had less than a week to get used to the weapon, particularly its programming system which was noted for its complexity. They then deployed to Tabuk towards the end of November where they practised flying in mixed packages of defence suppression and mud-moving Tornados. It was during these practices that the Standard Operating Procedures for the weapon was drafted. The Tornado force at Tabuk was also furnished with nine ALARM-capable aircraft which had been modified with the Mil-Std-1553B databus to communicate with the weapon, in addition to eight crews trained in deploying the ALARM.

The use of ALARM brought strike packages some time, as the radar operators would have to keep their equipment switched off while the missile was falling to the ground unless they wanted the missile to attack them. This had the added benefit of giving the package of aircraft time to unleash its strike. ALARM's first employment in combat came on the opening night of the air attacks. Two Tornados left Tabuk in Western Saudi Arabia at 02:10 local time, less than twenty minutes before Task Force Normandy would attack. The ALARM-equipped aircraft descended down to 200 ft (61 m) above the desert floor, skimming through the Arabian night to keep comfortably below Iraqi radar. The ALARM aircraft got the target, Al Asad airfield, west of Baghdad and launched their missiles at 03.50. These two aircraft were supporting a force of three Tornados which were attacking the airfield. Then on 21 January, the missile was used to support a strike package of F-15Es which was to attack a Scud missile storage depot at Al Qaim north-west of Baghdad. ALARM Tornados attacked the same site two days' later, again in support of F-15s performing another attack on the Scuds.

By 26 February a total of twenty-four ALARM missions had been flown. During these missions a total of 123 ALARM rounds were fired. The missiles supported attacks on a communications centre at Al Kufah south-central Iraq, the oil refinery at Bayji, northern Iraq; the Al Musayib power station south of Baghdad; ammunition dumps at Habbaniyah and Al Taqaddum in Central

Iraqi; the airfields of Al Asa, H-2 and H-3 and also the Al Iskandariyah and Qubaysah petrol-oil and lubrication depot.

By the 30 January, the impressive effects of the SEAD effort was becoming apparent. A briefing to reporters by General Schwarzkopf revealed that twenty-nine IADS nodes had been attacked with the result that the Iraqi IADS was paralysed. Coordination of Iraqi air defence over Kuwait and Iraq was now impossible. The radar kill tally was especially impressive. By the end of the first week of air combat, the Coalition claimed that all Iraq's air defence radar had been either destroyed or damaged, however it must be remembered that the Iraqis did succeed in placing around 20 per cent of these back into action.

Destroying the battlefield radar became the preserve of attack helicopters and CAS platforms such as the Fairchild A-10A Thunderbolt. These aircraft were able to use precision missiles to attack the radar, however threats still remained, most notably in the form of anti-aircraft guns. Systems such as the devastating ZSU-23-4 were to easy to attack, particularly given that its fire breathing 23-mm cannon could tear fuselage and airframe apart, as Soviet pilots had learned in Afghanistan.

The net effect was that the Iraqi air defenders went from being the hunters to the hunted. For them, the script was never supposed to have been written like this. They were the ones with the world's most robust, potent and well-connected air defences. It was them who should have been shooting Coalition aircraft out of the sky like grouse on the Glorious Twelfth. But the script had changed and the numbers spoke for themselves. The SEAD effort was so deliberate and effective that by the eighth day of the campaign, the Iraqis were moving those parts of their mobile air defences into mountain caves near the Iranian border to keep them 'out of HARM's way'. These missiles may have escaped destruction, but in a cave they could do little more than annoy bats unhappy with their new housemate. The presence and use of HARM also made them extremely reluctant to switch their radar on and begin a search for Coalition aircraft, which in turn prevented their air defences from being efficient and deadly. The Coalition mustered 112,756 sorties during the campaign, with fourteen aircraft being lost in combat, leading to an attrition rate of 0.06 per cent.

The Coalition also had the simple matter of geography on their side. The featureless desert terrain which played host to the air and land operations was perfect for SEAD. It gave the attacker a wide, uninterrupted view of the ground below while at the same time denying the defender locations to hide their SAMs and AAA.

It was true that the Iraqis had outfitted themselves with a potent air defence network, but that said, their employment and organisation of this system left a lot to be desired. Prior to Desert Storm kicking off, the Iraqis had organised their IADS with high and medium altitude threats in mind. However this left an obvious gap at low level. During the Iran-Iraq war, this was a gap that the Iranian air force was well-able to exploit by flying at low-level and penetrating the Iraqi air defence relatively unscathed. For their part, the Iraqis never truly addressed this gap and as a consequence they became extremely susceptible to Coalition ingress and egress at low altitude.

CHAPTER SEVEN

SEAD in the Balkans

The destruction of Iraq's strategic air defences was so profound that the threat from high-level SAMs seemed to have been severally chastened if not altogether eliminated. But that did not mean that the sky was now clear of air defences. Desert Storm, and operations over the corpse of Yugoslavia, would illustrate that AAA and MANPADS were still a significant threat, particularly for aircraft operating at low level. Higher altitudes were undoubtedly safer to operate in than they had been in the past, but the lower-level threat still remained and this would have profound consequences for the campaigns that NATO would fight in the Balkans during the 1990s. At the same time, the Serbian and Bosnian-Serb air defenders had learned valuable lessons from the devastation that was visited on the Iraqi air defence network. They worked hard to ensure that they would not fall prey to similar treatment, even if this meant curtailing their ability to engage Allied aircraft with as much enthusiasm as their systems would allow.

Enter Wild Weasel
As the F-4G had bowed out of Wild Weasel service in 1996, the USAF acquired a new aircraft to take to the fight. This aircraft was the F-16CJ, which was a variant of the F-16 Viper, entered service in 1994. The Wild Weasels from the 13th Panthers and 14th Fightin' Samurai FS, 35th Fighter Wing (FW) at Misawa AFB in Japan received 'WW' tail codes denoting their SEAD function. As the F-16CJ entered service between 1994 and 1997, ten squadrons of the aircraft were raised at four other bases: Shaw AFB, South Carolina, home of the 55th Fighting Fifty-Fifth, 77th Gamblers,

78th Bushmasters and 79th Tigers FS as part of the 20th FW; the 22nd Stingers and 23rd Fighting Hawks FS as part of the 52nd FW at Spangdahlem AFB, Germany; the 157th Swamp Foxes FS, part of the 169th FW, McEntire Air National Guard Base, South Carolina and the 366th Thunderbolts FS as part of the 366th Wing at Mountain Home AFB, Idaho.

The Wild Weasel features a General Electric F110-GE-129 engine throwing out 29,000 lb (13,152 kg) of thrust. The aircraft was based on the Block-50/52 Viper design and the electronics include the AN/ASQ-213 HTS, jokingly known as 'Weasel in a Can', because of its podded construction. This system watches the forward hemisphere of the aircraft for hostile radar sites.

The new aircraft were allied with new weaponry. From 1993, the AGM-88C HARM variant entered service. The missile was equipped with the WGU-2C/B blast-fragmentation warhead, while the missile's seeker had increased sensitivity and could guide itself to its target when fired in Target of Opportunity mode. The changes to the missile's seeker had come about because of a DoD competition to equip the missile with a new low-cost system resulting in Texas Instruments and Loral Aeronautics offering their respective C-1 and C-2 systems. Texas Instruments emerged as the victor and received a contract to build 2,041 AGM-88C-1 missiles which were procured largely to replace those missile fired during Operation Desert Storm.

The first major SEAD operation over the Balkans was Operation Deliberate Force (ODF) which saw a total of sixty-five AGM-88s being fired with EF-18 A/B Hornets from the *Ejército del Aire* (Spanish Air Force) firing two and US aircraft firing sixty-three, of which twenty-seven were fired in a reactive fashion after an aircraft was painted by a radar and thirty-six fired pre-emptively to neutralise radar threats which may have attempted to paint an incoming strike package. It was during ODF that US forces picked up most of the SEAD burden, flying 89 per cent of the missions, while the Spanish flew 7 per cent and the *Luftwaffe* 4 per cent. Of the American SEAD missions, the Navy picked up most of the burden, flying 395 sorties, while the USAF flew 244 and the United States Marine Corps (USMC) sixty-six.

It is worth back-tracking a little to understand how NATO operations in the Balkans came about. In 1991 Slovenia declared its independence from Yugoslavia and fought a short war with Belgrade. This was followed by the Croat-Serb war of 1991–1992 after Croatia's declaration of independence from the crumbling Yugoslav federation. However, it was the epicentre of Bosnia-Herzegovina which largely grabbed the western media's attention where Bosnian Muslims, Bosnian Serbs and Croats all fought for the independence of their respective areas. The Bosnian Serbs were insistent that their territory remained part of Yugoslavia and expelled Bosnian Muslims from their areas during a brutal campaign of ethnic cleansing which led to the deaths of thousands of Bosnian Muslims after the Bosnian government declared its independence in April 1992. The Bosnian Serbs responded by declaring their *Republika Srpska* (Serbian Republic) and began to expel and massacre Bosnian Muslims trapped in Bosnian Serb areas. The slaughter being meted out in this corner of Europe could be ignored no longer, especially as the Bosnian Serb Army (BSA) was able to pose an increasing threat to the Bosnian capital city of Sarajevo which was suffering appalling privations under siege by the Bosnian Serbs and where its population was being attacked by indiscriminate BSA shelling and sniper fire.

The initial response of NATO to the violence against the Bosnian Muslim population was to launch Operation Deny Flight on 12 April 1993. This campaign was intended to do exactly what it said on the tin, namely to prevent the airspace of Bosnia-Herzegovina being used for flights by fixed- or rotary-winged aircraft. Part and parcel of this operation was preventing Allied aircraft from coming under threat from BSA air defences.

Yugoslav Air Defences
The mid-1970s saw the extensive upgrade of Yugoslavia's air defences. The country acquired eight battalions of SA-2 missiles (around forty systems) along with six battalions of SA-3s, totalling sixty launchers. The missiles were reinforced with fifteen AAA regiments; a robust EW network and IADS command and control facilities were distributed across the country, increasing their redundancy and survivability. Political and military centres were well-protected with air defences, along with industrial facilities, airports and population centres.

Yugoslavia also received mobile SA-6 (around seventy launchers) and SA-11 systems which would prove to be particularly difficult for NATO to target. Smaller, mobile SA-9 and ZRK-BD Strela-10 (NATO codename SA-13 Gopher) launchers with a maximum engagement altitude of 11,500 ft (3,500 m) systems were available to the Serbians, along with SA-7, SA-16 and SA-18 MANPADS with similar engagement altitudes to the Gopher.

Before Yugoslavia imploded, the country had coordinated its air defences from a command centre in the Yugoslav capital Belgrade. This in turn was linked to a total of four command centres, each of which had responsibility for a specific sector. To make their air picture as comprehensive as possible, these centres could receive information from each other and also from observation posts lower down the network. Each sector operations centre would control a number of SAM units and also air defence fighters. Therefore, the organisation of the Yugoslav IADS was not altogether unlike the Iraqi system with air defence fighters and weapons coordinated by a single command, which borrowed heavily from Soviet air defence doctrine. In a nutshell, all of these components comprised the Yugoslav IADS. Yet there was a problem for the NATO air campaign planners. As the country had fallen apart so had the air defences, leaving bits and pieces of the now-disjointed system scattered around the various newly-independent parts of the Balkans. Inevitably, this meant that some of the Yugoslav air defences fell into Bosnian Serb hands and could thus threaten NATO aircraft.

The Alliance had to identify the parts which were in BSA possession, and as Deny Flight unfolded it became clear that the BSA had got its hands on SAMs (SA-2, SA-6 and SA-9/SA1-3) and MANPADS (SA-7/SA-14) along with AAA systems, the latter which was sufficient to compel the aircraft enforcing Deny Flight to operate at a minimum altitude of 10,000 ft (3,048 m). What was also worrying was the network of search, tracking and targeting radar with which the BSA could watch the skies.

As 1994 unfolded NATO aircraft were increasingly targeted by the BSA as they monitored and enforced compliance with UN Resolution 816 which had established the Bosnia-Herzegovina No-Fly Zone. NATO began to draw up concerted plans to attack and destroy the BSA IADS. The Combined Air Operations Centre (CAOC) at Vicenza, northern Italy, drew up plans to attack air defence sites including command and control and SAM systems in Bosnia-Herzegovina using electronic warfare and hard-kill weaponry. This formed the embryonic Dead Eye NATO SEAD effort. Echoing the work undertaken prior to Desert Storm, the NATO CAOC performed an analysis of the CoGs of the Bosnian Serb air defences and worked out strategies for degrading or, even better, eliminating the threat that they posed.

As the Dead Eye operations were being planned, Deny Flight continued although on 2 June 1995, an F-16C piloted by Captain Scott F. O'Grady flying near Banja Luka, northern Bosnia, was shot out of the sky, and the pilot later rescued. The attack was sufficient to trigger intensive preparations to get Operation Dead Eye ready for implementation. Dead Eye would provide a robust SEAD effort to accompany ongoing Deliberate Force operation, most importantly to ensure that NATO aircraft could operate in Bosnian skies with the minimum of interference from BSA defences. Dead Eye was to focus on targeting Bosnian Serb IADS communications systems, missile launch sites and also IADS logistics and support bases, These had been identified by NATO planners as being the key CoGs of the BSA air defence system. The operation focused on thirty-six identified targets.

The preparations for Dead Eye were being performed with a backdrop of worsening violence gripping Bosnia-Herzegovina. The UN had attempted to establish so-called Safe Havens where Bosnian Muslims would be safe from BSA attack but the policy was in ruins after the infamous events at Srebrenica which saw the deaths of around 8,000 Bosnian Muslims after Serb forces entered the town in July 1995, along with Zepa where the Bosnian Serbs had expelled the Bosnian Muslim population. Meanwhile Grozade, another safe haven, was under increasing threat of being overrun by the BSA. Time was running out for the international community to act and prevent the Bosnian Muslim areas from being destroyed.

Military action by NATO now seemed inevitable. The alliance was drafting plans to perform air strikes against BSA targets around the safe areas and the Dead Eye SEAD operations which had now been split into Dead Eye South-east and Dead Eye

North-west would provide a defence suppression effort to accompany NATO's air strikes.

NATO's justification for its attacks to begin crashed out of the August sky on 28th of that month into a market in Sarajevo killing thirty-eight civilians and injuring many others. Lieutenant-General Rupert Smith Commander of the UN Protection Force (UNPROFOR), and Admiral Leighton W. Smith Jr, Commander-in-Chief of US Naval Forces, Europe and Allied Forces Southern Europe agreed to begin air strikes after the British troops garrisoned as part of the UNPROFOR deployment in Gorazde headed out of the town to avoid being taken hostage by the BSA. The long and elastic patience of the international community had finally snapped after four years of war in the wreck of Yugoslavia: the Bosnian Serbs were about to pit themselves against the world's most advanced aircraft and most skilled air forces.

Deliberate Force
Deliberate Force was characterised by strict rules of engagement to ensure the minimum number of casualties, both military and civilian, on the ground. SEAD mission planning had to take a number of factors into account to perform defence suppression. This included giving adequate consideration to the avoidance of hitting unintended targets when firing a HARM at a radar and also to take into account the AGM-88's behaviour. Therefore, the SEAD effort was to be focused around aircraft using their own countermeasures and flight profile to frustrate the Bosnian Serb IADS. Kinetic self-defence was only authorised if the aircraft was unable to escape from the threat. HARMs were not permitted to be fired pre-emptively, unless authorised. Reactive HARM firing over Bosnia and Croatia was only permissible for the protection of a strike group, and the risk of collateral damage was minimal. HARMs could be fired if a SAM had been launched at a NATO aircraft.

As 29 August drew to a close, USAF KC-10 and KC-135 tanker aircraft took up their positions in orbit over the Adriatic close to the Croatian port of Split. They patiently waited for the first package of fourteen SEAD aircraft, along with three fighter-bombers to rendezvous to take a much needed drink of fuel after leaving Aviano. The package was a mixed bag of F-16Cs from the 510th FS, F/A-18s and EA-6B Prowlers and after taking on fuel it flew towards the campaign's first SEAD targets; SAM batteries and IADS C2 sites including the Han Pijesak communications relay station near the de facto Bosnian Serb capital of Pale which received the close attention of a pair of GBU-10 weapons. Other targets attacked that night by the SEAD package included the Mount Jahorina air defence control bunker, also near the Bosnian Serb capital along with an SA-6 site at Sokolac, and other air defence targets at Tuzla.

SEAD aircraft also supported the first strike packages to head for Bosnian Serb targets around the Bosnian Muslim capital which went into action one-and-three quarter hours after the Dead Eye South-east package had struck its aim points and left the theatre of operations. NATO's strike packages for the Sarajevo attacks were codenamed Alpha, Bravo, Charlie, Delta and Echo with their targets spread across Bosnian Serb logistics facilities and communication centres. The first strike package, Alpha, contained ten ground attack aircraft supported by four SEAD planes. The Bravo package was slightly larger with four SEAD aircraft and Fourteen ground attack planes hitting ammunition dumps around the city.

The opening attacks were joined by an all-arms SEAD effort as artillery deployed on the ground with the NATO Rapid Reaction Force hit BSA air defence targets around Mount Igman, outside Sarajevo. NATO planners had painted a clear picture of the BSA air defences that they were up against which included seven SA-2, six SA-6 and twelve SA-9 batteries, along with eleven AAA systems of between 0.78–2.75 in (20–76 mm) calibre, and an un-determined number of MANPADS. It was also expected that the BSA would obtain targeting information from the Yugoslav air defence network given their alliance with Belgrade.

A feint was provided in the form of AN/ADM-141 TALDs which were launched by the US Navy both in an attempt to convince the Bosnian Serbs that the armada approaching their air defences was bigger than it was and also to tempt them into acti-vating their radar to reveal themselves to the SEAD shooters. But, unlike the Iraqis three years before, on this occasion the Bosnian Serbs did not fall for the ruse.

So far so good, no NATO aircraft lost to Bosnian-Serb air defences. But NATO's luck would only last so long. Strike package Charlie picked up from where Bravo had left off and was sent to attack the logistics depot at Pale. However during the attack a French Air Force Mirage 2000N-K2 from EC2/3 Squadron was hit with an SA-7 sending the Mirage to the ground. The crew ejected and, unluckily for them, were picked up by a Bosnian Serb patrol and incarcerated until the end of December after the signing of the Dayton Peace Accords which concluded in late 1995 and effectively ended the conflict. However, the SEAD packages flown throughout the rest of the day kept the Bosnian Serb radar down. Even with SEAD support there was arguably not much that the HARM shooters could do about the AAA and MANPADS threat that lurked below and those BSA operators prepared to take a lucky shot.

As dawn broke over the Balkans follow-on packages of aircraft prepared to hit targets around Sarajevo which were supported by SEAD escorts. The SEAD support for Deliberate Force was intense because of the sheer number of aircraft and sorties which were operating over or near the Bosnian Herzegovina theatre of operations. This included aircraft providing reconnaissance and (BDA), airborne early warning and control, electronic warfare and CAPs. The result was 24 hour coverage over Bosnia and the Adriatic, this required SEAD which in turn forced the Bosnian Serbs to keep their heads down but meant that the SEAD shooters of the F-16CJ 23rd FS were in high demand as were the EC-130H Compass Call and EF-111A Raven aircraft which radiated their electrons to blind BSA radar and disrupt radio communications. Data on the electronic order-of-battle for the Bosnian Serb IADS was meanwhile gathered by the RC-135V/W Rivet Joint aircraft operating from RAF Mildenhall in Suffolk, UK.

The opening SEAD strikes by NATO aircraft did make an impression on the BSA air defences but did not destroy them outright. What the first night's attacks had achieved was breaking the air defence network up and shattering its connectivity but it was not yet on the canvas. NATO pilots still had to take the IADS threat very seriously when operating over Bosnia. The feeling at Aviano AFB, northern Italy, was that the opening attacks had a blinding but not a destructive effect according to one report. Part of the problem lay in the fact that the members of the BSA were far from ignorant. They were fully aware of the fact that to turn on one's radar could invite a HARM and they were clearly not ready to give their lives for Bosnian Serb glory just yet.

The effect of the Serbs' action was curious. Without radar, the chances that they could fire with anything like the accuracy that they were used to were, at best, minimal. However this meant that the BSA held onto its air defences. These could pose a nuisance value to NATO by forcing the Alliance to continue mounting SEAD missions for as long as these air defence systems remained intact.

Operations against Bosnian Serb positions and their accompanying SEAD strikes continued until 1 September when there was a pause in the NATO offensive to allow the BSA to withdraw heavy weapons from the vicinity of Sarajevo. Meanwhile NATO turned its thoughts to the air defences in north-west Bosnia. These IADS strikes would be codenamed Operation Dead Eye North-west. The concern was that the enemy had moved a large segment of their IADS into north-west Bosnia where they believed that they would not be attacked. However, this did not stop around five strike packages per day being sent over eastern Bosnia to attack bridges and ammunition dumps and after twelve of the former were attacked it dawned on senior NATO commanders that the target list for this part of Bosnia was growing decidedly thin. Moreover General Ratko Mladic, the BSA leader, had yet to agree to lift the siege of Sarajevo and move the BSA heavy weapons back to the 12 mile (20 km) minimum distance demanded by NATO.

The busiest time for the 23rd FS was between 8-9 September when the majority of HARM firings took place. Operation Deliberate Force saw the Wild Weasels firing off nine HARMs during some 160 sorties that the 23rd FS performed. The upshot of this effort was that there were no losses from Bosnian Serb SAMs when the unit was active. However, the Bosnian Serb air defenders were far from stupid and realised that the best way to preserve their lives was to leave their search and tracking radar switched off. That said, on 8 September, the squadron launched an AGM-88 after being painted by radar in the vicinity of Banja

Luka. At the time, the aircraft was escorting F-15E Strike Eagles tasked with hitting a communications centre with GBU-15 television/IR-guided bombs.

A typical SEAD sortie for the 23rd FS could see between eight and twelve F-16s supporting between three and five packages, each of which could include up to twenty aircraft. No NATO aircraft were permitted to operate over Bosnia-Herzegovina, termed 'feet dry', without SEAD support. The NATO CAOC would open a window of air operations over Bosnia-Herzegovina when the first SEAD aircraft arrived on station. The window would close when the last SEAD aircraft left. The strike packages would enter and exit the windows and SEAD aircraft were able to protect an average of around twelve windows per day, with each window remaining open for around two hours resulting in up to 24 hours of SEAD support being offered to the strike assets per day. SEAD platforms would also provide protected ingress and egress corridors for the aircraft entering or exiting Bosnia-Herzegovina.

When airborne, aircraft performing SEAD support would listen to their radios for requests for assistance from strike aircraft going 'feet dry'. A frequency was pre-selected for SEAD requests and any aircraft requesting such support could contact the duty SEAD assets. However, as well as providing this cab rank system, specific SEAD could also be provided. If, for example, a specific sortie was being undertaken for BDA or tactical reconnaissance in an area where a known SAM threat existed; then SEAD aircraft could be assigned to provide HARM support for the duration of the mission over Bosnia-Herzegovina.

SEAD aircraft were able to receive information on the BSA air defence electronic order of battle from aircraft such as the Rivet Joint as they prepared to take up SEAD station. SEAD aircraft could position themselves in a fixed orbit to provide cab rank style support to strike aircraft approaching the theatre of operations from a number of different routes, accompanying them to open an ingress corridor as they went 'feet dry' into the area of operations. That said, there were command and control issues during the SEAD operation. For example, coordination between SEAD packages and strike aircrews was at times problematic while the usual hazards of weather and Clausewitzian

'Fog of War' worked hard to cause problems for even the most thoroughly planned missions.

General Michael E. Ryan , Commander of Allied Air Forces, Southern Europe, had originally envisaged the SEAD campaign involving F-117A Nighthawk stealth fighters with six aircraft, along with accompanying crews, expected to be deployed from Holloman AFB, New Mexico to Aviano to remain there for up to a fortnight. The Nighthawk was the ideal low-visibility manned SEAD platform and the aircraft had proved its worth as an anti-air defence system during Operation Desert Storm, it could also attack from medium and high altitudes depending on the threat level. The use of the Nighthawks was based on the fact that General Ryan believed the Serbs to have deployed their air defences in a protective ring surrounding Banja Luka fortifying the city and posing a clear and present danger to Allied aircraft. In his own words, the danger that the 'formidable array of SAMs' posed to non-stealthy aircraft was 'very high'. The only way to reduce the risk in addition to using BGM-109 Tomahawk Land Attack Missiles (TLAMs) was to deploy the stealth fighters, noting that 'we should therefore pit our strengths against BSA weaknesses and that means using the F-117'. Ryan sent his request up the chain of command to US Marine Corps General George Joulwan, (Supreme Allied Commander Europe 1993–1997), and also asked the Italian Ministry of Defence for permission to deploy the aircraft at Aviano.

By 02.51 local time on 9 September, Ryan's request had been approved by US Defence Secretary William Perry and the aircraft from the 9th FS were cleared to deploy to Aviano for a maximum of 60 days. However, General Ryan was not yet out of the woods with his request. Diplomatic clearance for the aircraft's deployment had to be attained. Gen. Joulwan had to send a request to Commander-in-Chief US Atlantic Command, under whose jurisdiction the aircraft were placed, to release them to Ryan. Despite the fact that formal political approval for the F-117A deployment had yet to be obtained from the Italian government, personnel and *materiel* in support of the Nighthawk deployment began to arrive at Aviano that day. The political request was to be handled by Reginald Bartholomew, the US Ambassador to Italy. However, getting clearance from the Italian government was becoming increasingly difficult as the Prime Minister Lamberto

Dini was out of the country and Susanna Agnelli, the Foreign Minister was allegedly not treating the request with any sense of urgency. What resulted was Ms. Agnelli retorting that her government was 'tired of always saying yes to others while others always say no to Italy'. The Americans got their definitive answer on 11 September which informed them that the F-117 deployment was not permitted.

Stealth fighters notwithstanding, Ryan and his colleagues moved ahead with Dead Eye North-West, although the start of the operation was delayed for 24 hours until 9 September. This was done to give time for the targets to be double-checked and also to ensure that the weather was favourable for the attack. So it was that in the early hours as the F-117A request was being turned down, thirty SEAD aircraft fired thirty-three AGM-88s at SAM sites located at Majikici, Donji Vakuf and Sipovo in central Bosnia. The results were not quite as successful as had been hoped. The attack on the Banja Luka ring of steel had included a gaggle of AN/ADM-141 TALDs being fired towards the radar in a bid to get the BSA radar to show itself. Once these had flown towards their targets they were followed with an onslaught of AGM-88s fired by aircraft from the 23rd FS. The problem was that the BSA kept their radar down, making it hard for the HARMs to get a fix. That said, the 23rd FS did eventually bag a single SA-6 radar.

Undeterred NATO launched another series of SEAD strikes as part of Dead Eye North-east on 10 September, this time attacking the radio-relay station at Mount Svinjar just before midnight. Despite the fact that the Nighthawk deployment had not been agreed to, a force of thirty SEAD aircraft, eighteen fighter-bombers and thirteen BGM-109 TLAMs smashed into IADS targets at Lisina near Banja Luka and Mrkonjic; and a radio-relay site at Glamoc, both in western Bosnia. The AGM-84E Stand-off Land Attack Missile was brought into the fray for this target, although some of the weapons fired at the Glamoc facility experienced problems with their aircraft-to-missile datalinks which hampered the pilot's ability to transmit commands to the weapon. BDA analysts later concluded that all the weapons missed the radio relay station which presumably left it functioning and a proportion of the BSA IADS able to transmit commands and information.

This was not so for the TLAMs which hit the Lisina EW radar site. These missiles were launched from the USS *Normandy* and a total of seven of the weapons hit the installation. Here BDA showed that the facility had been wiped off the planet. Not only was the radar a thing of the past, so were its operations buildings and bunkers. Whether the BSA had activated this radar or not was largely academic as the United States Navy had the means of targeting the installation given the Terrain Contour Matching and Global Positioning guidance systems used by the TLAMs.

The Nighthawks were supposed to be thrown into the fray on the night of the 11-12 September, but with Italian permission not forthcoming, these plans were scotched in favour of another approach. What was to be called Dead Eye Part Three would see two F-15Es from the 494th FS taking GBU-15s for an attack on the Mrkonjic radio-relay station which was destroyed. Ingenuity had won the day, and even without the Nighthawks, the mission had been pressed home. Two days later, NATO planners decided to try their luck once again with the Lisina EW radar, radio-relay and television transmitter complex. This time the SLAMs played ball, with two missiles finding their mark. The laconic words of the BDA analysts termed the damage wrought on the facilities as 'severe' and at some points 'destroyed'. However, fate was to have other plans for further strikes, the bad weather on 14 September caused NATO planners to halt any further Dead Eye strikes in support of Deliberate Force.

The following day saw Sarajevo airport reopen and the Deliberate Force air strikes concluded. Nine air forces from Canada, France, Germany, Italy, the Netherlands, Norway, Portugal, Spain, Turkey, Ukraine, the UK and USA had flown a total of 3,515 sorties which included 750 attack sorties against fifty-six aim points, with a damage rate of 81 per cent inflicted. That said the operation was not entirely over. The BSA leadership was still in a belligerent mood. Matters came to a head on 4 October when a BSA missile guidance radar painted USMC EA-6B Prowlers which retaliated with a salvo of three HARMs. All the while US Ambassador Richard Holbrooke, Assistant Secretary of State for European and Canadian Affairs, and his colleagues were continuing to apply diplomatic pressure on the Bosnian Serb political and military leadership. His patience and hard work yielded results with the signing the Dayton Peace Accords, allowing the NATO Implementation Force (IFOR) to take over peacekeeping responsibilities from UNPROFOR which was done on 20 December 1996. No sooner was this done than the 5th Allied Tactical Air Force, under which the aircraft for the Deliberate Force and Dead Eye operations had been organised, changed its role to become the air power element of IFOR patrolling the skies of Bosnia and checking the air for infractions of the Dayton Peace Accords.

HARMs were fired during the campaign both reactively and pre-emptively, with US Navy F/A-18Cs performing thirty-three of the latter. Reactive HARM firings were performed after the ROE had been satisfied. This resulted in twenty-seven 'Magnum' reactive shots. The breakdown of HARM firings saw EA-6Bs firing ten, F/A-18Cs firing over thirty, F/A-18Ds firing four and F-16CJs firing nine; along with the two fired by Spanish EF-18As.

There were several star performers in the SEAD fight during Deliberate Force and the Navy in particular carried much of the SEAD burden. This is perhaps not surprising. Deliberate Force and its accompanying Dead Eye strikes were the kind of rapid ingress-egress air strikes that the US Navy's aviation elements were designed to support with SEAD aircraft flying off from the carriers, flying in with the mud-movers and trapping back on the flat tops as opposed to the USAF method which favoured a more free-ranging approach, looking over the battlefield for air defence targets of opportunity as they made their fatal mistake and activated their radar. The F/A-18C/Ds which operated from the USS *Theodore Roosevelt* and the USS *America*, from the 29 August–12 September in the *Roosevelt*'s case and from the 13 September in the case of the *America* could claim the biscuit as the hardest working SEAD assets, notching up 210 defence suppression missions. The Navy aviators were not the only Hornet drivers in theatre. From the VFMA 533rd FS the USMC had sent twelve F/A-18Ds to get stuck in, flying sixty-six SEAD sorties. The Spanish Air Force also sent eight EF-18A variants to Aviano and they flew fifty-two SEAD missions.

In second place was the venerable EA-6B Prowler. This self-contained wonder-plane with its HARMs and sharp electrons could mark 183 SEAD sorties in their squadron histories. Four units rotated between two and five aircraft through Aviano on a daily basis with the two squadrons on the *Theodore Roosevelt* and *America* amassing 183 SEAD sorties, with fifty-eight flown from the carriers and 125 from Aviano. Last but by no means least were the Wild Weasels from the 23rd FS. These aircraft made their combat debut during Deliberate Force and ten aircraft were sent from Spangdahlem in Germany to Aviano from which they flew 176 SEAD sorties. Finally, flying their first combat missions since World War II, the *Luftwaffe* sent eight Panavia Tornado ECR/IDS aircraft to Piacenza AFB, northern Italy. The aircraft flew with a mixed load out of two AGM-88s and a pair of AIM-9 air-to-air missiles performing twenty-eight SEAD sorties.

The primary means of electronic jamming available to NATO during Deliberate Force was provided by the USAF's EF-111A Ravens from the 429th Electronic Combat Squadron, performing sixty-eight SEAD sorties. These aircraft would perform stand-off jamming with their ALQ-99E system and were helped by similar equipment from the EA-6B Prowler. While the Ravens were ostensibly tasked with providing stand-off jamming, they would occasionally go 'downtown' to escort a strike package. The reason why this was not done more frequently was because the Ravens lacked the ability to deploy HARMs. However, this was not the case for the EA-6Bs. As a consequence, this aircraft performed more direct support and could get its feet dirty with the rest of a strike package. It is interesting to note that the Prowler and the Raven would jam in a different fashion, the latter directing its electrons from the front of the aircraft and the former from their wings. This allowed NATO air campaign planners to use the aircraft in concert with each other to direct their beams in such a way as to provide as much coverage as possible.

The RC-135V/W Rivet Joint ELINT aircraft flew staggeringly long sorties from RAF Mildenhall to maintain north-west–south-east 'feet wet' orbits over the Adriatic at high altitude listening carefully for the reactions of BSA air defence radar, flying twenty-one such missions. They were joined by the EC-130H Compass Call with four aircraft in total flying thirty-five sorties to provide communications jamming from Aviano. The unmanned assets such as the AN/ADM-141 TALDs also played their important part, with forty-seven rounds being expended to confuse BSA air defences.

Operation Allied Force
The Dayton Peace Accords did not bring the trials and tribulations of the Balkans to a conclusion. The break-up of the country called Yugoslavia was not yet complete and unbeknownst to the international community they would become involved once again in the troubled Balkans, this time dealing with the breakaway province of Kosovo. Despite the province having little involvement in Serbia's war with Croatia, Slovenia and Bosnia Herzegovina, in the 1990s, saw 1.8 million ethnic Albanians begin a campaign of passive resistance to assert their demand for an independent Kosovo. The tempo of violence increased as the *Ushtria Çlirimtare e Kosovës* (UÇK or Kosovar Liberation Army) began an armed struggle from February 1995 against Serbia's security apparatus including its *Specijalnih Jedinica Policije* (Special Police Units) and the Serbian Army. What began as isolated attacks soon developed into a steady campaign of violence.

As February 1999 unfolded, peace talks were held at Rambouillet outside Paris and included the Contact Group of France, Germany, Italy, Russia, UK and the USA, a Kosovar delegation and a delegation from the Serbian government. However, the talks concluded without the Serbians agreeing that 'NATO personnel shall enjoy, together with their vehicles, vessels, aircraft and equipment, free and unrestricted passage and unimpeded access throughout the Federal Republic of Yugoslavia, including associated airspace and territorial waters'. Something that the Serbian delegation felt unable to agree to.

That said, any armed intervention by NATO in Kosovo to stop the ethnic cleansing of the Albanian population would have to run the gauntlet of the robust Serbian IADS in theatre. The province was relatively small at 4,203 square miles (10,887 square km), with a high concentration of air defences which included a smattering of 0.78 in (20 mm) and 2.2 in (57 mm) anti-aircraft guns, an undetermined quantity of MANPADS, and SA-9/SA-13 systems, along with sixty-eight SA-6 mobile SAM systems that were operational throughout Yugoslavia, with a high concentration being positioned around Belgrade and around strategic targets such as military headquarters and command and control installations. Moreover, the Serbians could reinforce their SA-6s with SA-2 and SA-3A systems. However, the latter had a serious flaw: they were bereft of any night vision systems for the operators, which prevented them being fired without radar guidance, and radar guidance can invite an ARM. Moreover, as we shall see during the campaign, the Serbs did have a penchant for firing their SAMs ballistically, that is without radar guidance, in the hope of scoring a lucky hit. This was a desperate tactic given that several missiles were required to score a hit and this tactic thus becomes incredibly wasteful and ensures that stocks are depleted at a quicker pace than firing the missiles with radar guidance. Moreover, supplies might well be hard to come by once a country is at war, particularly if an arms embargo is in place. That said, a barrage of flying telegraph poles zooming around the sky with abandon is sufficient to cause a pilot to have an additional headache, so from this perspective it does offer the air defender a psychological advantage. It also caused NATO pilots to perform sudden evasive action such as jettisoning their fuel tanks and manoeuvring violently to avoid the missiles while also dispensing chaff. The Serbian MANPADS/AAA threat was evident throughout the conflict and extremely difficult to suppress, affording the Serbs some low-level cover at least.

Echoing the Desert Storm air war, the campaign was to be broken down into phases: Phase one would see the comprehensive destruction of the Yugoslav IADS. The first part of the SEAD phase was to include the destruction of Yugoslav long-range search radar which SEAD planners were concerned could hand off information to field units armed with AAA and MANPADS regarding the likely arrival time of NATO aircraft. Phase two would see the air interdiction of the Yugoslav army and security apparatus on the ground in Kosovo with a view to rolling back the campaign of ethnic cleansing. Initial operations during phase two would be performed below the 44th parallel; this area would become known as the Kosovo Theatre of Operations (KTO). However, phase two targets would be progressively expanded northwards during the campaign to include similar targets throughout the whole of Yugoslavia. For this phase to begin, the comprehensive destruction of the Yugoslav IADS would have to be completed. Therefore, SEAD became an indispensable part of the campaign which was to give Lieutenant General Michael C. Short, Combined Force Air Component Commander, and his staff at the CAOC in Vincenza endless headaches. Moreover, the Clinton administration and NATO were adamant that once Yugoslav President Slobodan Milosevic had tasted the wrath of allied air power he would throw in the towel and agree to withdraw his forces from the KTO and allow the entry of NATO peacekeepers.

Before the first shots were fired by NATO against Milosevic, the USAF got its SEAD assets well and truly in place. To this end, the 23rd FS F-16CJs from Spangdahlem AFB, Germany (this unit fired 150 HARMs in the first two months of operations) were deployed once again to Aviano, no doubt with a sense of *deja vu* from their days flying out of this base during Operation Deliberate Force. They arrived on the 21 February, the same day that F-117As from the 49th Fighter Wing bedded down at their Italian home. Other SEAD assets which joined the order of battle included the Vipers of the 78th FS from Shaw AFB.

The Wild Weasels were to perform missions in four-ship formations with two aircraft watching for radar threats in a specific area on one side, while another two aircraft performed a similar profile for the other. The reason for this was simple. The aircraft's HTS had a 180 degree field of view at the front of the aircraft, but with the four F-16s splitting up and monitoring the threat area from different directions they could provide complete coverage of a section of ground against any attempts to activate a search radar. The usual tactic was for the F-16s to arrive over a target area in advance of the main strike package. This would allow the area to be swept before the main package of aircraft arrived for an air-to-ground attack. If there was a clear threat, then the F-16CJs could relay this information back to the strike package to enable it to modify its ingress route accordingly. However, SEAD planners discovered that as the F-16CJs got more adept at detecting Yugoslav air defence threats, so the air defence operators got more adept at using their equipment in such a way as to reduce their chances of SEAD attack. The Vipers would be aloft 24 hours per day in order to provide continuous SEAD coverage and could provide the electronic order of battle as well as the air-ground situation as the attackers arrived in an area of operations.

SEAD assets available to NATO also included the EA-6Bs from eight different Navy and USMC squadrons positioned at Aviano, along with a single squadron of VAQ-141 Shadowhawks onboard the USS *Theodore Roosevelt*. These carrier-based SEAD aircraft would usually fly with two HARMs, although their counterparts operating from Aviano would eschew the HARMs, concentrating instead solely on their jamming role, because of the need to carry additional fuel on their longer route to the target area. The result of this for the Aviano based Prowlers was that they would operate closely with the F-16CJs and the *Luftwaffe* Tornado ECR/IDS at Piacenza and the *Aeronautica Militaire Italiana* (Italian Air Force) Tornado ECR/IDS at Giolle Del Colle AFB, which could carry HARMs. While the Prowler is undoubtedly an excellent SEAD platform, Allied Force underlined one of its failings which was its relatively slow cruising speed of 530 knots (982 km/h) compared with the strike packages of fast jets that it was escorting. Once again, the EC-130H Compass Calls from Aviano came into play in an effort to jam the communications systems for the Yugoslav air defence EW radar, in addition to the RC-135V/W Rivet Joint aircraft which would orbit beyond the range of the Yugoslav IADS to listen for reactions from the country's radar.

As the 24 March unfolded, preparations for Operation Allied Force (the NATO codename for the campaign) and Operation Noble Anvil (the codename for the US component of OAF) got underway. At RAF Fairford, subtly situated in the beautiful rolling countryside of the Cotswolds in Western England, B-52H Stratofortress crews from the 28th and 58th Bomb Wings were briefed on their targets. Outside, ground crews were preparing the aircraft. Matching them with their AGM-86C ALCMs that would be unleashed on targets throughout Serbia. In the Adriatic, Combat Information Centres on NATO warships and submarines were a hive of feverish and professional activity as BGM-109 TLAMs were checked and programmed with targeting information. An uneasy calm descended over Serbia as the country watched anxiously for the first signs of NATO activity.

The country fully expected an attack. The breakdown of talks in France had given President Slobodan Milosevic's government every indication that it could now expect a military response for its intransigence and to coerce it into accepting the terms laid out by the Contact Group. In preparation for the attack, Yugoslav military equipment such as armoured vehicles, artillery pieces, and mobile SAM systems were dispersed across the country. Milosevic seemed to be planning a strategy of absorbing the NATO air campaign while at the same time husbanding his military equipment. Meanwhile, Yugoslav air defenders at Zenum had ample warning that the attack was not far away. The rolling 24-hour news coverage that had chronicled war so dramatically since Desert Storm showed the B-52s heaving themselves into the crisp Gloucestershire sky. A few calculations and a look at Jane's *All the World's Aircraft* for the Stratofortresses' speed would give the Zenum occupants a rough idea as to what time the bombers would arrive.

In the skies to the west of Serbia, the Air Tasking Order sheet music choreographed the delicate aerial ballet which would organise SEAD aircraft, fighter-bombers and air-superiority fighters into strike packages that could enter Yugoslavia's airspace. These were supported by AWACS aircraft which could coordinate the packages while watching for hostile aircraft; tankers which would provide refuelling and electronic intelligence aircraft which would eavesdrop on the air waves to build the electronic order of battle of the Yugoslav air defence radar and IADS communications systems. Moreover, Combat Search and Rescue helicopters would stand ready to pluck out any aviators unlucky enough to be shot down by the Yugoslavs.

The bombardment began at 20.00 local time with twenty-three IADS installations across Yugoslavia being hit with the first salvo of cruise missiles which were fired form Allied warships, submarines and B-52s. Immediately after these missiles had scored their mark, they were followed by a second assault from strike packages of aircraft which attacked airfields, military command and control sites and other elements of the Yugoslav defences.

After the strikes, debrief rooms echoed with air crew relating the strengths of the Yugoslav air defences. SEAD assets had worked extremely hard in ensuring that no NATO combat aircraft were lost. To make matters even more difficult, unfamiliarity with some of the refuelling aircraft by some of the pilots made night-time tanking particularly challenging. The strength of the Yugoslav SEAD was such that NATO would initially only perform air strikes against Yugoslav targets at night, despite the SEAD aircraft that the Alliance had in theatre, although by late May, the air operations were continuing over a 24-hour period which was largely testament to the persistence and threat that the SEAD effort was able to pose.

The Serbs returned to firing volleys of SAMs ballistically into the night sky. Between 12–26 May, NATO pilots reported experiencing particularly heavy SAM barrages with thirty-six SAMs being fired into the air on the 12th and thirty-three being launched on the 26th. SEAD operations over Kosovo were a frustrating business at the best of times. Particularly hard to attack were the Serbian SA-3 Low Blow and SA-6 Straight Flush fire control radar of which there were around forty systems.

The refusal of the Yugoslav IADS to use their radar *en masse* during the conflict had some serious consequences for NATO SEAD planners. Most obviously, it made the radar much harder to attack given that their lack of emissions enhanced their invisibility to equipment such as the HTS. However, while most of the missile shots were thought to be ballistic around one-third may have been fired in a guided fashion. Part of the tactic of firing SAMs ballistically, with the occasional guided shot thrown in, was to get NATO aircraft out from higher altitudes and into the weeds where they could be engaged by the MANPADS and AAA which were much harder to target with the SEAD effort. Another favourite Serbian ruse was to fire SAMs at the last aircraft departing from an area of operations. It was thought that the Yugoslav theoretical underpinning for this initiative was that this aircraft would have relatively little protection from other aircraft, may be flown by a less experienced pilot or have inadequate fuel to perform evasive manoeuvres against the missile.

NATO had to contend with another issue: Quite obviously the Balkans was not the barren terrain where Desert Storm was performed. Iraq had relatively few areas to hide its air defence radar and SAM sites apart from those sent to the mountains near Iran. As such, SAM hunting was perhaps more straightforward for the SEAD effort. Kosovo could not have been more different. The province features mountains towards the south and southeast, which gives a good disguise to the E-8C JSTARS aircraft from the 12th Airborne Command and Control Squadron at Rhein-Main AFB, Germany that the USAF had deployed for ground target hunting. These planes carried both a synthetic aperture radar and a ground moving target indicator. However, when performing a ground search, if mountains were in the way of the radar when operating at an oblique angle, targets would not show up on the aircraft's sensors. Thus mobile SAM systems could be conveniently hidden behind millions of tonnes of rock. However, this did not protect them from the all-seeing eye of the U-2R photo-reconnaissance aircraft which would roam over the target area looking at the ground. That said, within the KTO the SEAD threat was relatively small compared to what the Alliance had to contend with in the rest of Serbia. Yugoslav IADS in Kosovo included only a single regiment of SA-6s.

The Yugoslavs had also taken great pains to harden their IADS communications systems. As well as subterranean communications lines, the Yugoslavs also had mobile communications relays which, because of their mobility, made them harder to target. One of the problems that NATO had to contend with was that EW radar in the north would feed data to air defences, notably AAA and MANPADS in the south, or throughout the rest of Yugoslavia, thus limiting the amount of radar that had to be active increasing their protection from HARM strikes, while also allowing lower-level air defences to continue posing a threat to NATO aircraft.

The stubbornness of the Yugoslavs to play the game and switch on their radar was perhaps understandable. A quick look at the history of air defence would have taught them that when the USAF or US Navy are operating, switching on a radar is equivalent to signing your own death warrant. Maintaining radar discipline may prohibit your range of action against attacking aircraft, but it allows you to pose a threat in other ways, either firing missiles ballistically or forcing aircraft down into the weeds where low-level air defences can then go to work. The Yugoslav radar discipline is evident from the fact that half of the HARM firings performed by NATO were said to be pre-emptive, usually when a strike package was entering an area of operations, which was intended to keep the air defenders' heads down while the bombs and missiles went to work. Details released at the end of the war spoke of many pre-emptive HARM firings being performed around Belgrade where the Yugoslav air defences were thought to be especially strong.

Yugoslav air defenders also had the annoying habit of switching on their air search radar for around 20 seconds to get a look at what was in the air and then abruptly shutting them down to avoid getting a HARM thrown in response. This allowed them to keep abreast of the air battle and possibly give them enough good information to allow them to fire off a SAM in the vague direction of a NATO aircraft while making themselves a fleeting target to the aircraft above. It seems that there were some questions as to the efficiency of the HARMs. Part of the problem seemed to be the amount of time that it would take an F-16CJ or an EA-6B to detect a hostile radar, fire a HARM and for the HARM to destroy the target. If a HARM was fired after a SAM had been launched, then the HARM's flight time would invariably be longer than that of the anti-aircraft missile. The result was that the aircraft that was being targeted would have to fend for itself in avoiding the SAM.

Unsurprisingly then, the Alliance favoured the destruction as opposed to the suppression of enemy air defences when at all possible; known as 'DEAD' rather than 'SEAD' in the trade. When IADS installations were discovered and plotted, NATO performed attacks using the F-15E Strike Eagles of either the 492nd or 494th FS at Aviano and RAF Lakenheath in the UK with their air-to-ground missiles (AGM-130) or laser guided bombs. Moreover, US Navy F/A-18Cs performed attacks using AGM-154 Joint Stand-Off Weapons which used the Global Positioning satellite system for guidance against enemy radar installations. However, DEAD missions against mobile radar were, at times, difficult given that the target had to be attacked while it was stationary.

Moreover, NATO had to stay continuously on the defensive to

protect strike packages from engagement by Yugoslav air defences and the possibility that the Yugoslavs might activate their radar at any point for a SAM attack. Moreover, the presence of the Yugoslav air defences also caused NATO to continue sending large packages of aircraft, which included SEAD platforms, into the KTO. This increased the planning burden on the CAOC which continually had to ensure that all aircraft were adequately protected. Finally, the continued existence of significant parts of the Yugoslav IADS served to keep some particularly valuable targets off-limits to NATO given the extent of the air defences which were thought to surround them.

To make matters worse for the Alliance some of the most valuable targets from a SEAD perspective were the EW radar systems in Montenegro. This country was bombed during OAF, although this was later stopped by NATO to shore-up the anti-Milosevic position of Montenegran President Milo Dukanoviæ, as such General John Jumper, Commander-in-Chief of US Air Forces in Europe and in overall command of OAF, could not get the necessary clearance from the NATO political leadership to go after the Montenegrin radar. The net effect was that these systems continued to give the Yugoslav IADS good warning time regarding the incoming packages of NATO aircraft.

Jumper and his colleagues also had to contend with strong political controls over the air campaign due to sensitivities over casualties in the KTO and Yugoslavia. The result of this was that the CAOC had to provide approval before a particular target could be struck. One report noted that 'the need for prior CAOC approval before attacking the fleeting IADS pop-up targets resulted in many lost opportunities and few hard kills of enemy SAM sites.

The net result of the air campaign over the KTO was that during an air war lasting for almost 78 days, in excess of 800 SAMs were fired. These included almost 500 SA-6s and 124 MANPADS systems. However, the majority of the SAMs that were launched were done so without any radar guidance. Two NATO aircraft were claimed including one F-117A from the 49th FW and an F-16C from the 31st FW. The F-117A was, of course, supposed to be incredibly difficult to shoot down because of its low-observable characteristics and the reasons for the aircraft's destruction are still hotly debated. Aircraft were also damaged including a second F-117A which was impacted from a nearby SA-3 detonation. Meanwhile, a pair of A-10As were hit by anti-aircraft fire. It seems that two MANPADS hit the same number of A-10s, although they bounced off the underside of the aircraft without doing any damage.

The NATO OAF SEAD response included 743 HARMs fired for a total of 38,000 sorties performed. This is almost one ARM for every SAM, although this had no effect against the low-level threats discussed above. The existence of these threats had a major impact for the Alliance, preventing it from operating below 15,000 ft (4,572 m) because of the threats to NATO air crew. The Alliance was acutely sensitive to both friendly military casualties and civilian casualties on the ground, realising that high numbers of either could have adverse effects on public support for a controversial war.

Keeping the aircraft at altitude had another important knock-on effect, namely challenging the effectiveness of the air campaign. Bombing from altitude became problematic with weather and strict ROE playing their part. Arguably, this caused the air campaign to take longer to achieve its desired effect than if the Serbians had been less effective at keeping the NATO aircraft at altitude.

The altitude issue, particularly in the KTO, also challenged NATO's reconnaissance efforts. SA-6 SAM systems could threaten NATO aircraft up to almost 78,000 ft (24,000 m) and therefore intelligence-gathering aircraft such as the E-8C JSTARS had to stand-off from the KTO in order to stay out of danger. NATO's difficulties were seen in the campaign statistics in the final weeks of OAF towards the end of May and early June, which saw the Alliance only being able to confirm a total of three SA-6 mobile system kills out of the twenty-five which the country possessed.

In essence what Yugoslav air defence did for a tactical advantage, that is to keep their air defences intact as much as possible, had a clear operational impact which caused the Alliance to adapt its behaviour to accommodate the threat and therefore degrade the efficiency of some of its systems such as reconnaissance assets which would have ramifications for the Alliance further down the line as air war planners sought to gather targeting information. Lt. Gen. Short noted that Allied aircrews fully expected a SAM threat on the scale of Desert Storm but 'it just never materialised. And then it began to dawn on us that they were going to try to survive as opposed to being willing to die to shoot down an airplane'.

There may also have been some significant USAF information operations against the Yugoslav IADS. Details surrounding such operations are still few and far between and for understandable reasons are probably kept well under wraps. Broadly speaking, information operations can be defined as: 'The integrated employment of the core capabilities of electronic warfare, computer network operations, psychological operations, military deception, and operations' security, in concert with specified supporting and related capabilities, to influence, disrupt, corrupt or usurp adversarial human and automated decision-making while protecting our own' according to the DoD. Such operations can include cyber attacks to implant viruses and other disruptive programmes into enemy computer systems to prevent them from working properly. It is doubtful whether USAF information operations were sufficiently advanced to implant viruses into the computers which controlled the actual air defence radars, although they may have found their way into computer systems which controlled the air defences at a higher level to disrupt the communications networks that the IADS relied on.

Allegations have been made that the information operations undertaken included implanting false targeting data into the computer systems controlling the Yugoslav air defences. However, this may have caused some conflicts of interest with those attacking the IADS using hard and soft-kill weaponry wishing to keep parts of the command and control systems intact to provide the staff building the electronic order of battle with enough information to construct a comprehensive jamming and electronic warfare plan. Napoleon's adage of 'never interrupting your enemy when they are making a mistake' springs to mind.

In short, this is all supposition and it will be many years before we know whether these information operations were performed and if so, their full extent. For the time being, we have to be content with the words of General Jumper who said that; 'we did more information warfare in this conflict than we have ever done before, and we proved the potential of it'. Whatever the behaviour of the Yugoslav IADS, the SEAD effort above all succeeded in its primary aim and that aim was to suppress Yugoslav air defences. These may not have been as comprehensively destroyed as originally hoped, but they were kept suitably subdued to keep Allied aircraft losses to a minimum.

CHAPTER EIGHT

SEAD During the Global War on Terror

Afghanistan

On the eve of Operation Enduring Freedom, mounted in response to the 9/11 terrorist attacks on the United States, Afghanistan had little in terms of technology including sophisticated air defence systems. That said the United States and its Allies had to be mindful of AAA as they began air operations against the Taliban and Al-Qaeda over the country from 7 October 2001. The militia's defences included an unknown number of ZSU-23-4 mobile systems, 3.9 in (100 mm) KS-19 AAA guns and ZPU-1/2/4 0.57 in (14.5 mm) weapons along with a smattering of SAM launchers.

The very first strikes against the Taliban infrastructure included attacks on EW radar systems with GBU-31 Joint Direct Attack Munition (JDAM) dropped by a B-2A Spirit stealth bomber from the 393rd Bomb Squadron on 7 October. Meanwhile, US Navy EA-6B Prowlers jammed the few other Taliban EW systems to ensure that the rag-tag militia could not get a look at the air armada coming for them. Moreover the air traffic control radar at Kandahar airport was hit during these initial strikes, possibly by the same B-2A. During the initial sorties, targeting Taliban air defences was essential to permit Coalition aircraft to have unimpeded access over the country to begin attacks on other Taliban and Al Qaeda sites.

During a press briefing at the Pentagon following these first strikes, a spokesman told reporters that: 'The only objective (of the opening strikes) was to kill obvious things out in the open (in order to) allow us to fly with impunity day and night, when we'll work on harder targets'. Defence Secretary Donald Rumsfeld followed this by saying that the opening attacks were 'to create conditions for sustained anti-terrorist and humanitarian relief operations in Afghanistan (which necessitated the removal of) the threat from air defences and from Taliban aircraft'.

These Taliban air defences did not stay idle during the opening strikes and some pilots reported shots from FIM-92A Stinger MANPADS that the militia had left over from the days of the Soviet Afghan war when they were covertly supplied by the Reagan Administration to the *Mujahideen*. AAA was also experienced by some pilots fired from the ZSU-23-4 systems that the Taliban had at their disposal, although generally speaking the environment was relatively safe for pilots operating above 20,000 ft (6,096 m). By 8 October, Rumsfeld felt bold enough to claim that the early SEAD efforts had neutralised the Taliban's air defences 'within the first fifteen minutes or so'. Despite the Secretary's claims, three SAM sites were detected and attacked on 9 October with a fourth SA-3 launcher being located but not judged as posing a threat to Coalition aircraft.

Back to Iraq
The end game in Iraq featured major SEAD operations both before and during Operation Iraqi Freedom, the US-led war which toppled Saddam Hussein in spring 2003. The intervening years between the conclusion of Operation Desert Storm and the start of this last battle, saw changes in the way that the United States Air Force thought about, and executed, SEAD. Operations in the Balkans and Iraq had shown that ARMs change the enemy's behaviour because they simply don't turn on their radar. To be fair, this was not so much of a new phenomenon. Even during World War II, German radar operators had realised that to allow themselves to be tracked was to invite attack. This was also the case for radar operators during the Vietnam War.

This was all well and good, and it is a testament to the AGM-88 that it has helped to promote this behavioural change in the enemies that the United States and its allies have faced. However, this only solved part of the problem. While a lack of air defence radar coverage was no doubt welcomed by pilots, radar has still remained very much alive, intact and able to function. As long as radar systems could do this, they remained a threat. In a sense, air defence radar is down but not out. Since Vietnam, SEAD has gone from being a mission in support of the main strike force, to a dedicated mission in its own right which has pulled in other parts of the armed forces, such as artillery units, which can hit air defences in their vicinity; as well as reconnaissance aircraft that can watch the ground below for radar and SAM systems; electronic warfare and intelligence aircraft which can disrupt the communications networks and radar systems of an adversaries' IADS and also conventional weapons such as cruise missiles which attack known air defences without depending on radar emissions to betray their location. The holistic nature of the SEAD effort, as far as Iraq was concerned, would be further sharpened as US, French and British aircraft patrolled the so-called No-Fly Zones (NFZs) over northern and southern Iraq prior to the violent conclusion to Saddam's rule.

NFZs

Although Saddam's air defences had received a serious battering during Desert Storm they were far from destroyed when hostilities ceased between the Coalition and his regime on 28 February 1991. One figure quoted the Coalition destroying only half of Saddam's air defences by the time that operations were concluded.

The international community had unfinished business with the Iraqi strongman. Persistent allegations and fears were expressed by the United States and her allies regarding Saddam's WMD. The elimination of these capabilities was made a high priority of the air war during Desert Storm, but it was suspected by the Bush Administration that not all his WMD stocks, delivery systems, storage and manufacturing facilities had been destroyed and that, as such, they could remain as a threat to the region and to allied forces in the future.

As part of the UN ceasefire which came into effect on 11 April 1991, Saddam agreed to get rid of his WMD capabilities. To oversee this, the UN established UNSCOM (UN Special Commission) on Iraq to inspect sites around the country for WMD stocks and manufacturing facilities, and to ensure that those which were found were destroyed. Originally, the United States, along with her Coalition partners in the Gulf, had planned to withdraw from the region following the conclusion of Desert Storm, but in many ways, this war was just the beginning of the US, British and French regional presence which would continue for the next eleven years. A force of American aircraft remained in theatre, including F-15C/E Eagles and Strike Eagles, F-4G Wild Weasels and F-16C Vipers housed at Al Dhahran AFB in eastern Saudi Arabia as part of the 4404th Provisional Wing.

The aircraft were not just there to keep a watch on Saddam's behaviour *vis-à-vis* the weapons inspectors, but were also present to keep an eye on his behaviour regarding Iraq's minority populations. Both the Shia Marsh Arabs located around Iraq's second city of Basrah and the country's Kurdish population, clustered around the north, had risen in open rebellion against Saddam exploiting the aftermath of the war when it was assumed by the Bush Administration that the Iraqi regime would be at its most fragile. To this end, the United States, together with the UK and France established the NFZs over southern Iraq below the 32nd parallel with Joint Task Force South-west Asia in charge of operations over this part of Iraq to interdict Iraqi army units which moved into the area to begin a brutal campaign of repression against the Marsh Arab population. The deployment would soon be known to the world as Operation Southern Watch and the brace of fast jets was reinforced with KC-135E tankers, E-3B/C Sentry AWACs and RC-135V/W Rivet Joint ELINT aircraft. The whole deployment soon had more than an air of permanence about it.

Given Saddam's oppressive activities in the north, a similar area of sanitized airspace was created as part of Operation Northern Watch which began on 1 January 1997 following the conclusion of Operation Provide Comfort which had been primarily focused on establishing an NFZ north of the 36th parallel. The upshot of both of these initiatives was that the Iraqi leader was forced to move his air defences into a strip of territory between these two NFZs. This did not stop these air defences continuing to be a hazard to Coalition pilots who were flying over the NFZs to interdict any Iraqi army units on the ground and to deter incursions by the *Al Quwwat Al Jawwiya Al Iraqiya* (Iraqi Air Force/IrAF) harassing the local population. The Iraqis used their own safe area to fire their SAMs towards Coalition aircraft and would often provocatively move their air defence systems into the NFZs to pose a direct threat to Coalition warplanes. For example, between December 1998 and August 2001, Iraqi air defenders performed over 1,000 attacks on Coalition aircraft monitoring the NFZs. It should be noted that many of these firings were ballistically-guided because to use radar would invite a HARM from the SEAD aircraft such as the Phantoms and later the F-16CJs, which would be escorting combat aircraft in the NFZs.

Confrontation with the West was a certainty and Saddam's efforts cost him a single MiG-25 downed by an F-16C on 27 December 1992. The air defences were dealt with on 13 January when a combined package of 100 Coalition aircraft went after Iraqi air-defence sites in the Southern NFZ (SnFZ). The Coalition had demanded that Saddam remove his SAMs from the area by 6 January, but with the Iraqi leader in a characteristically un-cooperative mood, a phalanx of aircraft including the US F-16s, together with British GR.1 Tornados and French Mirage 2000Cs smashed radar and SAM sites at Nasiriya and Samawa south-east of Baghdad, and Najaf and Al Amarah to the south of the city although only half the SAM sites that were present were said to have been struck, partly to make a 'political' point according to US officials. That said, the strikes on the air defences in the SNFZ continued for a week, before the Iraqi air defenders decided to move out.

The almost daily dance of death between the Coalition and the Iraqis always seemed to have similar steps. Coalition aircraft would begin a sortie over one of the NFZs. The Iraqis would paint the package of aircraft with a radar or worse, fire off SAMs or AAA at them from systems which had been covertly moved into the NFZ or from the strip of territory sandwiched in the middle. AGM-88s were the preferred means of destroying radar, alterna-tively conventional ordnance such as GBU laser-guided bombs or AGM-130 stand-off missiles could also pay them a visit. However, pilots flying in the NFZs were bound by strict ROEs as far as air-to-ground attacks were concerned, which included raids on the air defences. Only the air defences that were attacking them could be fired upon, but this could also include radar and C2 systems which were assisting the Iraqi air defenders at the time. There was an imperative to ensure that any ordnance hitting air defence targets hit just that, and collateral damage was kept to the bare minimum. The West had learnt early on about Saddam's penchant for exploiting civilian casualties and generally acting as the victim of Western aggression. That said, if the offending AAA or SAM battery was located in an area thick with civilian houses, shops, businesses, schools or hospitals then other air defence targets which were less well protected could be chosen for retaliation.

Saddam exploited the SEAD effort for every ounce of publicity that he could squeeze from it. To his people, the Iraqi air defenders were putting up a heroic fight against the odds and against the West. Yet close observation of the gunners on the rooftops of Iraqi buildings showed that more often than not they were blindly firing into the night sky at nothing in particular. Their may not have even been any Allied aircraft above them. Instead, their actions may have been to convince the population that the country was under continual attack. The Iraqi government also wasted no opportunity in highlighting the human cost that the Coalition's efforts to interdict Iraq's air defences were causing, claiming that 1,477 people had been killed and 1,358 injured between the imposition of the NFZs in the 1990s and 2002, although it was almost certain that the lion's share of these casualties were sustained by Iraq's Air Defence Command (ADC).

One thing that Iraq's air defenders were certainly not lacking was reckless bravado, particularly those who covertly infiltrated the NFZs with their weapons. They knew that the Coalition would leave no air defence action unpunished, but that said, they would occasionally switch their radar on or fire a ballistically-guided SAM regardless of the consequences. They were probably spurred on by a fear of failure and a desire to help Saddam score a propaganda coup by downing an American or British aircraft; something that they were unable to do for the entire duration of the NFZs' existence. The idea for Saddam was to maintain the air defence pressure on the Coalition and he no doubt hoped to put up a stiff enough defence to drive the aircraft from his airspace in the north and south, if only momentarily, so as to be able to launch a series of deadly strikes by his army against the dissident groups operating with relative impunity under the Coalition umbrella.

The status of air defenders in the Iraqi military structure improved dramatically in the years following Desert Storm. His air force's derisory performance during that war had caused it to fall dramatically out of favour as the IrAF flew its aircraft to Iran and its senior commanders ended their days before the firing squad. Iraq's air defence was removed from air force hands and placed under its own separate command. Those working for the new force enjoyed an increase in their salaries and better accommodation. They also got new equipment courtesy of Saddam's sanctions-busting efforts. This was despite the existence of the highly controversial 'oil-for-food' programme in which Iraq could sell its crude in return for food and humanitarian necessities such as medical supplies to reduce the privations suffered by the Iraqi populace in the wake of the sanctions imposed on the country following Desert Storm. Cash prizes were also on offer; $5,000 for the gun or missile crew that downed a Coalition aircraft, along with $2,500 for any Iraqi citizen capturing a downed pilot. Sanctions had done nothing to stop Saddam continuing to strengthen his air defences. By 2003, ADC was said to comprise around 17,000 personnel, although as this number was provided by Iraqi exiles it is possible that it may have been an exaggeration, although Saddam's desires and efforts to strengthen his defences were very real.

Air defenders were firing their missiles ballistically, which greatly reduced their chances of hitting a Coalition aircraft, but it had other effects. The SAM launcher was less likely to be hit by a HARM if the radar was switched off and this enhanced the operator's survival prospects. The launcher's ability to avoid the HARM may have also improved civilian morale as air defence would no longer be seen as such a futile task, though how much the Iraqi populace knew about successful attacks on the air defence network is doubtful, it would certainly not be a topic of discussion by the domestic media. The air defences that were clustered around Baghdad and the strip of 'sandwich filling' in which they were still allowed to operate never did destroy a Coalition aircraft during the 268,000 sorties that they performed.

The cat and mouse games continued well into the late 1990s, although the Coalition which by now only included the United States and Britain as France had pulled out of the NFZ patrols in 1996 after the SNFZ was moved further north to the 33rd parallel. This placed the line in the sand just south of the Iraqi capital. And was a response to a renewed round of repression by Saddam against the Kurdish population in the north. His efforts earned him Operation Desert Strike, launched on 3 September 1996 during which B-52H bombers of the 2nd Bomb Wing along with 27 BGM-109s attacked targets in southern Iraq as retaliation.

The tension between Washington, London and Baghdad, which was always high, was now reaching suffocating levels. The crux of the problem centred on Saddam's continued intransigence as far as the weapons inspections were concerned. A series of air strikes had been planned by the Coalition for March 1998 but a last minute diplomatic compromise between Iraq and the US and UK resulted in the plans being scrapped. The respite was short-lived and by the autumn confrontation once again seemed certain. By now, the United States had around 35,000 personnel in the region, with 9,000 drawn from the USAF. Saddam's defiance and prevarication as far as the weapons inspections were concerned continued and military action once again became a reality.

On 16 December 1998, a series of air strikes was orchestrated over four days mainly focusing on targets which were involved in Iraq's WMD industry. The task was taken up by aircraft from the USS *Enterprise* and B-52Hs firing AGM-86C/D ALCMs, flying from Diego Garcia in the Indian Ocean. These aircraft were joined by F-117As operating from Kuwait while B-1Bs performing their combat debut flew from Oman. The British lent their Tornado GR.1s to the effort. Needless to say, the strength of Iraq's air defences clustered in the sandwich filling gave the Coalition pause for thought and SEAD packages were flown to escort the strike packages from Incirlik AFB in Turkey as part of Operation Northern Watch.

Along with the 100 aimpoints struck during Desert Fox, which concluded on the 19 December, sixteen SAM installations suffered destruction and serious damage, meanwhile the critical junction points in the Iraqi IADS command and control system, known in the trade as the 'nodes', were also hit with thirteen being destroyed or damaged out of a total of eighteen. It was thought that during the entire four-day operation, the Iraqis only managed to launch a maximum of two SAMs. Admiral Thomas Wilson was the Director of Intelligence for the US Joint Chiefs of Staff and he noted that the suppression efforts on Iraq's air defences were working well: 'There really is no long term need to hit SAMs or integrated air defences for the sake of hitting integrated air defence systems. These systems are important to suppress, degrade, or in some cases destroy to support the strike'. Despite the UNSCOM weapons inspectors being refused entry back into Iraq after being evacuated prior to the attacks, perhaps an unsurprising conclusion, both British Prime Minister Tony Blair and US President Bill Clinton were quick to declare the Desert Fox missions a success. They might well have put the WMD programme back a few more years, but the air defences of Iraq were still very much present.

A Snapshot – Six Months in an Eleven-year War
Following Operation Desert Fox, engagements between Iraqi air defence and Coalition aircraft increased in frequency and ferocity. A summary of actions between December 1998 and June 1999 shows just how often US and British aircraft were performing SEAD operations against the Iraqi air defences which continued to threaten aircraft patrolling the Northern No-Fly Zone (NNFZ) and the Southern No-Fly Zone (SNFZ).

The SEAD units available to the Coalition for the first six months of 1999 included the 22nd FS which was equipped with F-16CJ Wild Weasels. These aircraft were reinforced by the F-15E Strike Eagles of the 494th FS and also the EA-6B Prowlers of Marine Tactical Electronic Warfare Squadron (MTEWS) VMAQ-1 which provided both kinetic and soft-kill SEAD. These aircraft were based at Incirlik as part of the 39th Air and Space Expeditionary Wing and were chiefly tasked with NFNZ SEAD missions.

Providing SEAD support to the SNFZ from Prince Sultan Air Base (PSAB) in Saudi Arabia were the F-15Es of the 335th and 336th FS together with the EA-6B Prowlers of the US Navy's VAQ-128 Tactical Electronic Warfare Squadron (TEWS); ELINT platforms including the RC-135V/W aircraft of the 763rd Expeditionary Reconnaissance Squadron and F-16CJs from the 20th FW as part of the 332nd Air Expeditionary Group based at Ahmed Al Jaber AFB, Kuwait,

In the Persian Gulf, SNFZ operations could also draw upon Carrier Air Wing-11 of the USS *Vinson* equipped with the F/A-18Cs of the VMFA-314 Black Knights Marine Fighter Attack Squadron (MFAS); similar aircraft from the US Navy's VFA-148 Blue Diamonds and the VFA-147 Argonauts FS plus the EA-6B Prowlers from the VAQ-138 Yellowjackets TEWS.

In March, units rotated in the Persian Gulf. The 22nd FS remained at Incirlik, while the 494th FS was replaced by the F-15Es of the 492nd FS. VAQ-128 Prowlers went 'feet dry' to PSAB to replace their VMAQ-1 counterparts. Afloat in the Persian Gulf SEAD assets were joined by Carrier Air Wing-3 of the USS *Enterprise* which included the F/A-18Cs of VFA-37 Ragin' Bulls FS, VFA-105 Gunslingers FS, and VMFA-115 MFAS along with the Prowlers from VAQ-130 Zappers TEWS. The USS *Vinson* later left the area in April leaving the *Enterprise* as the sole carrier in the Persian Gulf.

Later in April, the USS *Kitty Hawk* replaced the *Enterprise* with the SEAD assets of Carrier Air Wing-5 including the F/A-18Cs of the VFA-27 Royal Maces FS, the similar aircraft of the VFA-192 Golden Dragons and the VFA-195 Dambusters FS along with the EA-6B Prowlers of the VAQ-136 Gauntlets TEWS

These units saw almost daily action. For example, on 19 December at 03.00 Zulu (0300Z) a mix of thirty-two IADS and SAM sites in Iraq's southern Air Defence Sector (ADS), known as the 3rd ADS, were attacked with SA-2 and SA-3 batteries being hit particularly hard, with eleven suffering severe damage and destruction, and eight suffering lighter damage. A mere five days' later, Iraqi air defences engaged RAF Tornado GR.1 aircraft flying from Ali Al Salem AFB in Kuwait which attacked AAA targets in southern Iraq. An Iraqi spokesman claimed that, 'at (08.25Z) this morning formations of enemy planes attacked our air defence positions which confronted them and forced them to drop their load indiscriminately'. On the 28 December, US and RAF aircraft operating in the NNFZ engaged an Iraqi air defence target and meanwhile on the 30 December, up to eight SAMs were fired from the south-west of Talil AFB in southern Iraq at Coalition aircraft at around 03.00Z during a routine SNFZ patrol. A spokesman for US Central Command told reporters that: 'In response to that unprovoked attack, we responded by firing two HARM missiles and we dropped a number of GBU-12 500 lb (225 kg) precision-guided munitions at 07.15Z'. Iraq's account of the attack contained characteristic subtle understatement: 'Our brave air defenders have fired ground-to-air missiles at hostile formations forcing them to flee after it was almost certain that one of the planes was shot down. The criminals have once again violated our airspace in the southern region as formations of their hostile planes approached today at 06.24Z'.

By early 1999 it was becoming clear that the major concern of the Coalition was the mobile SA-6 systems which could be readied to fire in minutes. In contrast the SA-2 systems took longer to set up: 'They are moving their batteries around quite heavily. A concrete building is obviously easier to plan for and to hit than something that is mobile. They are difficult to hit and mobile. They are small targets ... And you don't always know where they are', said one US official.

The first major SEAD effort of 1999 occurred on the 7 January when a US F-16CJ fired an AGM-88 at a Roland battery which it was thought was preparing to fire. The missile launcher was believed to have been destroyed. Three days' later two F-15Es and an F-16CJ hit an Iraqi SAM system near Mosul in the NNFZ area. Air defences around Mosul continued to threaten US aircraft for the next four days, with radar sites being struck by HARMs, while F-15Es fired AGM-130 air-to-ground missiles at air defence targets near Mosul. On 25 January EA-6B Prowlers engaged an SA-2 site in the Northern NFZ with AGM-88s along with a second SA-2 site being hit by a HARM from an F-16CJ. Disaster would strike on the same day when an F-15E fired an AGM-130 against an air defence target near Basrah which missed and struck housing. On the 30 January, US warplanes performed a large SEAD strike with two F-15Es dropping GBU-12 bombs on an Iraqi Skyguard radar and two additional GBU-12s on an AAA system and its accompanying radar. Meanwhile an EA-6B struck another AAA site with a HARM which was followed up by a fourth site being hit with a pair of GBU-12s.

The first indication of a cash reward for air defence operators downing a Coalition aircraft came in early February when an Iraqi newspaper reported that: 'In accordance with the leader's order, the Presidential Office will grant 25 million Dinars to those who shoot down a hostile plane and 10 million (5,000 dollars) for gunning down a missile'. Saddam followed this by lavishing praise on his air defence troops: 'I salute your effort to defend the sovereignty of great Iraq. It's an irony when the Americans say they are defending themselves while they make an aggression on Iraq and air defence sites as if they are flying over Washington's skies, not Iraq's'.

Saddam was more than happy to use the NFZ SEAD effort for his own domestic political consumption and for international political grandstanding. As January came to a close, air defence targets in the Northern and Southern NFZs were hit particularly hard with Wild Weasels firing AGM-88s at radar near Mosul in Iraq's 4th ADC as part of a package of aircraft including F-15Es, Tornado GR.1 and E-3A Sentries. On 31 January, targets in the SNFZ were also struck. With two communications nodes at Talil and Al Amarah to the south-east of Baghdad being hit by a mixed package of Tornados, Hornets, Prowlers and Wild Weasels.

As February unfolded, Coalition aircraft had one of their busiest SEAD days since Desert Storm with F-15Es dropping two GBU-12 bombs on an AAA site near Mosul while an SA-2 radar was struck by an AGM-88 fired from a Prowler. A further two GBU-12s were dropped on AAA systems by Strike Eagles followed by a further Paveway-II attack against other anti-aircraft guns. Interestingly, a day later Iraq moved some of its SAM launchers from the NFZ areas back into Central Iraq. This did not stop the Coalition performing a robust strike on 11th with two communications systems, the same number of missile launchers and a radar being hit around Mosul. Pentagon spokesman Captain Michael Doubleday told reporters that: 'We believe we have been effective in hitting the targets threatening Coalition forces and our intention is that as long as they (Iraq) continue these provocative actions we will continue to respond'. Demonstrating DoD resolve, a day later, an F-15E dropped a GBU-12 on an AAA site to the north of Mosul.

Matters remained relatively quiet until 21 February when

communications nodes at Talil and Al-Amarah in the SNFZ were struck. Meanwhile, F-15Es dropped a total of eleven bombs on separate AAA sites around Mosul, other southern targets hit included communications facilities near Basrah attacked by F-15Es and Tornado GR.1 aircraft. These attacks were followed by heavy strikes on the 23rd which saw F-15E Strike Eagles drop GBU-10 2,000 lb (907 kg) bombs on a bunker near Mosul, possibly the 4th ADC Intercept Operations Center also attacked missile launchers with GBU-12 weapons in response to an attack from Iraqi AAA units. The following day, F-15E and Navy F/A-18C jets attacked two mobile SAM launchers south of Baghdad at Al Iskandariyah. An air defence radar near Talil was also hit by two AGM-88s from an F-16CJ. On 27 February the Coalition claimed that it had been attacked in the SNFZ by Iraqi air defence weapons on ninety separate occasions since the conclusion of Operation Desert Fox and responded with attacks against thirty-five air defence targets. The following day, Mosul was again the focus of NNFZ attacks during which F-15Es hit an air defence command and control site and radio relay station with a barrage of AGM-130 and GBU-12 weapons after they came under fire from Iraqi AAA.

As March unfolded, and the United States, together with its NATO Allies prepared air strikes against Serbia, Secretary of State for Defence William Cohen told journalists that the ROEs for Coalition pilots performing SEAD in the NFZs had been adapted to allow them to hit a range of air defence targets, not just those that were firing at them. If they came under attack from Iraqi weapons: 'Pilots have been given greater flexibility to attack those systems that place them in jeopardy. They are not simply going to respond to an AAA site or to a SAM site…They can go after command and control and communications centres as well that allow Saddam Hussein to try to target them and put them in jeopardy. So they have some flexibility and they will continue to have that flexibility'.

A day later following Mr. Cohen's comments, British Tornados attacked radar sites south of Basrah and at As Shuaybah as part of SNFZ operations after the jets were painted by an Iraqi radar. On 6 March, a series of major strikes in both the NFZs saw five AAA systems destroyed, while in the south two communications

facilities and a single missile launcher were hit in the vicinity of
Basrah. Speaking at Incirlik, a USAF spokesman reflected on the
missions of the previous few days and hinted at tactical changes
being adopted by the Iraqis: 'What it seems has been happening
in the last few days is (that the) Iraqis have been changing their
positions...We have simply widened the definition of what a
threat system is from a specific system to (an) integrated system
and all the things attached to that site . . . The systems they are
using and the way they are forced to use them because of our
tactics means they have a very low probability of hitting any of
our aircraft'. This seemed to be a rather cryptic and long-winded
way of saying that the ROE have widened the number of targets
that could be struck, reiterating Cohen's earlier comments, while
the Iraqis may be increasingly reluctant to activate their radar for
fear of receiving an attack from a HARM, although they did not
completely refrain from painting Coalition aircraft.

No sooner had reporters digested these comments than a large
series of attacks reflected the new Coalition tactics. A clutch of
AAA sites were attacked by Strike Eagles in the NNFZ while radar,
a communications relay and missile launchers were attacked in the
SNFZ. On the 12 March, a Prowler fired an AGM-88 at a site to the
north of Mosul, joined by an F-15E dropping a GBU-12. F-15E
strikes continued the following day with AAA sites north of Mosul
being hit by GBU-12s concluding on 15th when additional anti-
aircraft guns were hit. To the south SNFZ aircraft smashed a
communications relay and radar to the south-east of Baghdad.
Mosul AAA defences continued to be a problem for the Coalition
throughout mid-March with Strike Eagles once again unloading
GBU-12s on AAA sites to the north of Mosul.

Coalition aircraft were not just under threat from Iraqi air
defences. The NFZs would also be periodically 'buzzed' by IrAF
aircraft although the response from the Coalition could include
attacks on air defence installations as retaliation. Such an incident
occurred on 19 March when a radar near As Shuaybah was
attacked along with a communications facility at Muzalbah in
response to an incursion from an unidentified Iraqi MiG.

Not coincidentally, reports emerged in late March that the
Iraqis had received a delegation of Yugoslav air defence experts
which met with their Iraqi counterparts. A Pentagon source told

the press that the meetings were thought to revolve around discussions on British and American tactics in the NFZs and defence cooperation between the two states. Such cooperation would have seemed logical because both countries used similar styles of Soviet air defence systems. Officially the DoD stayed tight-lipped on the subject with spokesman Kenneth Bacon saying that: 'These are two countries both subject to attack by forces within NATO, they both have primarily Soviet-built or purchased air defence systems, and they are both subject to international embargoes. So they might obviously look for ways to work together'.

On 1 April, SAM launchers were attacked by Vipers, Hornets and Tornados in the SNFZ, along with two communications facilities, after the F-16s were painted by Iraqi radar during an SNFZ patrol. Pentagon officials said that since Desert Fox there have been 160 Iraqi air defence actions and aircraft incursions in the SNFZ. Fifteen days later, a radar near Talil was hit by Tornado GR1s and a day later in the NNFZ, a clutch of F-15E, F-16CJ and EA-6B Prowlers hit AAA sites north of Mosul with attacks continuing on the anti-aircraft guns during 21st, hitting a radar in the city's vicinity on the 22nd and returning to attack the AAA sites five days later.

In early May, Mosul continued to endure attacks against AAA sites around the city with F-15Es dropping GBU-12s on 2nd followed with AGM-130 and F-16CJ AGM-88 HARM attacks on SAM launchers. The Pentagon admitted that the NFZ enforcement was something of a cat-and-mouse game and that one of Saddam's favoured tactics was to move air defence into civilian areas to frustrate Coalition retaliation: '[Saddam] is constantly looking for ways to shoot down a US plane and [is] therefore recalibrating his air defence and other systems better to enable him to do that. That's just speculation, but the pattern appears to be that he challenges for a while, we whack him day after day in response to his challenges, and then he pulls back and goes down for a period and does nothing. And then he comes back up and presents a new series of challenges, sometimes with slightly different tactics. One of his tactics now may be to place his air defence systems in civilian neighbourhoods, thinking that he can challenge us with impunity, because he's done that'.

The dark game continued as GR.1s, together with F-16Cs hit Iraqi air defences around Basrah after they were engaged by AAA on 11 May. On 25 May GBU-12s and GBU-10 bombs were dropped by F-15Es on communications facilities thought to be used by Iraq's air defenders. The strikes continue into June with GBU-12s hitting a communications facility to the east of Mosul following an engagement by Iraqi AAA systems.

These incidents were just snapshots of the almost daily actions in which US and British aircraft were involved during the NFZ enforcement. They are merely a drop-in-the-ocean compared with the number of engagements of Coalition aircraft by Iraq's air defences and subsequent retaliation which occurred during the entire period following Desert Storm prior to Iraqi Freedom. However, they do give an indication both of the intensity of the Coalition SEAD effort and also the extent of Iraq's air defences.

The Eve of the War

By the time that Operation Iraqi Freedom (OIF) began in March 2003, Saddam was still thought to have up to 210 SAMs, 150 EW radar systems and a working C2 network as the clouds of war gathered overhead. To make matters worse, most of the SAM systems were reckoned to be operational. It is impossible to give precise numbers as to how many air defence systems US, British and Australian aviators faced as they prepared to fight Saddam during a second war in Arabia. What was known was that they faced a *smorgasbord* of defences, including the ubiquitous SA-2 of which Saddam was thought to have between twenty to thirty batteries, along with up to fifty batteries of SA-3 Goa launchers and between thirty-six to fifty-five SA-6 Gainful launchers. While it was unknown how many were operational, it was understood that the Iraqis had the means to repair their air defence systems when necessary and even produce replacement missiles.

Below the missiles the same deadly AAA menace that pilots had faced during Desert Storm was still in abundance. This included around 4,000 AAA weapons of between 0.5 in (12.7 mm) to 0.9 in (23 mm). Add to this a plethora of IR-guided vehicle-mounted and MANPADS systems including SA-7, SA-8, SA-9 and SA-16 weapons. All of this was commanded and controlled from the Air Defence Operations Centre (ADOC) bunker below

Al Muthana AFB in Baghdad. This facility was linked by fibre-optic communications to other regional air defence facilities around the country. Although the fibre optics were purchased during the mid-1980s, the Clinton Administration had accused Chinese contractors of helping to maintain and upgrade Iraq's IADS communications system throughout the 1990s. It was from these centres that the activities of the Air Defence Command were coordinated.

The ADC was split into the following sectors: Based at Taji in the north-west outskirts of Baghdad was the 1st Sector Operations Centre (SOC) for the 1st Air Defence Sector (ADS) which had jurisdiction for defending the airspace over central Iraq and was joined by the Taqqadam, Mukhayb, Najaf, Salman Pak and Taji Intercept Operations Centres (IOC) located around Baghdad in an anti-clockwise fashion. The 2nd ADS was to the west with the SOC located at the H-3 airfield with the H-3, Ar Rufbah and H-1 IOCs stretching from west to east. In the south the 3rd ADS was located with the SOC at Talil and IOCs clockwise at Al Amarah, Talil, Az Zubayr and As Salman. Finally, the northern part of the country was controlled by the 4th ADS with the SOC at Karkuk and IOCs at Mosul in the north-west and Karkuk to the east. Most of Iraq's air defences were located under the command of the 1st ADS protecting the Iraqi capital and key strategic sites such as military bases, presidential residences and WMD facilities.

The order of battle for the 1st ADS included sixteen SA-2 and SA-3 batteries along with SA-6 and Roland systems. Aircraft operating in the southern NFZ were watched and challenged by the 3rd ADS which had one SAM brigade and an unknown number of AAA systems. Meanwhile, the 4th SOC had around six SA-2 and SA-6 batteries to threaten aircraft operating over the NNFZ. Linking this network together with fibre optics gave the Iraqis an important advantage as information could be passed from one AOC to the other; crucially, this could include radar and targeting information. Aircraft could be spotted with radar in one sector but could be engaged with air defence systems in another, saving the latter the danger of having to activate their radar until the last moment to guide their SAMs, although this still carried the risk of interception by a HARM.

Air Defence Command also jury-rigged their SA-2 weapons in an effort to extend their engagement altitude apparently in a bid to target U-2Rs performing reconnaissance. Despite the existence of both the SOCs and IOCs in the air defence sectors, it should be noted that Iraqi air defenders became accustomed to operating their weapons systems in a decentralised fashion, that is firing their missiles and then moving their systems to reduce the risk of being attacked by British or American aircraft. Moreover, operating in more of a freelance capacity probably reduced the amount of damage that Coalition attempts to frustrate the communications between C2 centres and air defence units in the field could have. However, the use of fibre optics by the Iraqis was thought to have reduced the amount of electronic emissions that electronic intelligence aircraft were able to gather to prepare an electronic warfare order of battle as part of the SEAD campaign.

Before the war SEAD efforts reached their zenith on the eve of Operation Iraqi Freedom. Dubbed Operation Southern Focus, British and American aircraft launched a series of robust attacks against Iraqi AAA and air defence targets in response to repeated violations of the NFZs. The rationale behind the plan was a last-minute softening-up of Iraqi air defences prior to the war kicking off. Publicly the motive was given that Iraq was acting in an increasingly provocative fashion targeting Coalition aircraft performing their missions over the SNFZ and that this had left the Coalition little choice but to go after the air defences that were harassing them. Lieutenant General Michael 'Buzz' Moseley, who would command the Coalition air war during OIF, was in charge of the Southern Focus operations in his capacity as Commander, Ninth Air Force, US Central Command. He brought the power of his assets in the region to bear on the air defence targets which also included communications links as well as weapons systems. For the duration of Southern Focus from June 2002 until the start of OIF, Allied aircraft flew 21,736 sorties hitting 345 targets, the result was that the Iraqi air defences in the south and west, principally in the 2nd and 3rd ADSs, were rendered ineffective.

Operation Iraqi Freedom

As Iraq and the Coalition moved to what seemed like inevitable war, the SEAD capabilities of the combined American, British and Australian air forces in theatre were further reinforced. For example, as Operation Southern Focus was in full swing during January 2003, the 23rd FS deployed its F-16CJs from Spangdahlem AFB, Germany in anticipation of escorting strike packages as they went 'downtown' into the so-called SuperMEZ (Super Missile Engagement Zone) which ring-fenced the Iraqi capital in a protective network of concentrated SAM and AAA systems.

In fact SEAD was to be a major priority in the opening stages of the war. A high emphasis was placed by Moseley and his staff on attacking the crucial CoGs in Iraq's air defence network. Not only would the Wild Weasels join the fight, but they would be reinforced with US Navy and Marine Corps F/A-18 Hornets and EA-6B Prowlers. The F-16CJs of the 23rd FS were joined by similar aircraft from the 77th FS from Shaw AFB, South Carolina, which were sent to PSAB, while Wild Weasels from the 14th FS, Misawa AFB, Japan were deployed to Saudi. F-16CJs from the 22nd FS, also from Spangdahlam, were originally to provide SEAD cover over northern Iraq from Incirlik, Turkey, but this became an impossibility because of Turkish opposition to OIF, instead they were moved to Al Udeid AFB, Qatar. These aircraft joined the 157th FS Wild Weasels also at Al Udeid

It is interesting to note that it was not just SEAD that the F-16CJs were tasked with. Prior to the war, the Wild Weasels were also performing Night Time Intelligence Surveillance and Reconnaissance missions, known in the trade as NTISR. Thanks to the AN/AAQ-28 Litening-II targeting pods that the aircraft carried along with their HARM Targeting Systems, they assisted the intelligence gathering operation focused on locating Saddam's theatre ballistic missile force. The Coalition had concerns that the Iraqi dictator would once again try to bring Israel into the war by hitting the country with either Scud-B, *Al Hussein, Al Abbas, Al Hijarah, Al Sammound, Al Abadil*, BADR-2000 or *Al Abid* missiles. As it was, three Iraqi missiles were launched at Kuwait with two being intercepted by PAC-3 Patriot SAMs. The F-16CJs were to gather this information which could then be handed to special forces troops to allow them to attack the TBMs in the north. The aircraft were also used to build a picture of surviving EW radar and observation posts in northern Iraq to aid the aircraft which would be infiltrating Coalition special forces once the war began. The NTISR efforts got underway in February and with the information that these aircraft had gathered B-52H, B-1B and F-15Es hit air defence targets near Iraq's border with Jordan which could pose a threat to the infiltrating aircraft.

Up until the last moments of uneasy peace, OSW NFZ missions were being flown. Aircraft from the 77th FS escorted U-2R aircraft in late February as they flew near the SuperMEZ to build an increasingly detailed picture of the defences that the Coalition faced. OSW would officially come to rest on 19 March at 03.00Z when ingress and egress routes out of the area, operating altitudes and codenames were changed in anticipation of the war that was only hours away. The last combat action of OSW was to be a SEAD sortie in which an F-15E dropped a GBU-28 laser-guided bomb onto the IOC at H-3.

Two days before the famed Shock-and-Awe attacks on Baghdad, which began at 17.00Z on 21 March, the United States military had launched an unsuccessful attack to kill Saddam Hussein and his two sons Uday and Qusay. They were thought to be meeting at a location called Doura Farms in the southern outskirts of Baghdad. Two F-117As from the 8th FS at Al Udeid were despatched to attack the location with Enhanced-GBU-27 Paveway-III laser-guided bombs. Much to the frustration of the Coalition, it appeared that the Iraqi leader and his offspring slipped away moments before the Nighthawks attacked. SEAD was provided in the form of EA-6B Prowlers and also accompanying F-16CJs. Joining these aircraft were forty BQM-109 cruise missiles fired from the USS *Milius, Donald Cook, Bunker Hill* and *Cowpens* cruisers and destroyers and the USS *Montpelier* and *Cheyenne* nuclear submarines positioned in the Persian Gulf and the Red Sea.

Yet the intensive bombardment that signalled the start of the Shock-and-Awe phase of Iraqi Freedom would not get going until the 21 March. The pictures of this macabre fireworks display were transmitted around the world as television cameras in downtown Baghdad were dazzled with orange explosion plumes and earth-shuddering percussions. The military campaign to the south of Baghdad got underway as ground troops together with air support got moving from their jump-off locations in Kuwait. SEAD targets included an EW radar and C2 centre in the 2nd Air Defence Sector along with an air traffic control radar on the outskirts of Iraq's second city Basrah. The reason for this site being attacked was that is was said to provide targeting information for Iraqi AAA guns in the 3rd ADC and possibly in other ADCs also.

The whole panoply of Iraq's air defences was attacked including command centres, radars, batteries and communications systems and it was not just the United States that was lifting the SEAD burden, British Royal Air Force Tornado GR.4s fired Storm Shadow cruise missiles against air defence targets, fitted with the BROACH (Bomb Royal Ordnance Augmented CHarge) warhead system which increased the missile's penetration strength when attacking hardened facilities. BGM-34 Firebee drones were also thrown into the fray and these were used both to fool Iraqi radar in their characteristic fashion and also to sow the air with chaff.

The deception effort included large numbers of AN/ADM-141 TALDS which were used to try to tempt the Iraqis into activating their radar. Along with the AGM-88s, the RAF also deployed the ALARM anti-radar missile as they had eleven years earlier for the first time during Desert Storm. Not one Allied aircraft was lost during these opening strikes. This was of great consolation to the respective air forces which took part, given that the defences of the SuperMEZ were thought to bristle with sea urchin-like defences which could wreak havoc on the Coalition strike packages flying over the city.

Having said that, Coalition pilots did report that Baghdad was alive with AAA and SAMs flying through the air with the latter fired ballistically, and the former arcing through the sky but failing to score accurate hits. The problem that the Iraqis had with flak was its altitude limitations and instead the Coalition aircraft could just fly straight over it. The missiles were another matter, but the Iraqi's reluctance to use their radar meant that the accuracy of these shots left a lot to be desired. Moreover, as the war unfolded, the levels of air defence faced by the Coalition was said to diminish, perhaps the Iraqis just lost their heart for a fight. Certainly for the SAM operations, the power of the anti-radiation missiles probably helped to persuade them that using their radar could be a death sentence. The result of this diminishing performance was that the head of the Iraqi ADC was sacked. The total number of missile launches faced by the Coalition during the war included 1,660 SAM firings and 1,224 AAA attacks, along with 436 radar illuminations, these still failed to down a single Coalition aircraft. In terms of taking the SEAD war to the Iraqis, the Coalition struck 1,441 so-called air supremacy targets which would have included a high proportion of air defence aim points. However, unlike Desert Storm it was said that the Coalition did not try to destroy Iraq's airfields with runway denial munitions. Probably a prudent measure given that they would be needed for logistics and forward basing as the Coalition advanced into Iraqi territory. Therefore, the figure that we have of 1,441 air supremacy targets can reasonably be assumed to have contained a high level of air defence sites.

The SEAD campaign throughout the rest of the war would retain the appearance of the cat-and-mouse game that British and American pilots had played during the days of the NFZs. In other words, British and American aircraft would pursue all the elements of Iraq's ADC including the command and control systems, weapons, radar and communications while the Iraqis would do their best to frustrate their plans by hiding and disguising their systems as much as they could. They had probably not bargained on the heavy use of ELINT by the Coalition which included RC-135V/W Rivet Joint aircraft from the 55th Wing operating out of PSAB, along with RAF Nimrod R.1s of 51 Squadron probably operating from Ali Al Salem AFB in Kuwait and EP-3 Aries-II aircraft from the VA-1 World Watchers squadron of the US Navy. These aircraft were tasked with eavesdropping on Iraqi radar and communications emissions and then downloading this information both to E-3A Sentries and also to the CAOC at Al Udeid where the information would then be turned into aim points for Coalition aircraft.

It was expected by Moseley and his staff that the SEAD platforms, including the USAF F-16CJs and the Navy and USMC/US Navy EA-6Bs and F/A-18C/D/E would be among the most heavily tasked aircraft in the conflict, but after the first few days of operations it became clear that Iraq's air defences, while still posing a threat, were becoming increasingly un-coordinated and its operators taking strenuous efforts to enhance their own survival by keeping their radar switched off. From the 24 March, the Wild Weasels were carrying free-fall bombs in addition to their AGM-88s to assist troops on the ground with CAS and also to hit time-sensitive targets. In addition, the EA-6Bs downsized their electronic jamming role in favour of communi-cations disruption of the Iraqi forces on the ground. SEAD platforms would also perform 'Lane SEAD' in which they would sweep a corridor into and out of Iraqi air space for strike pack-ages in a similar fashion to the role they had performed during the Balkans campaigns and during operation Eldorado Canyon. Like Desert Storm, Iraqi Freedom was using both a Manoeuvrist and a mass approach to SEAD.

When escorting strike packages, the Wild Weasels would usually carry a pair off AGM-88s and would work closely with the strike package to detect radar emissions as the force flew towards its objective. As well as the HARMs being fired pre-emptively, it was possible to pre-programme the missile to hit a location where suspected radar existed, regardless of whether or not it was radiating. Deft timing was also an imperative, with the HARMs programmed to be flying through the air at precisely the moment the rest of the strike package was attacking its target i.e. when it was at its most vulnerable.

Furthermore, in an echo back to the days of CAS during Desert Storm, the airspace of Iraq was divided into so-called 'Kill Boxes'. These were squares of territory measuring 11.5 miles by 11.5 miles (18 km x 18 km) over which Coalition aircraft could roam to provide CAS. SEAD aircraft such as the F-16CJs would provide 'on-call' SEAD for any aircraft operating in the kill boxes as and when they needed it. The rationale was that the SEAD shooters would sanitize the ground of air defences to assist the CAS aircraft as they provided support to ground units advancing northwards to Baghdad. Moreover, the F-16s were called upon to move their missions from the realm of SEAD to DEAD. The imperative here was to bring hard kill free-fall ordnance to the fight against the air defences as well as the AGM-88s which were being employed. Such weapons included CBU-103 Wind Corrected Munitions Dispenser cluster weapons and GBU-31 2,000 lb (907 kg) GPS-guided Joint Direct Attack Munitions. AGM-165 Maverick air-to-ground missiles were also brought to the fight. Iraqi air defences were not just to be suppressed but to be wiped from the kill boxes once and for all. The end result was that the Iraqis may have realised that using their SAMs was just not worth the effort. To remain stationary, perform a radar fix and then launch a SAM would invite an AGM-88 as the response and the Iraqis had evidently decided that this was point-less. Furthermore, they had to remain on the move and hidden which further degraded their abilities to challenge Coalition aircraft.

During Iraqi Freedom, there was a total of 408 AGM-88 firings. From the 21–26 March these missiles were fired pre-emptively, that is in anticipation of a radar threat. Iraqi radar operators were often wisely keeping their radar off the air and because of this it was essential for the SEAD assets to take no chances as they accompanied the attacking aircraft downtown. The missile would be employed in this fashion in areas where radar was known or strongly suspected to be operating.

AGM-88 and ALARM were both very much traditional anti-radar weapons, but a new system was brought into the SEAD fight, namely the UAV. These pilotless aircraft have long been seen as a promising future technology for SEAD as they take the pilot out of the cockpit for what is a very dangerous mission. Their drone cousins have also found a valuable niche in spoofing air defence systems regarding the number of attacking aircraft that they are facing. However on the 23 March at 13.00Z, a General Atomics RQ-1A Predator UAV despatched an AGM-141K Hellfire-II air-to-ground missile at a ZSU-23-4 AAA system located at Al Amarah, near Basrah. The USAF reported that this was the first time that a UAV has ever performed such a mission and it is possible that this may yet be remembered as a key moment in SEAD; the first occasion that a pilot was taken out of the cockpit to perform a kinetic SEAD attack. What is also interesting is that AAA systems such as the Shikla have in the past proved fiendishly difficult to engage thanks to their furious rates of fire and the need to get in low to attack them. The use of the

Predator offers a possible means by which these systems can be engaged in the future.

Artillery was also brought into the SEAD fight along with the UAVs. The US Army's employment of artillery systems was led by units such as the 214th Field Artillery Brigade (214th FA) which used its M-39 Army Tactical Missile System (ATACMS) weapons in support of the SEAD effort on 23 March. M-39 operations in support of the SEAD effort began at 21.00Z when the unit fired twenty-nine Block 1 along with three Block 1A missiles at Iraqi battlefield air defences in support of the 11th Attack Helicopter Regiment's AH-64 Apache strike against Iraqi Army targets to the west of As Samawah, 124 miles (200 km) south-east of Baghdad. The 214th were joined by their colleagues from the 41st FA which attacked the field air defences of the Republican Guard Medina Division around Karbala, south-west of Baghdad, Al Hillah and Al Haswah, central Iraq, in support of the 101st Airborne Division's Apaches. Later on 30 March, the 214th FA attacked two radars at Najaf with M-39 missiles.

The 41st FA brought its M-39 systems to the fight once more on 5 April when it fired ten Block 1A M-39 missiles in support of the 11th Aviation Group against AAA positions near the Buhayrat Ar Razzazah Lake south-west of Baghdad. On the same day at 13.57Z the units switched its attacks, firing fifteen Block 1 M-39s at air defence targets in support of the 101st Airborne Division's aviation as it engaged the Medina Division around Fallujah to the west of Baghdad.

At the other end of the spectrum, B-52H bombers from the 93rd Bomb Squadron entered the SEAD fight on 11 April smashing a radar and command and control centre at Al Sahra to the north-west of Tikrit. What made this strike unique was that it was the first time that the B-52 had used the Litening-II targeting pod for an attack which allowed it to drop a single GBU-12 Paveway-II laser guided bomb on this facility.

The Coalition managed to establish air superiority over Iraq by early April: around ten days after the start of the campaign. The Coalition enjoyed this superiority over 95 per cent of Iraq's air space; the remaining five per cent was contested by Iraqi SAM systems.

The SEAD effort during the NFZ enforcement, Operation Desert Fox and OIF had several important effects on Iraq's air defences. First and foremost, the defences never recovered from Desert Storm. Crucially, Saddam did not change his air defence doctrine. True, he established the ADC, but the command and control of the system was still orchestrated along Soviet lines and therefore highly centralised. Secondly, the NFZ enforcement had resulted in a 'death from a thousand cuts' for the Iraqis. Every time they were threatened, Coalition aircraft would attack Iraqi air defence, this led to their progressive destruction, although the Iraqis did adapt in this respect and performed maintenance of the IADS at home and may have illegally imported replacement parts and upgrades for their IADS where they could. Moreover, the Iraqis learned that there was simply not too much that they could do about the Coalition's tactics of monitoring their radar emissions, jamming their radar and communications and firing HARMs at their SAM systems. They learned that the most effective means of survival was simply not to turn their radar on and to stay well-hidden which of course degraded the effectiveness of their weapons systems.

CHAPTER NINE

Future SEAD

The ways and means of SEAD have evolved in almost seventy years since the *Luftwaffe* attacks on the Chain Home radar. Specialist missiles and aircraft now characterise the SEAD fight. Along with new concepts of defeating anti-access strategies, of which robust air defences are a key element. Unsurprisingly, the United States is leading from the front. New Concepts of Operations or ConOps are dedicated to negating the danger that enemy air defences can pose to an attacking force. Meanwhile, new SEAD aircraft and weaponry are on the near horizon and further into the 21st century we may see a situation where a significant part of the SEAD burden is absorbed by UAVs.

Global Strike ConOps

New technology and airframes have led the USAF to think afresh about circumventing the potent air defence systems that they may face in future wars. At the cornerstone is the stealthy F-22A Raptor air-superiority fighters with groups of Raptors protecting a formation of B-2A Spirit stealth bombers as they fly towards their targets: firstly destroying SAM systems such as the Russian-built S-300MPU/SA-10 (NATO codename Grumble), S-300V/SA-12 Giant and S-400/SA-20 Triumpf, together with their accompanying C2 equipment. The aircraft's attentions will then be turned to high-value, immobile leadership targets and other C2 installations.

Their mission will be to deliver a short, sharp shock to the enemy's military infrastructure so as to render it incapable of effective retaliation and to allow the entry of 'follow-on' forces to begin unimpeded attacks against other targets. This duo of stealthy aircraft, coupled with sophisticated command and control systems will be known as the USAF Global Strike Concept of Operations (GSConOps). Although it may sound like science fiction, the GSConOps is, according to Colonel David Gerber, GSConOps Champion at the Pentagon's Directorate of Operational Capability Requirements, 'already up and running'.

The GSConOps takes lessons from history. During Operation Desert Storm air power fragmented the command of Iraq's military machine and softened up army units in the field before the ground war to liberate Kuwait began. Over the Balkans, air power was used during operations Deliberate Force and Allied Force. During the latter, it was hoped that NATO bombing would persuade the Serbian leadership to invite NATO peacekeepers into Kosovo. As events turned out, it took longer for Belgrade to capitulate.

The former Chief of the USAF Air Combat Command (ACC) General John Jumper, the architect of the GSConOps argued that Allied Force taught an important lesson: 'we should never start a limited operation if the enemy can turn it into a sustained conflict'. Rather than conduct a graduated increase of bombing, such as that undertaken in Operation Rolling Thunder during the Vietnam war, the USAF will begin its air campaigns with a sudden and focused bombing campaign, such as that seen during the Shock and Awe attacks at the start of Operation Iraqi Freedom; as Col. Gerber says: 'The whole (GSConOps) idea is pulled from the history of the last 50 years'.

The use of stealth aircraft with precision weapons such as the JDAM and the forthcoming GBU-39 Small Diameter Bomb (SDB) will allow USAF aircraft to outmanoeuvre their enemy. After all, why attack an enemy's strong points, when you can smash its weak points?

Rather than hitting massed formations of troops in the field, surrounded by heavy air defences, the C2 nervous systems which control these forces will be attacked, paralysing the enemy early on in the fight. Gen. Jumper is confident that: 'stealth applied to bombers and manoeuvrable fighters, all-weather precision-guided munitions (PGMs), and UAVs will

allow us to manoeuvre over, around, and through or to stand-
off outside (the) advanced defensive systems and networks
already available to potential adversaries'. It is hoped that the
GSConOps will provide the, 'maximum shock during the first
stage of the battle'. Such a display might even persuade an
adversary that 'resistance is futile' and encourage them to sue
for peace rather than endure more attacks. Col. Gerber stresses
that, 'the point of strategy and war is to force the adversary to
their mind'. Moreover, the stealthy qualities of the Raptors and
Spirits will be almost impossible to defend against.

A typical GSConOps attack would begin with a clutch of B-2s
and F-22s entering enemy airspace, while B-52 bombers armed
with cruise missiles loiter beyond the enemy's borders. Between
them, they will deliver a devastating initial attack against the
enemy's fixed SAM sites and C2 installations. Meanwhile
the Raptors will defend the bombers should the enemy's air
force try to engage.

Once the initial strike is complete and the anti-aircraft threat
has been degraded, follow-on forces of less stealthy aircraft such
as the F-35 and the US Navy's F/A-18E/F will conduct precision attacks from around 15,000 ft (4,572 m) on, or around, the
third day of the conflict. Although these aircraft are not as
invisible as their cousins, the F-35 reportedly has a radar signature which is the size of a golf ball. The Super Hornet's radar
signature, when it is armed with external ordnance on its hard
points, is said to be the size of a 3 ft (0.91 m) sphere.

With the initial attacks complete, the Spirits will begin combat
air patrols in a 'cab rank', waiting for orders to attack time-
critical and fixed targets as they are identified by reconnaissance
aircraft. Meanwhile, UAVs armed with missiles will attack
heavily fortified targets which present too much of a threat to
the crewed aircraft.

The USAF's F-22A Raptor will be an integral part of the
GSConOps. It is a 'first-look, first-shot, first-kill' air-superiority
fighter, which is designed to outclass the advanced fighters and
SAMs which US forces may encounter in future conflicts. Its
angular appearance is said to give the aircraft a radar signature
which is the size of an aluminium marble, while it can cruise at
Mach 1.5 at altitudes of 40,000 ft (12,192 m). Such speeds and

altitudes combined with the size of its radar signature, would mean that anti-aircraft radars would have a tough time trying to find the aircraft. The Raptor even has an internal weapons bay to reduce the radar returns reflected by external stores.

When teamed with the B-2 bomber, the Raptor-Spirit combination will be a potent one. Four stealth bombers and forty-eight Raptors all carrying SBDs could hit 380 targets in only fifty-two sorties. According to Major-General David Deptula, former Director of Plans and Programs at ACC, this combination allows the USAF to create the 'effects of mass (bombing) without massing'.

Once the force is operating, the Airborne Laser, a USAF 747 armed with a powerful laser beam, will vaporise any ballistic missiles which the enemy may launch as retaliation against US or allied forces stationed beyond its borders. Command and control of the GSConOps will be provided by a mixed bag of E-3 Sentry AWACS aircraft, which can watch the skies and direct friendly warplanes to and from their targets; E-8C JSTARS which will watch the ground for enemy movements and U-2C Dragon Lady reconnaissance aircraft that can provide high-altitude, all-weather surveillance along with RQ-4A Global Hawk UAVS. Meanwhile RQ-1 Predator UAVs will strike heavily guarded targets, operating with special forces behind enemy lines.

The entire force will be co-ordinated thousands of miles away from the 'battlespace' at the ACC's new CAOC at Langley Air Force Base, Virginia. Using state-of-the-art technology, the CAOC will collect information from the force's reconnaissance assets, identify 'aim points' for the attack aircraft and then transmit this information to the force. Gen. Jumper hopes that this will result in time-critical targets being struck in less than ten minutes from their detection, helping to reduce the all-important 'sensor-to-shooter' gap.

Furthermore, the USAF's future tanker aircraft will give the force a global reach. While this can already be achieved with the force's KC-135E Stratotanker and KC-10 Extender aircraft, these tankers are ageing. Refuelling the force will eliminate the need to negotiate basing and over-flight rights from countries which may be hostile to the United States. Although aircraft carriers can negate the need for overseas basing, they can be vulnerable to anti-shipping missiles and many of their aircraft do not have the payload capacity of aircraft such as the Spirit.

The GSConOps is designed to eliminate many of the challenges seen in recent air operations involving US forces. It will do away with the need for overseas airbases on the doorstep of an adversary such as those used in Saudi Arabia, Bahrain and the United Arab Emirates during Desert Storm. The precision weapons that the force will deploy should help to minimise civilian casualties and collateral damage on the ground. The stealthiness of the force will render it largely invulnerable to air-to-air and SAM threats, while a relatively small force will be able to inflict a level of damage far outstripping its size. Advanced command and control systems will allow time-critical targets to be struck, while keeping an eagle-eye on the battlefield and the skies above it. Finally, the all-weather capabilities of the force will mean that the foul conditions that were occasionally seen during operations Desert Storm and Allied Force will not necessarily ground the GSConOp force.

The only thing that seems to be missing from the equation is a new electronic warfare platform that can blast enemy air defences with noise to ease the passage of the opening strikes and successive attacks. The USAF has taken a tortuous route in developing an electronic attack aircraft for tomorrow's wars. Since the retirement of the EF-111 Ravens in 1998, the force has been without a dedicated electronic warfare system and has primarily relied on the EA-6B Prowlers of the US Navy and USMC.

The USAF assessed its electronic warfare options in 2000–2001 conducting the Analysis of Alternatives initiative to study possible platforms for electronic attack from 2010. The following year the Pentagon gave the nod to a cross-service initiative in which three services (USAF, US Navy and USMC) would develop a common platform for electronic warfare given that the Prowler was also looking towards its retirement. For a while, the solution looked set to be Stratofortresses tricked-up with electronic attack black boxes which could work as stand-off jammers, while EA-18G Growler F/A-18E/F Hornet derivatives would fly off the carrier to go 'downtown' with the strike force supplying electronic attack and also kinetic kill with AGM-88 HARMs in support of the attack. However, only one half of this one-two punch was to become a reality. The B-52 stand-off jammer was abandoned in 2005 because of cost issues and the service remains without a dedicated electronic attack system.

EA-18G Growler

There is not a problem for the US Navy however. Soon to roll off the production line at Boeing's factory in St. Louis, Missouri, is the EA-18G Growler electronic warfare aircraft which was one of the results of the Pentagon's Analysis of Alternatives and can trace its birth back to the early 1990s. According to Mike Gibbons, Boeing Program Manager of the EA-18G: 'The actual idea had its genesis in 1993. The Navy had contacted McDonnell Douglas (prior to the company's purchase by Boeing) and asked to do a quick study of making the Super Hornet platform into an electronic attack aircraft. We concluded that it was feasible. The programme got momentum from 2002 and the Navy put us under a Systems Development and Demonstration contract'.

The Growler has a vital role to play and its missions will include offensive electronic emission monitoring, detection, classification and jamming, as well as supporting electronic and physical SEAD. The Navy and USMC EA-6B Prowlers are not getting any younger, and are also slow compared to the two services' F/A-18 Hornet planes, the former trundling along at around Mach 0.72. One report noted that the aircraft was; 'like an elderly grandfather on Halloween escorting trick-or-treaters on a sugar high'. The Prowler has almost four decades of service under its belt and has played a hugely important role in spoofing enemy electronic communications and radar systems in conflicts involving the United States right up to the Global War On Terror. However, things aren't quite done with the Prowler. It will remain in service until around 2010.

So far, the Navy has been the only taker for the Growler, but Boeing is ready to build the aircraft for other customers should the need arise. 'Our only customer is the Navy. The Marines and the Air Force are conducting their own studies (into future

EW aircraft), but we've got the capacity to build extra aircraft if so required', notes Mr. Gibbons.

It was in 2001 that Boeing demonstrated to the Navy that the F/A-18 Hornet design could carry the under-wing pods housing the equipment necessary for the electronic warfare mission. During tests an F/A-18F Super Hornet carried three AN/ALQ-99 jamming pods along with two fuel tanks on its hard points and all went well. Fast-forward two years and Boeing was awarded the Systems Development and Demonstration contract to transform a variant of the Super Hornet into the Growler.

In terms of the aircraft's systems, the Block 1 design of the airframe will include an ALQ-218(V)2 receiver. In addition, there will be an AN/ALQ-227 communications counter-measures system and the ALQ-99 pods which house high- and low- frequency detection and jamming equipment. The net effect of these systems is that the Growler will have improved capabilities enabling it to identify, classify and locate electronic signals which can then be jammed. However, these powerful electronic systems will not interrupt the aircraft's own communications. This will mean that the EA-18G can use its Link-16 and its Mode 5 Identification Friend or Foe system while it conducts the jamming mission. Meanwhile, the cockpit of the aircraft will have the same F/A-18F Block 2 avionics fit.

Outwardly, the Growler is recognisable by the large pods located beneath the wings and on the central station, but apart from that there is little to tell the EA-18G apart from its Super Hornet sibling. This is deliberate on the manufacturers' part. The Navy was very keen to have an aircraft which has a high degree of commonality with its existing Hornet fleet. Mike Gibbons comments that: 'We have maintained so much commonality with the F (i.e. the F/A-18E/F) aircraft that in some cases we've even changed the design of the F going forward to keep as much commonality as we can between the F and G versions. That's going to have savings not only in production, but it will also allow the Navy to operate a single type (of fast jet) and will help them with their logistics costs as well. This aircraft maintains all the capabilities of the F, with pretty much the only exception being that the Growler doesn't carry a gun. Other differences include the wing tip weapons stations which will have receiving antennae. Where the gun is positioned on the Super Hornet, an LR-700 receiver and satellite communications system which connects with the AN/ALQ-99 system will instead be installed.

The ALQ-218 is a particularly interesting system in that it can perform reactive electronic jamming, that is when a threat has been discovered, or alternatively it can perform pre-emptive jamming i.e. switching on the noise before the enemy even realises that there is a Growler in their midst. Meanwhile the AN/ALQ-99 pods will listen out for hostile radar emissions. The pods can work out the strength and position of hostile radar and can then decide how much energy is needed to put them out of business. What is more, these pods can be operated autonomously, semi-autonomously or manually by the crew. The AN/ALQ-99 has the ability to be programmed to listen out for a specific frequency which is assumed to be hostile and respond if radar emissions on that frequency are detected. It is also possible that the aircraft's electronic warfare systems could double-up as RWRs to protect the aircraft.

Another arrow in the Growler's quiver is the AN/APG-79 Active Electronically Scanned Array (AESA) which will allow the aircraft to attack ground targets thanks to the AESA's synthetic aperture radar system, including non-emitting air defence installations; this was something that the Prowler was unable to do this because its radar lacked the appropriate fidelity. This will also put an end to an adversary trying to harass US and Allied aircraft by blind-firing their surface-to-air missiles or anti-aircraft guns in the hope of scoring a lucky hit.

SEAD can be performed not only with the electronic systems onboard the aircraft, but the Growler will also have the where-withal to deploy kinetic weaponry if a hostile air defence site is detected. In particular it can fire AGM-88s which makes the aircraft into a completely self-contained Wild Weasel system. In addition CBU-87 Combined Effects Munition can be carried for anti-personnel, soft-target and light-armour kills.

So where are we now and when will the aircraft enter service? Initial Operational Capability is expected for 2009. The aircraft has already been rolled out; on 5 August 2006 to be precise, and took its maiden flight eleven days later. During the ceremony at Boeing's St. Louis plant, Chief of Naval Operations, Admiral Michael G. Mullen commented that: 'It is clear the demand for electronic warfare is not only going to remain high, but it's going to grow. The Growler was designed and built to answer that call. Its speed, range and robust self-defence systems will serve as a force multiplier for naval aviation and greatly strengthen the entire joint force'.

The acquisition of the Growler has implications for the rest of the United States armed forces. Current predictions say that, for the near future, it will remain the only dedicated electronic warfare aircraft in the joint fleet once the Prowler is retired. The next effect of this is that the aircraft may find itself particularly heavily tasked; called on to protect not only United States Air Force and USMC strike packages, but also those of allied countries during multinational operations. This begs the question as to whether there will be enough Growlers to go around. Current plans call for the Navy to acquire around ninety airframes. However, it is entirely possible that other services may get their electronic attack house in order and buy their own platforms. Meanwhile, the USMC may decide to develop a dedicated electronic warfare version of the F-35 Lightning II. Whatever happens, the Navy hopes to have around fifty Growlers in service by 2012, with the rest completing the order thereafter. Mr Gibbons and his team can build extra aircraft if needed, and the USMC and the USAF may yet come knocking.

EA-6B Prowler ICAP-III
For the time being, some extra life will be squeezed out of the EA-6B Prowler. This aircraft, nicknamed the Fat Kid, has become a highly versatile platform. The Global War on Terror has seen the Prowler used not only for SEAD but also to jam communications systems being used by insurgents in Iraq. Prowlers equip four USMC squadrons and fourteen US Navy units; however their electronic attack capabilities place the aircraft in high demand. But the EA-6B is not getting any younger. Wear and tear means that the Prowler's availability is becoming an increasing problem. This translates into around sixty Prowlers being available on an average day out of a fleet of

over 100 aircraft. Arguably, the Prowler now is more in demand than ever and it has played a pivotal role in protecting strike aircraft during conflicts in the Balkans and the Middle East.

The first unit to receive the EA-6B was the VAQ-129 Vikings at Whidbey Island, Washington State in 1971 and twenty years later the last production aircraft was delivered. No sooner had the Prowler entered service than it underwent an upgrade in the form of the Extended Capability programme, followed by the ICAP-I six years later.

Looking afresh at the Prowler's capabilities and helping to extend its life until the entry into service of the Growler, the US Navy has ordered the Improved Capability III (ICAP-III) upgrade with Northrop Grumman, the aircraft's builder, as the prime contractor for the upgrade which began in 1998 with an order for two aircraft upgraded to ICAP-III standard. A second contract was won by the company in March 2006 to convert a further five aircraft to the ICAP-III configuration. Since then, fifteen aircraft have been delivered to the VAQ-139 Cougars and VAQ-137 Rooks electronic attack squadrons.

The ICAP-III brings some important improvements to the Prowler's capabilities. The aircraft retain their AN/ALQ-99 Tactical Jamming Systems while the AN/ALQ-218 digital receiver system will monitor the spectrum for threats. The AN/ALQ-218 can monitor signals and measure threats across a wide bandwidth in a much quicker fashion than the Onboard System contained in the AN/ALQ-99 was able to. The Digital Receiver System works by capturing a signal of interest with its accompanying characteristics transmitted to another receiver on the aircraft which performs a more detailed analysis of the transmission. Once the signal has been analysed it can then be jammed. It is at this point when one of the ECM officers would decide on the most appropriate jamming response to the threat. The benefits of having a second receiver on the aircraft has another advantage in that the aircraft can jam a specific area while performing a detailed search for threats in another. The main thing that this system brings to the fight is a much more accurate measurement of the position and characteristics of a hostile emitter. This will sharpen up the aircraft's abilities to perform the surgical jamming of hostile radar.

Meanwhile, the aircraft has gained a glass cockpit with the AN/ASN-123 navigation system removed and replaced by modern Multi-Functional Displays which give the crew a clear picture of the emitter situation below them. Other additions to the aircraft under the ICAP-III upgrade include an AN/USQ-113 communications jammer, satellite communications and the Multi-Mission Advanced Tactical Terminal, the latter of which fuses the data arriving from the aircraft's communications jammer, satellite links and Integrated Data Modem (IDM) at one location via the AN/ALQ-218 system. The IDM is especially important to the SEAD fight as it allows the EA-6B to share targeting data with the F-16CJs which, along with the Prowler, can fire HARMs at the hostile radar.

AGM-88 HARM

Toward late February 2006 Raytheon, the US defence contractor that built the seminal AGM-88 HARM, flight tested that latest incarnation of their radar killer, known as the AGM-88 Advanced Anti-Radiation Guided Missile (AAGM). The new weapon is the result of the HARM Destruction of enemy air defence Attack Module (HDAM) upgrade to the missile's seeker system which primes the weapon to make the lives of air defence personnel even more miserable well into this century.

The latest series of tests were flown against a low-power radar emitter. The test was the final one in a series of evaluations which have tested the missile's hitting power. Previous versions of the HARM would have found a low-powered radar transmitter particularly difficult to hit, given the strong air defence radar emissions that the weapon needed to use in order to home in on, and kill, the system.

US Navy officials described the final test, which occurred on 21 February, as the most challenging they had performed as part of the AGM-88 AAGM programme. The missile was carried aloft by an F-16 Block 50 aircraft, before it was launched 18 miles (29Km) from the target, while the aircraft was flying at 0.8 Mach. The missile hit the target with no problem whatsoever. Jeff Wadsworth, HARM programme manager at Raytheon told reporters that: 'the test has clearly demonstrated the extended capabilities of the HDAM. The three successful

HDAM flight tests concluded the highly successful cooperate research and development agreement providing the air force with an opportunity to upgrade its existing inventory with a system that can be utilized as a suppression or destruction of enemy air defences weapon with additional capability as a high-speed strike weapon'. HDAM can be a new, multi-role arrow in the Air Force warfighter's quiver.

Since 1983, when the AGM-88 entered production, 22,500 HARMs have been delivered and they have equipped the USAF, US Navy and US Marine Corps, in addition to a score of foreign operators. Mr. Wadsworth described the HDAM improvements as a: 'hardware and software upgrade to the HARM missile system'. Much has been made in the press of the Global Positioning System jammers which are available on the international market which have the propensity to disrupt military operations depending on such technology. Mr Wadsworth adds that the missile; 'will work with GPS or in environments where GPS is denied. It gives the weapon a much more accurate position than it had before'.

The HDAM improvements could also potentially solve another problem. One SEAD tactic is to fire a number of HARM missiles pre-emptively towards a suspected SAM site in the hope that the radar will be activated and guide the HARMs to their target, before the radar has a chance to plot a fire solution against a friendly aircraft. For example, of the fifty-six HARMs that were fired during Operation Deliberate Force, thirty-three of them were fired in this fashion. Firing pre-emptive HARMs has two drawbacks: firstly, the missiles are not exactly cheap, at around $250,000 a shot and secondly should the missile not detect enemy radar, there is a risk that it may lock-on to friendly emissions and destroy the wrong target. Lt. Gen. Short USAF, Commander Allied Air Forces Southern Europe, noted that; '(During) the pre-emptive HARM shot, when it opens its eyes and there is nothing for it to see, (it can) take off like a "mad dog"'. It was during the Kosovo campaign that six HARMs that had been fired ended up over the Bulgarian border by mistake.

The HDAM upgrade will allow the missile only to engage targets within a preset area thanks to its GPS/INS addition. According to Jeff Wadsworth, this should make the suppression of enemy air defence job more straightforward and maybe even remove the need to fire HARMs pre-emptively: 'Your rules of engagement should be a little easier to fulfil because now you can define areas where you want the missile to attack and areas where you do not want the missile to attack'. He goes on to say that; 'inside an area where you do military operations, there may be specific sub-areas where you do not want the missile to engage; a hospital for instance. With this weapon you can define the area where you do want the missile to look for targets that it can engage and you can define zones of exclusion where the missile is not allowed to engage. It does give the aircrew a tremendous amount of flexibility in employing the weapon even if there are stringent ROEs.

This feature was put to the test during the first series of trials in August 2005, when an AGM-88 with the modifications described above, was launched from an F-16CJ aircraft. The missile was presented with two radar sources at the China Lake Test Range in California in order to select the correct one. Once the missile was launched, the first radar emitter, beyond the Missile's Impact Zone (MIZ) was activated. This was detected by the weapon, which noted that this target was beyond its MIZ. A second radar emitter was then activated which the missile determined was within its MIZ and was destroyed.

The addition of the GPS/INS package will also allow the weapon to operate as a *de-facto* air-to-surface missile against ground targets; even in the absence of emitting radar. This is because the upgrade will make the missile compatible with the MIL-STD-1553 data bus which means that it can be programmed with coordinates while in flight: 'Now it becomes a point-to-point supersonic strike weapon and a time-critical target weapon it you know the target's location', comments Jeff Wadsworth.

At present, the HDAM initiative is a cooperative research and development programme with the USAF, but Mr. Wadsworth and his colleagues hope that it will be turned into a fully-fledged procurement initiative: 'We are hopeful that the USAF will procure the weapon, however at this point we have no contract with them to do so'. There is also the potential that the HDAM upgrade may find its way abroad: 'It's designed to go on the Tornado, F/A-18 and EA-6B as well as the F-16. There is the potential for a very active Allied participation'.

The HDAM upgrade will also allow other improvements to be made to the weapon in the future: 'Our premise here is that SEAD is a needed capability, but the more missions a weapon can handle the better, and it's cheaper to upgrade an existing weapon than it is to develop a new one. Along with the HDAM upgrade, we have given that some thought as to how you would upgrade that further if the nation required that upgrade. HDAM is made to be easily programmable. In addition to that we have looked at seeker upgrades that could be done to further enhance the mission, and propulsion upgrades that could be done to increase the range of the weapon'.

UAVs

The use of UAVs for the SEAD mission is nothing new. The Israelis wrote the rule book in this respect with their deployment of unmanned aircraft at the start of Operation Peace for Galilee. This baton was later taken up by the Americans during Desert Storm when customised target-drones were pressed into service as part of the Scathe Mean initiative. When employed with imagination, these aircraft can fool even the most well-trained air defender into thinking that the drone is a manned aircraft. This, as we have seen, has the added benefit of betraying the behaviour of an air defence system to the attacking force. Put simply, the UAV can be the embodiment of the all-important feint in the SEAD operations.

Anyone visiting a defence conference over the past ten years who has seen a presentation from a company specialising in UAVs will be in no doubt as to the potential of these pilotless aircraft in keeping aircrew out of harm's way. 'Dull, dangerous and dirty' – the 3D mission – is the oft. repeated mantra of the UAV community in summarising what their designs bring to the fight. It is no surprise then that one of the most frequently highlighted applications for UAV technology as it matures is SEAD. Defence suppression falls squarely within the second category of the 3D mission, and as air defences grow in sop_histication year by year, ways of taking the human out of this dangerous environment are being studied more closely.

However, the application of UAVs to the SEAD fight is by no means a new phenomenon. In the dark and chilly days of the Cold War, the USAF wrestled with how to protect their B-52G Stratofortresses against attack from SAMs. The menace that they had to contend with back then was the SA-2, which was specifically designed to wreck bomber formations. The solution was the ADM-20B Quail air-launched decoy constructed by McDonnell Douglas which was designed to fit into the bomb-bay of the giant aircraft. Anyone visiting Duxford Air Museum in the United Kingdom will have a very good idea just how big the weapons bay of a Stratofortress is, but once filled up with nuclear weapons, space is at a premium and the Quail was designed with folding wings and a tail to allow eight decoys to be carried per bomber with each measuring 155 x 29 x 26 inches (3.94 x 0.74 x 0.66 m), however the usual quantity of decoys carried per aircraft was around four located right at the back of the bomber's weapons bay. Once in flight, Quail would be dropped into the slipstream of the bomber as it approached heavily defended parts of Soviet airspace, i.e. the outskirts of Moscow, other major cities and defence installations. Once dropped from the aircraft, the Quail's wings and tail assembly unfolded and the AGM-20A J85-GE-7 turbojet engine would ignite. Not only did the Quail carry chaff and flares but also a radar reflector in the drone's fuselage that spat out electrons to convince the ground-based air defences that the Quail and not its parent bomber was the real target.

Had it ever come to war, it is doubtful how effective Quail would have been. The drone was programmed by autopilot but the capacity of this system did not stretch beyond two turns and a single speed change along its 455 nautical mile (825 km) flight, and the Soviets would no doubt only fall for the ruse for so long. The limitations of Quail were not discovered before around 500 were built for Strategic Air Command. Another variant of Quail was constructed for low-altitude manoeuvres and this entered service in 1960 when the first production systems were delivered and one year later, the first B-52G unit was outfitted with the decoy. In 1961, a low-level variant of the Quail, ADM-20B was produced as the USAF began to think about low-level ingress into the Soviet Union as a means of mitigating the air defence threat.

Quail was not a panacea and had shortcomings. The drone had reliability issues and trials in the early 1970s showed that USAF radar operators could distinguish between the bomber and the decoy on 98 per cent of occasions. The result was that the ADM-20A/B was put out to pasture and followed by the Model 150 which was the brainchild of the Brunswick Corporation in California. Known as the Maxi Decoy this drone was a step up from the Quail design and could perform the chaff and flare missions in addition to jamming and even intelligence gathering. However, unlike Quail, the Model 150 was bereft of an engine and could be released as a glider from its host aircraft, carried on a hardpoint until the time that it was needed. Generally speaking, it was expected that the Model-150 would have a range in the region of 90 miles (144 km) with a gliding speed of 460 mph (740 km/h). The rationale was the same; to sow confusion into the enemy's radar system.

Brunswick Defence Corporation did later produce a powered version of the Model 150 known as the Model-150P. Brunswick installed a rocket motor which gave the missile a flight time of around 5 minutes. However, despite the ingenuity in developing the Model-150/P systems, the USAF elected not to buy any of the decoys, with the SEAD burden remaining squarely on the shoulders of the F-4G Wild Weasels and the air force's own electronic warfare aircraft. However, the Israelis were interested in the design and some types were said to have been purchased for use as the basis for that country's Samson UAV.

The major breakthrough in designing UAVs for the SEAD mission came for the USAF in the 1970s with the development of the BGM-34B Firebee. Experiments were performed with the drone outfitted with a single AGM-65 Maverick air-to-ground missiles and Mk.82 gravity bombs, the logic being for the drone to fly towards the air defences and then to attack them with their weapons. Despite the combination being used experimentally during the Vietnam War, the design was too late for that conflict. The Israelis however were once again quick to see an opportunity and experimented with their own BGM-34A drones carrying the Maverick and sending back TV pictures of possible targets. These same pictures were also sent to the

Mavericks' guidance system. The Maverick-Firebee combination had several applications and one of these was SEAD.

There is no doubt that the UAV has much to offer the SEAD mission; its disposability being one of its key attributes. If UAVs can be produced *en masse* for the SEAD role, it may be possible to deploy huge quantities to swarm them over an enemy's air defences and overwhelm them. For this to become a reality, the technology has to be as least as reliable as current manned SEAD platforms, if not more so, and also cheaper. What is more, UAVs performing the SEAD mission would have to accommodate intricate software capable of making the correct decision on what is an air defence site and what is not, and to then attack in a timely manner. Such software could prove fiendishly expensive to develop and may become more expensive than designing a SEAD equivalent of an existing combat aircraft. Datalinks to other SEAD platforms would have to be robust to ensure that the SEAD UAV could share its information with other aircraft and individuals. The SEAD UAV will need to be able to shoot ARMs, look for hostile emitters, and prioritise the most dangerous; it will also need to hand-off targets to other platforms, receive and action information arriving from other sources or platforms and stay in touch with their controllers. It may need to perform many, if not all of these tasks simultaneously in an environment where the enemy may well be doing their level best to saturate the air with hostile electrons to crash communications links between the UAVs and other SEAD platforms. The reliability of these SEAD UAV's would also have to be extremely high. In cost terms, there is one factor that could play into a SEAD UAV's favour. Such an aircraft could theoretically be packed away into a storage container until it was needed and then unpacked ready for its mission. Operator proficiency could be maintained by the use of simulators of increasing fidelity rather than having to take an aircraft aloft regularly to maintain pilot's ability to fly demanding high-g manoeuvres, thus eliminating the wear and tear that a manned aircraft suffers. Containerising a SEAD UAV would also allow the aircraft to be taken closer to a theatre of operations and to be deployed from there so as to reduce flight times. True, this can also be done with a manned SEAD aircraft, but a pre-packed

UAV pre-equipped with anti-radar missiles would not need the same army of supporting personnel, only those individuals who would unpack the aircraft and ready it for the mission. Communications datalinks could then allow the UAV to be flown from a ground control station miles away from the danger zone.

The precedence for UAV usage for SEAD has already been set, not only with the Israeli and USAF experience but most recently with the use of Predator UAVs to attack anti-aircraft guns during Operation Iraq Freedom. There are some moral and legal issues to be resolved before a UAV becomes a staple part of the SEAD structure. A pilot flying in support of a UN-mandated No Fly Zone over a particular country can make an almost instant decision in accordance with their ROEs if they are suddenly painted by an enemy radar or fired at by an enemy SAM. They can make the judgement as to whether evasive action or a retaliatory shot with an ARM is the most appropriate response for their particular situation.

There are, however, a number of questions that need to be answered before UAVs are deployed. Who would decide on the appropriate level of force to be used if an unmanned aircraft was performing this mission? The UAV's operator or the aircraft itself? Is an operator based thousands of miles from the action in the control centre able to accumulate enough inform-ation to make a rapid, informed and ultimately correct choice as to what level of response is appropriate? What if this decision is taken out of human hands and the UAV decided to launch a missile against the radar system, but the missile goes awry and hits a school. Who is responsible for such a mistake? The air force owning the UAV? The UAV's operator? The missile's manufacturer? The government in command of the air force, or all four? At present, the individual responsible for an aircraft is the pilot in command. Will this still be the case with UAVs performing SEAD? Moreover, would it be appropriate for the UAV to launch a SEAD missile when it would ultimately be extinguishing human life for the defence of a machine? Is not the idea of the SEAD UAV that it would be expendable?

These debates are arguably for some time in the future as the SEAD UAV is still not yet a reality, but as the use of the

Predator has illustrated, it may not be as far away as we think. Eventually, defence planners, strategists, pilots, lawyers and politicians will be faced with the armed UAV and they will have to work out a means of employment for such an aircraft which is both legally and morally acceptable and in accordance with the rules of war.

Until then, there are technical challenges that will have to be surmounted along with the software challenges discussed above. Wild Weasel aircraft are called upon to perform tight and difficult manoeuvres as they engage a SAM launcher and avoid being shot down themselves. Dextrous aircraft handling, lightning reflexes and quick decision-making are prerequisites for the pilot, while the SEAD UAV will have to retain airmanship that is at least as good if not better than the human pilot and be able to perform such manoeuvres without error. Though on the positive side, the absence of a pilot no longer inhibits the g-forces that an aircraft can perform. One possible compromise in any future manned versus unmanned SEAD argument could be to have the UAVs performing the electronic attack and intelligence-gathering portion of the mission, while the pilot still flies the aircraft and performs the kinetic kill.

Other design challenges include the ordnance required to perform the mission. With the exception of the Global Hawk, current UAVs are not exactly large yet a SEAD UAV would need to carry the array of electronic countermeasures, HARM Targeting System, or equivalent, and the anti-radar missiles that their manned cousins currently carry, although future miniaturisation of ordnance may reduce the size of the electronics required for the mission thus alleviating this problem.

We can already see one glimpse into the future possibilities of the SEAD UAV. There is a pan-European project called nEUROn involving a cluster of European aviation contractors to develop a technology demonstrator to prove a number of concepts for a future unmanned strike aircraft. The programme involves Dassault, EADS and Thales of France, Saab of Sweden, Alenia Aeronautica of Italy, EADS CASA of Spain, EAB of Greece, RUAG of Switzerland. Concept drawings for the aircraft display a Manta-Ray shape with a recessed air intake and the first flights of the technology demonstrator are expected in early

2010. The project has defence suppression as one of its key concepts. The shape and materials used for the nEUROn make it particularly stealthy which is of course a great benefit in performing the SEAD mission. However, the main aim of nEUROn is not to build a concept aircraft capable of performing single missions and the SEAD role is one that will be subsumed into a number of air-to-ground operations which the UCAV could reasonably be expected to perform. Not only is the programme intended to develop the air-to-ground concept for a stealthy UAV but also to demonstrate that it can be done at a reasonable cost. Should nEUROn become a reality then it is possible that some of the SEAD burden could be taken up by this design should it ever become a production aircraft.

Nearly seventy years of SEAD have shown some intriguing changes and some intriguing constants. When radar operators are threatened with attack, they switch off their radar. This is unlikely to change in the near future, although the development of the upgrade for the latest incarnation of HARM could go some way to negate this with the use of GPS for targeting, Meanwhile the mission remains as dangerous as ever and the flying skills which it requires are still demanding. The SAM may not have been tamed, but the sacrifices of pilots in World War II, Korea and Vietnam helped to pave the way for innovative tactics which can at least momentarily reduce its dangers. At the same time, the SEAD fight has grown into an all-arms affair – arguably it always was as the commando raids during World War II illustrated. But no longer is the SEAD effort an addition to the prosecution of a wider air campaign, in some cases, notably Bekaa Valley, it has been the air campaign, at least at the start of the fighting. SEAD support is a prerequisite for any offensive air operation be it in the form of electronic attack or kinetic missile kill.

Air defences will of course grow in sophistication. SAMs which can fire on the move could become especially difficult to pinpoint and attack but technological advances will catch up and the advantage that these systems retain through agility will be neutralised. Most importantly, the SEAD fight has shown that a country cannot rely on SAMs alone to prevent its adversary attaining air superiority. SAMs can inflict damage as well as AAA, but as operations over Iraq and the Balkans have shown most recently, missile launches may lack guidance and air defenders may spend much of their time contemplating how to stay alive in the face of an adversary with a robust SEAD force. In this respect SEAD initiatives have worked very well over the past years in forcing an adversary to change their behaviour to the benefit of the attacking force. Nobody knows how SEAD will change in the future, what new tactics, weapons and platforms may be applied to the fight, but one thing remains certain: the game of cat and mouse will continue.

Glossary

AAA	Anti-aircraft Artillery
ACC	Air Combat Command
ADC	Air Defence Command
AdlA	French Air Force
ADOC	Air Defence Operations Centre
ADS	Air Defence Sector
AESA	Active Electronically-Scanned Array
AFB	Air Force Base
AAGM	Advanced Anti-Radiation Guided Missile
ALARM	Air-Launched Anti-Radiation Missile
ALCM	Air-Launched Cruise Missile
APC	Armoured Personnel Carrier
ATACMS	Air TACtical Missile System
BDA	Battle Damage Assessment
BRoach	Bomb Royal Ordance Augmented CHarge
BSA	Bosnian-Serb Army
C2	Command and Control
CAOC	Combined Air Operations Centre
CAP	Combat Air Patrol
CAR	Central African Republic
CAS	Close Air Support
CENTAF	Central Command Air Forces
CIA	Central Intelligence Agency
CoG	Centres of Gravity
CRT	Cathode Ray Tube
DMZ	DeMilitarized Zone
DoD	Department of Defense (US)
ECM	Electronic Countermeasure

EEPROM	Electronically Erasable/Programmable Read Only Memory
EW	Early Warning
ELINT	ELectronic INTelligence
FAN	Forces Armêe du Nord
FEBA	Forward Edge of the Battle Area
FW	Fighter Wing
GBAD	Ground-Based Air Defence
GSConOps	Global Strike Concept of Operations
HARM	High-speed Anti-Radiation Missile
HDAM	HARM Destruction of enemy air defence Attack Module
HTS	HARM Targeting System
HUMINT	HUman INTelligence
IAF	Indian Air Force
IAFADC	Iraqi Air Force Air Defence Command
IADS	Integrated Air Defence System
ICAP	Improved CAPability
IDF/AF	Israeli Defence Force/Air Force
IDM	Integrated Data Modem
IFOR	Implementation Force
IGB	Inner German Border
IOC	Intercept Operations Centre
IR	Infra-Red
IrAF	Iraqi Air Force
ISR	Intelligence Surveillance Reconnaissance
JDAM	Joint Direct Attack Munition
KTO	Kosovo Theatre of Operations
LANTIRN	Low-Altitude Navigation and Targeting Infra-Red for Night
MANPADS	Man-Portable Air Defence System
MARTEL	Missile Anti-Radar Television
MFAS	Marine Fighter Attack Squadron
MIZ	Missile Impact Zone
MoD	Ministry of Defence (UK)
MRCA	Multi-Role Combat Aircraft
MRD	Motorised Rifle Division
MTEWS	Marine Tactical Electronic Warfare Squadron
NFZ	No-Fly Zone

NNFZ	Northern No-Fly Zone
ODF	Operation Deliberate Force
OIF	Operation Iraqi Freedom
PAVN	People's Army of Vietnam
PAF	Pakistan Air Force
PGM	Precision Guided Munition
PLO	Palestinian Liberation Organisation
PRU	Photo-Reconnaissance Unit
PSAB	Prince Sultan Air Base
RAF	Royal Air Force
RHAWS	Radar Homing and Warning System
ROE	Rules of Engagement
RWR	Radar Warning Receiver
SADF	South African Defence Force
SADS	Soviet Air Defence Simulator
SAM	Surface-to-Air Missile
SDB	Small Diameter Bomb
SEAD	Suppression of Enemy Air Defence
SNFZ	Southern No-Fly Zone
SoAAF	South African Air Force
SOC	Sector Operations Centre
SOF	Special Operations Forces
SLCM	Sea-Launched Cruise Missile
SuperMEZ	Super Missile Engagement Zone
SWAPO	South West Africa People's Organisation
SWP	Surprise-Weight-Persistence
TEWS	Tactical Electronic Warfare Squadron
TFW	Tactical Fighter Wing
TLAM	Tomahawk Land Attack Missile
TOO	Target of Opportunity
UAV	Unmanned Air Vehicle
UCAV	Unmanned Combat Air Vehicle
UCK	Kosovar Liberation Army
UN	United Nations
UNPROFOR	UN Protection Force
UNSCOM	United Nations Special Commission
USAAF	United States Army Air Force
USAF	United States Air Force
USMC	United States Marine Corps

USN	United States Navy
VVS	Soviet Air Force
WARPAC	WARsaw Pact
WMD	Weapons of Mass Destruction
WWS	Wild Weasel Squadron
Z	Zulu (Greenwich Mean) time

Index

101st Airborne Division, US Army;149, 213

1025th Fighter Squadron Libyan Air Force; 133

11th Attack Helicopter Regiment, US Army; 213

11th Aviation Group, US Army; 213

12th Airborne Command and Control Squadron, US Air Force; 183

12th Tactical Fighter Wing, US Air Force; 60

13th 'Panthers' Fighter Squadron USAF; 162

13th Tactical Fighter Squadron, USAF; 52, 54

14th 'Fightin' Samurai' Fighter Squadron, USAF; 162, 207

157th Fighter Squadron, USAF; 163, 207

15th Tactical Fighter Wing, USAF; 36

16 Squadron, Indian Air Force; 117

169th Fighter Wing, USAF; 163

16th Reconnaissance Squadron, US Army Air Force; 22, 29

17th 'Wild Weasel' Tactical Fighter Squadron, USAF; 59, 60, 64

20 Squadron, RAF; 159

20th Fighter Wing, USAF; 138,163, 198

20th Special Operation Squadron, USAF; 149

214th Field Artillery Brigade, US Army; 213

22nd 'Stingers' Fighter Squadron, USAF; 163, 197, 198, 207

23rd 'Fighting Hawks' Fighter

Squadron, USAF; 163, 169, 170, 171, 173, 176, 179, 207

28th Bomb Wing, USAF; 180

2nd Air Division, USAF; 43

32 Fighter Ground Attack Wing, Pakistan Air Force; 118

332nd Air Expeditionary Group, USAF; 198

335th Fighter Squadron, USAF; 197

336th Fighter Squadron, USAF; 197

347th Tactical Fighter Wing, USAF; 61

354th Tactical Fighter Squadron, USAF; 54

354th Tactical Fighter Squadron, USAF; 54, 59

355th Tactical Fighter Wing, USAF;41, 59, 60

357th Tactical Fighter Squadron, USAF; 54, 55

35th Tactical Fighter Wing, USAF; 64, 162

366th 'Thunderbolts' Fighter Squadron, USAF; 60, 163

37th Tactical Fighter Wing, USAF; 110, 150

388th Tactical Fighter Wing, USAF; 41, 52, 59

393rd Bomb Squadron, USAF;189

39th Air and Space Expeditionary Wing, USAF; 110, 197

415th Tactical Fighter Squadron, USAF; 150

42nd Electronic Combat Squadron, USAF; 138

4404th Provisional Wing; 192

44th Tactical Fighter Squadron, USAF; 59

4537th Fighter Weapons School, USAF; 50, 61

48th Tactical Fighter Wing, USAF; 138

492nd Fighter Squadron, USAF; 184, 198

494th Fighter Squadron, USAF; 174, 184, 197, 198

49th Fighter Wing, USAF; 179, 185

51 Squadron, RAF; 18, 210

52nd Fighter Wing, USAF; 163

52nd Tactical Fighter Wing, USAF; 163

55th Wing, USAF; 162, 210

561st Tactical Fighter Squadron, USAF; 60, 64

561st Tactical Fighter Squadron, USAF; 60, 64, 110

562nd Tactical Fighter Squadron, USAF; 64, 110

57th Fighter Weapons Wing, USAF; 61

58th Bomb Wing, USAF; 180

596th Bomb Squadron, USAF; 151

5N62 'Square Pair' radar; 133, 134

5th Allied Tactical Air Force;175

6010th Provisional Wild Weasel Squadron, USAF; 59

6234th Tactical Fighter Wing Wild Weasel Detachment, USAF; 41, 42, 43, 52

66th Fighter Weapons School, USAF; 61

763rd Expeditionary Reconnaissance Squadron, USAF; 198

77th 'Gamblers' Fighter Squadron, USAF; 162, 207, 208

78th 'Bushmasters' Fighter Squadron, USAF; 163, 179

79th 'Tigers' Fighter
Squadron, USAF; 163
80th Tactical Fighter
Squadron, USAF; 61
81st Tactical Fighter
Squadron, USAF; 106, 110
90th Tactical Fighter
Squadron, USAF; 110, 111
93rd Bomb Squadron, USAF;
213
98th Reconnaissance Wing,
Soviet Air Force; 101
9K31 Strela/SA-9 'Gaskin'
Surface-to-Air Missile; 83,
105, 123, 127, 146, 165, 168,
177, 204
9K310 Igla-1/SA-16 'Gimlet'
Surface-to-Air Missile; 146,
165, 204
9K32 Strela/SA-7 Surface-to-
Air Missile; 73, 74, 75, 83,
105, 122, 127, 146, 165, 169,
204
9K33 Osa/SA-8 'Gecko'
Surface-to-Air Missile; 82,
87, 105, 131, 136, 146, 204
9M714U Totshka/SS-21
'Scarab' Surface-to-Surface
Missile; 99
Abu Nidal; 80, 81, 135
Abu Suweir; 67
Achille Lauro; 135
Adan, General Abraham;
Israeli Army; 77
Adler Tag; 16
Aero L-29 Delfin; 78
Afghanistan; 10, 63, 76, 101,
160, 189, 190
AGM-114 Hellfire Air-to-
Ground Missile; 149, 150,
212
AGM-130 air-to-ground
missile; 184, 193, 199, 201,
203
AGM-154 Joint Stand-Off
Weapon; 184
AGM-45 Shrike Anti-
Radiation Missile; 40, 46,
47, 49, 51, 52, 53, 54, 55, 61,
74, 76, 95, 103, 109, 124,
125, 139, 142
AGM-65 Maverick air-to-
ground missile; 85, 108,
109, 110, 212, 230, 231
AGM-78 'Standard' Anti-
Radiation Missile; 40, 43,
49, 54, 58, 85, 103, 107, 109,
115, 159
AGM-84 Harpoon Anti-Ship
Missile; 134
AGM-86 Conventional Air
Launched Cruise Missile;
151, 180, 196

AGM-88 HARM Destruction
of enemy air defence
Attack Module (HDAM);
225, 226, 227, 228
AGM-88 High-speed Anti-
Radiation Missile; 2, 3,
101, 104, 108, 109, 112, 113,
114, 138, 139, 140, 142, 153,
154, 155, 157, 160, 163, 167,
169, 170, 171, 175, 183, 184,
190, 193, 195, 199, 200, 202,
203, 205, 207, 212, 225, 226,
227, 233, 234
Agnellia, Susanna, Italian
Foreign Minister; 173
Agra AFB, India; 118, 120
Ahmed Al Jaber AFB, Kuwait;
198
AIM-7 Sparrow Air-to-Air
Missile, 46, 108
AIM-9 Sidewinder Air-to-Air
Missile; 56, 108, 176
Airborne Laser, 218
Air-Launched Anti-Radiation
Missile (ALARM); 158,
159, 209, 212
Ajlun, Jordan; 68
Akwal, Pakistan; 117
Al Amarah, Iraq; 193, 200, 205,
212
Al Asa AFB, Iraq; 160
Al Asad AFB, Iraq; 159
Al Dhahran AFB, Saudi
Arabia; 192
Al Haswah, Iraq; 213
Al Iskandariyah, Iraq; 160, 201
Al Kark, Iraq; 155
Al Kufah, Iraq; 159
Al Minya, Egypt; 68
Al Musayib, Iraq; 159
Al Qaim, Iraq 159
Al Sadat, Muhammad Anwar,
Egyptian President; 70
Al Taqaddum, 155, 159
Al Udeid AFB, Qatar; 207, 208,
210
Al-Assad, Hafez , Syrian
President; 80
Al-Aziziyah, Libya; 139, 141
Alexandria, Egypt; 71
Ali Al Salem, Kuwait; 198, 210
Al-Qaeda; 189
Al-Sadat, Muhammad Anwar,
Vice President of Egypt; 70
Ambala AFB, India; 120
Amman, Jordan; 68
Amritsar AFB, India; 120
AN/AAQ-28 Litening-II
Targeting Pod; 207
AN/AAQ-28 Litening-II
Targeting pod; 207, 213
AN/ADM-141 Tactical Air-

Launched Decoy; 156, 168,
173, 176, 209
AN/ALE-20 Flare Dispenser;
62
AN/ALQ-101 Electronic
Countermeasures pod; 57
AN/ALQ-101 Electronic
Countermeasures pod; 71
AN/ALQ-105 Electronic
Countermeasures pod, 57
AN/ALQ-119V-17 Electronic
Countermeasures system;
110
AN/ALQ-131 Electronic
Countermeasures system;
110
AN/ALQ-218 Digital Reciever
system; 224, 225
AN/ALQ-227
Communications
Countermeasures system;
221
AN/ALQ-99 Tactical
Jamming System; 112, 142,
176, 221, 222, 224
AN/ALR-18 Reciever system;
62
AN/ALR-31
Countermeasures
Receiving system; 51, 108
AN/ALR-53
Countermeasures
Receiving system; 107
AN/ALR-74 Radar Warning
Reciever; 107
AN/ALT-22 Jamming system;
62
AN/ALT-32L Electronic
Countermeasures system;
62
AN/ALT-6B Multi-Band
Jammer; 62
AN/APG-79 Active
Electronically Scanned
Array radar; 222
AN/APR-25 Radar Signal
Detecting set; 40, 41, 50,
51, 53, 57, 60, 62
AN/APR-26 Surface-to-Air
Missile Launch Warning
Set; 38, 50, 52
AN/APR-31 Radar Homing
and Warning System; 57
AN/APR-38 Radar Homing
and Warning System; 108,
109, 114, 140
AN/APR-47 Radar Homing
and Warning System; 108,
114, 157
AN/APR-47 Radar Homing
And Warning System; 114,
115
AN/APS-107

Countermeasures system; 54, 107
AN/ASN-123 Tactical Doppler/Inertial Navigation set; 225
AN/ASQ-213 HARM Targeting System; 101, 163, 233
AN/AVQ-26 PAVE TACK Targeting system; 112
AN/AWG-25 Command Launch Computer, 113
AN/MPQ-33 radar; 103
AN/MPQ-34 Radar, 103
AN/MPQ-39 Radar, 103
AN/MPQ-46 Radar, 103
AN/MPQ-48 Radar, 103
AN/MPQ-53 Radar, 104
AN/TPS-43 Radar; 104, 124
AN/TPS-44 Radar; 104, 124
AN/USQ-113 Communications Jammer; 225
Anderson AFB, Guam; 41
Angola; 121, 122, 123
Antonov An-12C/D; 99
Argentine Air Force; 123
Argentine Naval Aviation; 123
Argov, Shlomo, Israeli Ambassador to the United Kingdom; 81
Armstrong Whitworth-Whitley, 18
AS 37 Martel Anti-Radiation Missile; 124, 129, 130, 131, 132
As Salman, Iraq; 205
As Samawah, Iraq; 213
As Shuaybah, Iraq; 201, 202
AS-30 Air-to-Ground Missile; 123
Aswan Dam, Egypt; 71
Australia; 148
Aviano AFB, Italy; 168, 169, 172, 175, 176, 179, 180, 184
Avro Lancaster, 17, 19
Avro Vulcan, 124, 125, 126
Awantipur AFB, India; 120
Az Zubayr, Iraq; 205
AZ-EL radar location system; 50

Badin, Pakistan; 117, 119
BAE Systems Nimrod R1; 158
BAE Systems/McDonnell Douglas Harrier GR3; 94, 124, 125
Baghdad, Iraq; 115, 150, 153, 154, 155, 156, 158, 159, 193, 195, 196, 200, 201, 202, 205, 208, 209, 211, 213
Bahrain; 147, 219

Baldwin, Stanley, British Prime Minister; 17
Bangui AFB, Central African Republic; 128, 130, 131
Banja Luka, Bosnia; 166, 173
Bareilly AFB, India; 117
Bartholomew, Reginald, US Ambassador to Italy;172
Basrah, Iraq; 154, 192, 199, 201, 202, 204, 212
Battle of Britain; 15, 16
Begin, Menachem, Israeli Prime Minister; 81
Beirut, Lebanon; 81, 82, 83, 86, 87, 126
Bekaa Valley, Lebanon; 63, 81, 82, 83, 84, 85, 86, 87, 88, 89, 90, 115, 137, 142, 152, 154, 234
Belgrade, Yugoslavia/Serbia;164, 165, 168, 178, 184, 216
Benghazi, 136, 138, 139, 142
Benina AFB, Libya; 137, 139, 140
Berlin, Germany; 16, 135
BGM-109 Tomahawk Land Attack Missile; 172, 173, 180, 208
BGM-34 Firebee drone; 76, 209
Bhuj AFB, India; 118
Bikaner AFB, India; 120
Bilbeis AFB, Egypt; 68
Bir Gifgafa AFB, Egypt; 67
Bir Thamada AFB, Egypt; 67
Blackburn Buccaneer; 122
Blair, Tony, British Prime Minister; 197
BLU-107 Durandel Anti-Runway bomb; 67
Boeing B-17 Flying Fortress; 17, 22, 23
Boeing B-52 Stratofortress; 49, 60, 61, 62, 63, 151, 158, 180, 181, 196, 208, 213, 217, 220, 229
Boeing E-3 Sentry; 210, 218
Boeing E-8C JSTARS; 183, 186, 218
Boeing EA-18G Growler; 219, 220, 221
Boeing KC-135 Stratotanker; 167, 192
Boeing RC-707; 83
Bosnia; 115, 164, 165, 166, 167, 169, 170, 171, 173, 175, 177
Bosnian Serb Army (BSA); 164, 165, 166, 167, 168, 169, 170, 171, 172, 173, 174, 176, 177
BQM-74C Chukar drone; 154, 156
Brazilian Air Force; 125

Breguet Atlantique; 128, 130
Brezhnev, Leonid, Soviet President; 79
Brown, Harold, Secretary of the US Air Force; 41
Bruneval, France; 18
Brunswick Corporation Model 150 decoy; 230
Buhayrat Ar Razzazah Lake, Iraq; 212
Bulgaria, 92
Bungress, James R, author of Suppression of Enemy Air Defenses and Joint War Fighting in an Uncertain World; 152
Bush, George W, US President; 191, 192

C-10035 Control Indicator; 113
C-160 Transall; 122, 128, 130
Cairo International Airport, Egypt; 68
Cairo West AFB, Egypt; 67
Cairo, Egypt; 67, 68, 69, 71, 78
Calais, France; 20
Cambodia; 33, 59
Canada; 147, 174
CARPET; 21, 22
Carrier Air Wing-11, US Navy; 198
Carrier Air Wing-5, US Navy; 198
Castle, Flight Lieutenant Dave, RAF; 126
CBU-24 Cluster Bomb; 45, 56
Central African Republic (CAR); 128
Central Front, Germany; 92, 93, 106, 111
Chad;128, 130, 131
Chaff; 20
Chain Home radar; 16, 215
Chak Jhumra AFB, Pakistan; 117
Chhamb Salient, Pakistan; 117
China; 28, 33, 46, 112, 227
Choc Ta Rie, North Korea; 111
Chouf Mountains, Lebanon; 83
Churchill, Winston, British Prime Minister; 19
Clark, Captain Donald, USAF; 43
Clausewitz, Carl von, Prussian Theorist; 5
Clinton, Bill, US President; 179, 197, 205
Cohen, William, US Secretary of State for Defence; 201
Colmar AFB, France; 129
Cox, Charles, Flight Sergeant, RAF; 18

CP-1269 Command Launch Computer; 113
Croatia; 164, 167, 177
Crotale Surface-to-Air Missile; 136, 137, 140
Crowe, Admiral William J, US Chairman of the Joint Chiefs of Staff; 135
Cuba; 32, 35
Cuban Missile Crisis; 32, 34
Czechoslovakia; 92, 98

Dahshur, Egypt; 71
Damascus, Syria; 74, 76, 79, 81, 86, 126
Dassault Mirage; 78, 123, 128, 129, 130, 132, 136, 147, 169, 193
Dassault nEUROn UAV; 233, 234
Dassault Super Etendard; 123
Dawson, Captain Clyde, USAF; 43
Dayan, Moshe, Israeli Defence Minister; 78
Dayton Accords; 169, 175, 177
DBAP-100 Anti-Runway Bomb; 128
Dempster, General KC, USAF; 37, 38, 50
Deptula, Major General David, USAFAir Combat Command Director of Plans and Programs; 218
Destruction of Enemy Air Defences (DEAD); 45, 88, 184, 211
Dijon AFB, France; 129
Dini, Lamberto, Italian Prime Minister; 173
Donji Vakuf, Bosnia; 173
Donovan, Captain Jack, USAF; 41, 42, 50, 51
Dougherty, Major Stanley J, USAF; 4, 7, 8, 9, 10, 12, 13
Douglas A-1 Skyraider; 37
Douglas A-4 Skyhawk; 36, 37, 123
Douglas C-47 Skytrain; 24, 67
Douglas DC-8; 130
Douglas EA-1 Skyraider; 48
Douglas EA-3B Skywarrior; 55
Douglas EB-66 Destroyer; 36, 41, 49, 55, 62
Dover, United Kingdom; 16
Dukanovi?, Milo, President of the Republic of Montenegro; 185 Dunkirk, France; 16 Düppel; 21
EC2/3 Squadron, French Air Force; 169 Edwards AFB, USA; 39 Eglin AFB, USA; 39, 40, 41, 51, 56

Egypt; 66, 67, 68, 69, 70, 71, 72, 73, 74, 76, 77, 78, 82, 90, 121, 136

Egyptian Air Defence Force (ADF); 68, 69, 72
Egyptian Air Force; 67
Eighth Air Force, US Army Air Force; 20, 21, 24
Eisenhower, Dwight D, US President; 33
Eitan, General Rafael, Israeli Chief of Staff; 80
El Arish AFB, Egypt;67
El Qantara, Egypt; 79
Electronic Intelligence (ELINT); 1, 58, 83, 84, 131, 176, 192, 197, 210
Electronically Erasable/Programmable, Read-Only Memory (EEPROM); 113
English Electric Canberra; 117, 118, 119, 122
ER-142 Reciever; 54, 57, 60, 107
Exercise Green Flag; 151
Exercise Red Flag; 111

Fairchild A-10A Thunderbolt; 25, 94, 111, 160
Fairchild AC-119K Stinger; 59
Fairford AFB, United Kingdom; 180
Falkland Islands; 89, 124
Fallujah, Iraq; 213
Falouga, Lebanon; 126
Fan Song' radar; 36, 39, 42, 44, 46, 52, 53
Fantasmagoria Electronic Warfare pod: 104
Fayid AFB, Egypt; 67
Fletcher, Yvonne, British Police Officer; 134
Forces Armêe du Nord (FAN); 128
Ford, Sergeant Kenneth, La Belle Nightclub casualty; 135
FPS-6 radar; 118
France; 16, 24, 26, 132, 147, 152, 174, 177, 181, 192, 196, 233
French Air Force; 127, 128, 129, 130, 131, 132, 136, 169
Freya radar; 17, 18, 21, 28
Fricke, Captain Maurice, USAF; 41
Friedrichshafen, Germany; 19
Fulda Gap, Germany; 105

Gabon; 130
Gaddaffi, Colonel Muammar,

Libyan leader; 127, 128, 132, 133, 134, 135, 138, 141, 144
Gardner, Brian, Flight Lieutenant, RAF; 126
GBU-10 Laser-Guided Bomb; 150, 168, 201, 204
GBU-12 Laser-Guided Bomb; 151, 199, 200, 201, 202, 213
GBU-15 Television/Infra-Red Guided Bomb; 171, 174
GBU-27 Laser Guided Bomb; 208
GBU-28 Laser Guided Bomb; 208
GBU-31 Joint Direct Attack Munition; 189, 212, 216
General Atomics RQ-1A Predator Unmanned Aerial Vehicle; 212
General Dynamics EF-111A, 112, 138, 155, 156, 169, 176
General Dynamics F-111 Aardvark; 112, 142
General Dynamics F-16 Fighting Falcon; 2, 81, 87, 101, 106, 162, 169, 184, 197, 201, 203, 225, 227, 228
George AFB, USA; 64, 110
Gepard Short-Range Air Defence System; 97
Gerber, Colonel David, USAF Global Strike Concept of Operations Champion; 216
Germany; 17, 18, 21, 24, 26, 27, 28, 30, 90, 92, 93, 96, 99, 105, 106, 110, 141, 152, 159, 163, 174, 176, 177, 179, 183, 207
Giolle Del Colle AFB, Italy; 180
Glamoc, Bosnia; 173
Global Strike Concept of Operations, USAF; 215, 216
Glosson, Brigadier General 'Buster', USAF Central Command Air Forces Director of Campaign Plans; 148
Gloster Meteor; 80
Goins, Sergeant James, La Belle Nightclub casualty 135
Golan Heights, Israel; 74
Goodman, Richard, USAF Bombardier/Navigator; 127
Great Bitter Lake, Egypt; 77
Griffin Laser Guided Bomb; 85
Grozade, Bosnia; 166
Grumman A-6 Intruder; 54, 37, 126

Grumman E-2C Hawkeye; 83
Grumman EA-6B Prowler; 3,
  112, 114, 133, 155, 156, 168,
  174, 175, 176, 180, 184, 189,
  197, 198, 199, 200, 203, 207,
  208, 219, 220, 223, 224, 225,
  228
Grumman F-14 Tomcat; 126,
  133
Gulf of Sidra, Libya; 113, 133,
  134, 136, 141
Gulf of Tonkin, Vietnam; 33,
  39

H-2 AFB, Iraq; 160
H-3 AFB, Iraq; 160, 208
Habbaniyah, Iraq; 159
Habré, Hissene, Leader of
  Forces Armêe du Nord;
  128
Haiphong, Vietnam; 35, 61, 63
Halwara AFB, India; 120
Hamburg, Germany; 20
Hammana, Lebanon; 126, 127
Hannay, Nermin; La Belle
  nightclub casualty 135
Hanoi, Vietnam; 33, 35, 36, 42,
  55, 61, 63
Hawthorne Test Range, USA;
  40, 49
Helwan AFB, Egypt; 68, 71
Henry, Lieutenant Larry
  'Poohah', USAF; 148
Herghada AFB, Egypt; 68
Hickham AFB, USA; 41
Holbrooke, Richard , Assistant
  Secretary of State for
  European and Canadian
  Affairs: 174
Holloman AFB, USA; 172
Horner, Lieutenant General
  Charles 'Chuck', USAF
  Commander Central
  Command Air Forces; 148,
  156, 158
Human Intelligence
  (HUMINT); 6
Hungary; 92
Hussein, Qusay, son of
  Saddam Hussein; 208
Hussein, Saddam, Iraqi
  President; 89, 145, 146, 149,
  190, 201, 208
Hussein, Uday, son of Saddam
  Hussein; 208

IAI Kfir; 85
IMI Mastiff Unmanned Aerial
  Vehicle; 84
Inchas AFB, Egypt; 67
Incirlik AFB, Turkey; 196, 197,
  198, 202, 207
India; 116, 117, 120

Indian Air Force; 86, 117, 118,
  120, 121
Inner German Border (IGB);
  92, 95, 98, 105, 106, 111
IR-133 Panoramic Scan
  Reciever; 38, 41, 50, 52
Iraq, 15, 59, 63, 68, 73, 74, 141,
  145, 146, 147, 148, 149, 150,
  151, 152, 153, 154, 155, 156,
  157, 158, 159, 160, 161, 162,
  165, 190, 191, 192, 193, 194,
  195, 196, 197, 198, 199, 200,
  201, 202, 203, 204, 205, 206,
  207, 208, 209, 210, 211, 212,
  213, 214, 216
Iraqi Air Defence Command
  (ADC); 194, 195, 200, 201,
  205, 209, 210, 214
Iraqi Air Force (IrAF); 147,
  192, 195, 202
Iraqi Air Force Air Defence
  Command (IRAFADC);
  146
Iron Hand; 42, 45, 63
IS-91 'Straight Flush' radar; 3,
  72, 131, 182
Islamabad, Pakistan; 119
Ismailia, Egypt;, 72
Israel; 66, 67, 69, 70, 71, 72, 74,
  75, 78, 79, 80, 81, 82, 85, 87,
  88, 89, 115, 121, 126, 207
Israeli Army; 66, 75, 79, 86
Israeli Defence Force/Air
  Force (IDF/AF); 66, 67, 68,
  69, 70, 71, 72, 73, 74, 75, 76,
  77, 78, 79, 81, 83, 84, 86, 87,
  88, 89, 120, 123
Italian Air Force; 180
Italy; 23, 147, 166, 169, 172,
  173, 174, 176, 177, 233

Jabal al Knaisse, Lebanon; 126
Jaisalmer AFB, India; 118, 120
Jammu, India; 116
Jamnagar AFB, India; 118
Japan; 28, 29, 31, 61, 111, 162,
  207
Jebel Libni AFB; Egypt; 67
Jodhpur AFB, India; 120
Johnson, Captain Harold,
  USAF; 54
Johnson, Lyndon B, US
  President; 34, 58, 59, 60
Jordan; 66, 67, 68, 69, 70, 71,
  73, 208
Jumper, General John, USAF
  Chief of Staff; 185, 216

KA-71 Motion Picture
  Camera; 50
Kabrit AFB, Egypt; 67
Kadena AFB, Japan; 61, 111

Kandahar, Afghanistan; 101,
  189
KARI Iraqi Air Defence
  system; 147
Karkuk, Iraq; 205
Kashmir, India; 116, 117
Kep AFB, Vietnam; 42
Kerr, Captain George, USAF;
  41, 50
Kh-23/AS-7 'Kerry' Air-to-
  Ground Missile; 103
Kh-24 Air-to-Ground Missile;
  102, 103
Kh-25 Air-to-Ground Missile;
  102, 103
Kh-27/AS-10 'Karen' Anti-
  Radiation Missile; 102, 103
Kh-28/AS-9 'Kyle' Anti-
  Radiation Missile; 95, 100,
  102
Kh-31AS-17 'Krypton' Anti-
  Radiation Missile; 101, 104
Kh-58/AS-11 'Kilter' Anti-
  Radiation Missile; 101,
  103, 104, 105
Khamis Mushait AFB, Saudi
  Arabia; 150
Khan, Mohammad Ayub,
  Prime Minister of
  Pakistan; 116
Khost, Afghanistan; 101
Klinghoffer, Leon, Achille
  Lauro passenger; 135
Korat AFB, Thailand; 41, 51,
  52, 55, 59, 60
Kosovo Theatre of Operations
  (KTO); 178, 179, 183, 185,
  186
Kosovo; 177, 178, 182, 183, 216,
  226
Kropuik, Colonel Kim, USAF;
  40
KS-19 Anti-Aircraft Artillery;
  39, 189
Kuwait; 145, 147, 148, 149, 154,
  157, 160, 196, 198, 207, 209,
  210, 216

La Belle Nightclub, Germany;
  135
Laarbruch, Germany; 159
Lackman, Flight Officer Chris,
  RAF; 126
Lakenheath AFB, United
  Kingdom; 138, 184
Lamb, Captain Al, USAF; 41,
  42, 50
Land Roll' radar; 82
Lange, Lieutenant Mark A.,
  US Navy; 127
Laos; 33, 59
LAU-3 Rocket; 42, 52
Le Havre, France; 18

Lebanon; 80, 81, 82, 83, 86, 87, 89, 126, 135, 144
Libreville, Gabon; 130
Libya; 113, 114, 127, 128, 132, 133, 135, 136, 137, 138, 142, 143, 144, 152
Libyan Air Force; 133, 136
Liddell-Hart, Basil, British military theorist; 7, 8
Lifsey, Captain Walt, USAF; 41, 50
Lisina, Bosnia; 173, 174
Litani River, Lebanon; 82
Lockheed AC-130U Spooky, 59
Lockheed C-5A Galaxy; 132
Lockheed EC-121 Warning Star; 55
Lockheed EC-130 Compass Call; 151, 155, 156, 169, 176, 180, 189
Lockheed EP-3 Aries-II; 210
Lockheed F-104A Starfighter; 120
Lockheed F-117A Nighthawk; 12, 150, 155, 171, 172, 173, 174, 185, 186, 198
Lockheed Martin F -22A Raptor; 12, 215, 217, 218
Lockheed Martin F-35 Lightning-II; 12, 217, 223
Lockheed SR-71A Blackbird; 111
Lockheed U-2; 31, 32, 46, 218
London, United Kingdom; 16, 81, 134, 196
Lorence, Captain Paul F. USAF;141
Low Blow' radar; 58, 70, 182
Luftwaffe; 15, 16, 17, 20, 22, 27, 163, 176, 180, 215
Luxor AFB, Egypt; 68
Luxueil AFB, France 129

M117 Bomb; 71
M230 Chain Gun; 150
M260, 150
M270 'Hydra' Rocket; 152
M-39 Army Tactical Missile System; 213
M61 Gatling Gun; 51, 54
Madden, Captain Donald, USAF; 41
Mafraq AFB, Jordan; 68
Mahmoud, Lieutenant General Sidqi, Egyptian Air Force Chief of Staff; 67
Majikici, Bosnia; 173
MANDRELL; 22
Manoeuvrist Approach to SEAD; 7, 8, 9, 10, 11, 13, 14, 94, 148, 151, 153, 211
Mansura AFB, Egypt; 68

Masroor AFB, Pakistan; 118
McConnell AFB, USA; 49, 60
McDonnell Douglas ADM-20B Quail, 229
McDonnell Douglas AH-64 Apache; 149, 151, 213
McDonnell Douglas F/A-18 Hornet; 114, 134, 155, 163, 175, 184, 198, 200, 203, 207, 217, 219, 220, 221, 222, 228
McDonnell Douglas F-15; 87, 106, 159, 171, 174, 198
McDonnell Douglas F-4 Phantom; 36, 37, 50, 51, 59, 60, 63, 64, 69, 71, 72, 74, 75, 83, 85, 87, 100, 106, 107, 108, 109, 110, 111, 112, 114, 141, 157, 162, 192, 230
McDonnell Douglas F-4G Advanced Wild Weasel; 64, 107
McDonnell Douglas KC-10 Extender; 167, 218
McDougall, Squadron Leader Neil, RAF; 125, 126
McEntire AFB, USA; 163
McNamara, Robert, US Secretary of State for Defence; 35
Mghite, Lebanon; 126
MiG-17, 54
MiG-19, 69
MiG-21, 69, 82
MiG-23; 82, 103, 140
MiG-25; 100, 101, 104, 133, 147, 193,
MiG-27; 102
MiG-27; 102, 103
MiG-29; 105, 147
Mil Mi-8; 78, 81
Mildenhall AFB, United Kingdom; 169, 176
Milosevic, Slobodan, President of Yugoslavia and Serbia; 89, 179, 181
MIM-104 Patriot Surface-to-Air Missile; 104, 207
MIM-14 Nike Hercules Surface-to-Air Missile; 27, 97
MIM-23 Hawk Surface-to-Air Missile; 23, 37, 55, 74, 97, 98, 100, 103, 104, 146, 233
Minh, Ho Chi, President of North Vietnam; 33, 34, 35
Misawa AFB, Japan; 162, 207
Mitterrand, Francois, French President; 127
Mk.82 Bomb; 45, 126, 139, 230
Mladic, Najor General Ratko, Bosnian Serb Army Chief of Staff; 170

Mohawk Midgetape 400 Tape Recorder; 38
Moltke, Field Marshall Helmuth von Moltke, Military theorist; 9
Monchegorsk, Soviet Union/Russia; 101
Mont-de-Marsan AFB, France; 132
Moseley, Lieutenant-General Michael 'Buzz' , USAF; 206
Mosul, Iraq; 199, 200, 201, 202, 203, 204, 205
Mount Hermon, Lebanon; 82
Mount Igman, Bosnia; 168
Mount Jahorina, Bosnia; 168
Mount Svinjar, Bosnia; 173
Mountain Home AFB, USA; 163
Mrkonjic, Bosnia; 173, 174
Mujahideen; 76, 101, 190
Mukhayb, Iraq; 205
Mullen, Admiral Michael G., US Navy Chief of Naval Operations; 223
Murat Sidi Bilal, Libya; 139, 141
Murmansk, Russia/Soviet Union; 101
Muzalbah, Iraq; 202

N'Djamena, Chad; 128, 130, 131, 132
Nabatieh, Lebanon; 82
Najaf, Iraq; 193, 205, 213
Namibia; 121
Nancy AFB, France; 129, 130
Nasiriya, Iraq; 193
NATO Implementation Force (IFOR); 175
Nellis AFB, USA; 49, 50, 51, 52, 61, 64, 110, 111, 132, 152
Netherlands; 24, 174
Nickel Grass; 80
Nixon, Richard M, US President; 58, 59, 61, 63, 79
No Fly Zone (NFZ); 191, 192, 193, 196, 197, 198, 199, 200, 203, 204, 205, 206, 208, 210, 214
North American F-100F Super Sabre; 37, 41, 42, 44, 51, 64
North American T-39F; 40, 49
North Atlantic Treaty Organisation (NATO); 3, 31, 72, 82, 90, 92, 93, 94, 95, 96, 97, 98, 99, 100, 101, 102, 103, 105, 106, 112, 137, 162, 163, 164, 165, 166, 167, 168, 169, 170, 171, 173, 174, 175, 176, 177, 178, 179, 180, 181, 182, 183, 184, 185, 186, 201, 203, 215, 216

North Vietnamese Army (NVA); 35, 36, 39, 49, 52, 54, 57, 59, 60
Northrop B-2A Spirit; 12, 189, 215
Northrop Grumman RQ-4A Global Hawk Unmanned Aerial Vehicle; 218
Norway; 174
Nukhayb, Iraq; 150

O'Grady, Captain Scott F. USAF; 166
Oman; 196
Operation Allied Force; 76, 177, 180, 216, 219
Operation Attain Document; 133
Operation Badr; 74
Operation Black Buck; 123
Operation Dead Eye; 166, 168, 170, 173, 174, 175
Operation Deliberate Force; 76, 163, 170, 179, 226
Operation Deny Flight; 164
Operation Desert Fox; 196, 197, 201, 214
Operation Desert Shield; 148
Operation Desert Storm;15, 26, 76, 77, 114, 146, 148, 150, 151, 152, 154, 161, 162, 163, 166, 172, 178, 181, 182, 187, 190, 191, 192, 195, 200, 204, 209, 210, 211, 214, 216, 219, 228
Operation Dugman; 74
Operation Eldorado Canyon; 114, 135
Operation Enduring Freedom; 63, 189
Operation Focus; 67
Operation Iraqi Freedom; 15, 190, 204, 206, 207, 214, 216
Operation Linebacker; 60, 61, 62, 64, 65
Operation Mivtza Moked; 67
Operation Noble Anvil; 180
Operation Northern Watch; 192, 196
Operation Overlord; 20
Operation Peace for Galilee; 66, 80, 81, 85, 87, 88, 89, 90, 228
Operation Protea; 123
Operation Provide Comfort; 192
Operation Reindeer; 122
Operation Rolling Thunder; 34, 36, 37, 42, 216
Operation Scathe Mean; 153, 154, 228
Operation Senior Surprise; 151

Operation Southern Focus; 206, 207
Oslo Report; 18
Ouaddi Doum, Chad; 128, 130, 133
Oum Chalouba, Chad; 128

P-12 'Spoon Rest' radar; 36, 70, 72, 137, 150
P-14 'Tall King' radar; 137, 138, 139
P-15/-19 'Flat Face' radar; 57, 58, 70, 72, 131, 132, 137, 140, 150
P-15M(2) 'Squat Eye' radar; 149
P-35/-37 'Bar Lock' radar; 120, 122, 137, 140
P-37 radar; 137
P-40 'Long Track' radar; 72
Pakistan Air Force (PAF); 117, 118, 119, 120, 121
Pakistan; 32, 101, 102, 116, 117, 118, 119, 120
Palestinian Liberation Organisation (PLO); 80
Panavia Tornado; 158, 159, 176, 180, 196, 198, 200, 201, 203, 209, 228
Parachute Regiment, British Army; 18
Pathankot AFB, India; 120
People's Army of Vietnam (PAVN); 34, 36, 37, 38, 39, 42, 43, 44, 45, 47, 48, 53, 54, 57, 58, 60, 61, 62, 63
Perry, William, US Secretary of State for Defence; 172
Pevensey, United Kingdom; 16
Photo Recconaissance Unit, RAF; 18, 19
Piacenza AFB, Italy; 176, 180
Pickard, Wing Commander PC, RAF; 18
Pitchford, Captain John, USAF; 41, 42, 43
POLYGONE EW Range, France/Germany; 152
Port Said, Egypt; 77, 78, 79
Portugal; 174
Prince Sultan AFB, Saudi Arabia; 197, 198, 207, 210
PRV-11 'Side Net' radar; 57, 70, 72

Qatar; 147, 207
QRC-253-2 Radar Homing system; 37
QRC-317A SEE-SAMS system; 51
Qubaysah, Iraq; 160

Rambouillet, France;177
Rann of Kutch, India; 116
Rapier Surface-to-Air Missile; 97
Ras Banas AFB, Egypt; 68
Ras el Sadat, Egypt; 69
Ras Gharib, Egypt; 70
RC-135V, 169, 176, 180, 192, 198, 210
Reagan, Ronald, US President;126, 133, 135, 190
Red Sea, Egypt; 71, 208
Republic F-105 Thunderchief; 37, 42, 43, 44, 49, 50, 51, 52, 54, 55, 56, 57, 59, 60, 63, 64, 106, 107, 108
Rhein-Main AFB, Germany; 183
Ribas-Dominicci, Major Fernando L, USAF; 141
Robinson, Major Bill, USAF; 53
Rogers, William, US Secretary of State; 71
Roland Surface-to-Air Missile; 97, 146, 147, 199, 205
Romania; 92
Royal Air Force (RAF); 15, 16, 18, 19, 23, 29, 94, 123, 124, 138, 158, 169, 176, 180, 184, 198, 209, 210
Royal Jordanian Air Force; 68
Royal Navy; 123
RPK-2 'Gun Dish' radar; 73, 123
Rumsfeld, Donald, US Secretary of State for Defence; 190
Ryan, General Michael E., USAF Commander Allied Air Forces, Southern Europe; 172
Rye, United Kingdom; 16

S-125/SA-3 'Goa' Surface-to-Air Missile; 57, 70, 71, 72, 82, 121, 122, 131, 133, 134, 136, 140, 146, 158, 164, 182, 186, 190, 198, 204, 205
S-200VE/SA-5 'Gammon' Surface-to-Air Missile; 133, 134, 136, 140
S-300MPU/SA-10 'Grumble' Surface-to-Air Missile; 215
S-300V/SA-12 'Giant' Surface-to-Air Missile; 215
S-400/SA-20 'Triumpf' Surface-to-Air Missile; 215
S-75/SA-2 'Guideline' Surface-to-Air Missile; 31, 32, 35, 36, 37, 38, 46, 47, 53, 57, 67, 68, 69, 70, 71, 73, 74, 82, 111, 122, 131, 132, 134, 136,

140, 146, 158, 164, 165, 168, 178, 198, 199, 200, 204, 205, 206, 229
Saigon, Vietnam; 33
Sakesar, Pakistan; 117, 119
Salman Pak, Iraq; 205
Samawa, Iraq; 193
Samson Unmanned Aerial Vehicle; 84, 85, 230
Sandilius, Captiain Ed, USAF; 41
Sarajevo, Bosnia; 164, 167, 168, 169, 170, 174
Sargodha, Pakistan; 117
Saudi Arabia; 67, 147, 150, 154, 159, 192, 197, 219
Schwarzkopf, General Norman N, US Army; 148, 160
Score Board radar; 72
Scout Unmanned Aerial Vehicle; 84
SEPECAT Jaguar; 128, 130, 131
Serbia; 177, 180, 181, 183, 201
Serbian Army; 177
Sharon, General Ariel, Israeli Army; 77
Shastri, Lal Bahadur, Indian Prime Ministeri, 116
Shaw AFB, USA; 31, 162, 179, 207
Short, Lieutenant General Michael C., USAF Commander Allied Forces Southern Europe; 179, 187, 226
Sidon, Lebanon; 82
Signals Intelligence (SIGINT); 95, 130, 131, 143, 144
Sikorsky CH-53D Sea Stallion; 70
Sikorsky MH-53J PAVE LOW; 149
Sikorsky SH-3H Sea King; 127
Sinai Desert, Egypt; 67, 68
Sindh, Pakistan; 117
Singh, Hari, Maharaja; 116
Sipovo, Bosnia; 173
Sirte, Libya; 134, 136, 140
Six Day War; 66, 67, 68, 69, 88, 90, 120
SkyGuard radar; 124
Slovenia; 163, 177
Smith, Admiral Leighton W, Commander-in-Chief US Naval Forces Europe and Allied Forces Southern Europe; 167
Smith, Barry, Flight Lieutenant, RAF; 126
Smith, Lieutenant General Rupert, United Nations

Protection Force Commander; 167
SON-9 'Fire Can' radar, 42, 122
South African Air Force (SoAAF); 121
South African Defence Force; 121
South Korea; 115
South West Africa People's Organisation (SWAPO); 121, 122, 123
Soviet Air Defence Simulator (SADS); 40, 49, 64
Soviet Air Force (VVS); 92, 93, 94, 95, 96, 97, 98, 99, 101, 102
Soviet Union (USSR); 27, 29, 31, 32, 33, 34, 57, 61, 65, 68, 70, 71, 79, 90, 92, 105, 133, 145, 146, 158, 229
Spain; 138, 174, 233
Spangdahlem AFB, Germany; 106, 110, 141, 163, 176, 179, 207
Spanish Air Force, 163, 175
Split, Croatia; 167
SPS-141 Jamming system; 103
SPS-142 Jamming system; 103
SPS-143 Jamming system; 103
Srebrenica, Bosnia; 166
Srinagar, India; 120
SS-1 'Scud' Surface-to-Surface Missile; 149, 155, 159, 207
St. George, AFB, USA; 49
Stancil-Hoffman Tape Recorder; 50
Storm Shadow Cruise Missile; 209
Strategic Air Command (SAC), USAF; 63, 229
Suez Canal, Egypt; 68, 69, 70, 71, 73, 77, 78, 79, 90
Sukhoi Su-24; 101, 103, 105
Super Missile Enagagement Zone (SuperMEZ); 207, 208, 209
Super Oerlikon Anti-Aircraft Artillery; 124
Supermarine Spitfire, 18
Syria; 66, 67, 73, 74, 79, 80, 81, 85, 86, 89
Syrian Arab Air Force (SAAF); 80, 81, 86, 123

Tabuk, Saudi Arabia; 159
Tactical Air Command (TAC), USAF; 31, 63
Taji, Iraq; 155, 158, 205
Takhli AFB, Thailand; 54
Taliban; 189, 190
Talil, Iraq; 199, 200, 201, 203, 205

Taqqadam, Iraq; 155, 159, 205
Task Force Normandy; 149, 150, 159
Tet Offensive; 60
Thailand; 41, 54, 59
Thin Skin' radar; 72
Thunderbird Surface-to-Air Missile; 102
Tikrit, Iraq;145, 213
Tobruk, 136
Tonkin Gulf Resolution; 34
Torodoum, Chad; 128
Trevaskus, 126
Trier, Captain Bob, USAF; 41, 42, 43
Tripoli, Libya; 136, 137, 138, 139, 140, 141, 142, 143
Tsouprake, Flight Lieutenant Rod, RAF; 53
Tupolev Tu-16 'Badger', 95, 97, 100, 101
Tupolev Tu-22 'Blinder', 95
Turkey; 174, 196, 207

Ukraine; 174
United Arab Emirates; 148
United Kingdom; 16, 19, 21, 24, 33, 81, 138, 169, 174, 177, 184, 192, 196, 299;
United Nations (UN); 79, 116, 121, 148, 149, 165, 166, 167, 191, 232
United Nations Protection Force (UNPROFOR); 167, 175
United Nations Special Commission (UNSCOM); 191, 197
United States Air Force; 2, 3, 4, 12, 29, 30, 31, 34, 36, 37, 38, 45, 48, 49, 50, 52, 55, 56, 59, 60, 62, 63, 64, 66, 76, 88, 92, 94, 100, 105, 106, 107, 112, 115, 120, 123, 132, 136, 137, 140, 141, 142, 144, 147, 151, 152, 156, 157, 162, 163, 167, 175, 176, 179, 183, 187, 196, 202, 210, 212, 215, 216, 217, 218, 219, 223, 226, 227, 229, 230, 232
United States Army Air Force; 17, 20, 21, 22, 23, 25, 28, 29
United States Marine Corps; 3, 29, 63, 65, 163, 174, 175, 180, 210, 219, 220, 226, 223
United States Navy; 3, 33, 36, 37, 46, 54, 63, 65, 92, 107, 112, 114, 115, 123, 126, 127, 132, 133, 134, 136, 138, 142, 144, 155, 156, 168, 175, 183, 184, 189, 197, 198, 207, 210, 217, 219, 220, 223, 224, 225, 226

United States of America; 2, 17, 27, 29, 31, 32, 33, 34, 58, 60, 62, 69, 70, 71, 76, 79, 80, 88, 89, 90, 106, 118, 121, 124, 126, 127, 134, 147, 163, 174, 177, 189, 190, 191, 192, 196, 201, 208, 209, 215, 218, 220, 223

Unmanned Aerial Vehicle (UAV); 76, 81, 83, 84, 85, 89, 142, 212, 213, 215, 216, 217, 218, 228, 229, 230, 231, 232, 233, 234

Upper Heyford AFB, United Kingdom; 138

USS America, 114, 133, 175

USS Bunker Hill, 208

USS Cheyenne, 208

USS Coral Sea; 114, 134, 139

USS Cowpens, 208

USS Donald Cook, 208

USS Enterprise, 196, 198

USS John F. Kennedy, 126

USS Kitty Hawk, 198

USS Maddox, 33

USS Milius, 208

USS Montpelier, 208

USS Saratoga, 134

USS Theodore Roosevelt, 175, 180

USS Turner Joy; 33

USS Vinson, 198

Uttarlai, AFB, India; 118, 120

VA-1 'World Watchers' Squadron, US Navy; 210

VA-15 'Valions' Squadron, US Navy; 126

VA-176 'Thunderbolts' Squadron, US Navy; 126

VA-34 'Blue Blasters' Squadron, US Navy; 139

VA-46 'Clansmen' Squadron, US Navy; 139

VA-55 'Warhorses' Squadron, US Navy; 139

VA-72 'Blue Hawks' Squadron, US Navy; 139

VA-75 'The Sunday Punchers' Squadron, US Navy; 55

VA-83 'Rampagers' Squadron, US Navy; 134

VA-85 'Black Falcons' Squadron, US Navy; 126

VA-87 'Golden Warriors' Squadron, US Navy; 126

VAQ-128 Squadron, US Navy; 197, 198

VAQ-129 'Vikings' Squadron, US Navy; 224

VAQ-130 'Zappers' Squadron, US Navy; 198

VAQ-131 'Lancers' Squadron, US Navy; 114

VAQ-135 'Black Ravens' Squadron, US Navy; 139

VAQ-136 'Gauntlets' Squadron, US Navy; 198

VAQ-137 'Rooks' Squadron, US Navy; 224

VAQ-138 'Yellowjackets' Squadron, US Navy; 198

VAQ-139 'Cougars' Squadron, US Navy; 224

VAQ-141 'Shadowhawks' Squadron, US Navy; 180

Vector IV Radar Homing And Warning System; 38

VF-102 'Diamondbacks' Squadron, US Navy; 133

VF-33 'Starfighters' Squadron, US Navy; 133

VFA-105 'Gunslingers' Squadron, US Navy; 198

VFA-132 'Privateers' Squadron, US Navy; 139

VFA-147 'Argonauts' Squadron, US Navy; 198

VFA-148 'Blue Diamonds' Squadron, US Navy; 198

VFA-27 'Royal Maces' Squadron, US Navy; 198

VFA-37 'Ragin' Bulls' Squadron, US Navy; 198

VFMA-533 US Marine Squadron; 175

Vicenza, AFB, Italy; 166

Vickers Wellington; 18

Victor Jones, Reginald, British Assistant Director of Intelligence (Science); 18

Viet Cong; 33, 36, 60

Vietnam; 2, 3, 23, 29, 32, 33, 34, 35, 37, 38, 39, 49, 53, 54, 55, 56, 58, 60, 62, 63, 64, 88, 90, 92, 93, 95, 98, 105, 106, 108, 112, 115, 141, 144, 148, 151, 190, 191, 216, 230, 234

VMAQ-1 US Marine Squadron; 197, 198

VMAQ-2 'Playboys' US Marine Squadron; 139

VMFA-115 US Marine Squadron; 198

VMFA-314 'Black Knights' US Marine Squadron; 198

VMFA-323 'Death Rattlers' US Marine Squadron; 139

Vought A-7 Corsair; 114, 126, 127, 134, 142

Vought F-8 Crusader; 36, 46

War of Attrition; 69, 72

Warsaw Pact (WARPAC); 90, 92, 96, 97, 98, 99

Watt, Sir Robert Watson; 16

Weinberger, Casper W, US Secretary of Defence; 135

Wheeler, General Earle Gilmore, US Army Chairman of the Joint Chiefs of Staff; 34

White, Captain Ed, USAF; 41, 50

Wideawake AFB, Ascension Island; 124, 125

Wild Weasel; 3, 23, 29, 38, 39, 40, 41, 42, 43, 44, 45, 46, 47, 49, 50, 51, 53, 54, 59, 60, 63, 64, 100, 101, 106, 107, 108, 110, 114, 148, 157, 162, 163, 222, 233

Wiliard, Major Garry, USAF; 40

Wilson, Admiral Thomas, Director of Intelligence for the US Joint Chiefs of Staff, 197

WINDOW; 20, 21, 30

World War Two, 1, 15, 17, 28, 29, 31, 34, 66, 88, 91, 176, 190, 234

WR-300 Reciever; 38

Würzberg radar; 17

Yakovlev Yak-28; 95, 100, 102

Yakovlev Yak-28 'Brewer'; 95, 100, 102

Yen Bai, Vietnam; 42

Yom Kippur War; 73, 76, 77, 80, 81, 82, 83, 88, 89, 90, 112, 121

Yugoslavia; 141, 162, 164, 165, 167, 177, 179, 181, 183, 185

Zahal, Lebanon; 81

Zepa, Bosnia; 166

ZPU-1/2/4 Anti-Aircraft Artillery; 189

ZRK-BD Strela/SA-13 'Gopher' Surface-to-Air Missile; 146, 165, 177

ZRK-SD Kub 3M/SA-6 'Gainful' Surface-to-Air Missile; 3, 72, 75, 81, 82, 85, 87, 105, 123, 131, 132, 136, 146, 158, 165, 168, 173, 177, 182, 186, 199, 204, 205

ZSU-23-4 Anti-Aircraft Artillery; 73, 74, 75, 82, 105, 111, 122, 123, 136, 146, 147, 160, 189, 190, 212